T0013366

INTO
THE
TOWER

A choose-your-own-path book

Hari Conner

With illustrations by Hari Conner,
Tiffany Baxter, Anine Bösenberg, Alexander Chacón,
Kateřina Čupová, Shazleen Khan, Ashley McCammon,
Rowan MacColl, Felix Miall, Sajan Rai, Faye Stacey,
Danielle Taphanel, Korinna Mei Veropoulou,
Peter Violini, Letty Wilson, and Val / Bishop Wise

Andrews McMeel
PUBLISHING®

HOW TO PLAY

This book will tell you how to play and what to do. All you need to play is a pencil.

The book is designed to be played multiple times—it has many different paths and endings that will uncover different parts of the story.

QUICK START

- **Find character sheets** on <u>page 306,</u> or online at **hari-illustration.com/itt**
  You can rip these pages out, print copies or make your own versions.

  There are four characters with different skills that will let you access different routes through the tower. Each character has at least two unique endings. You can find an **achievements** checklist on <u>page 310</u> to track which you've unlocked.

- **If your stamina reaches zero or 'your journey ends', it's game over.**
  Turn back to the start to try again or play a new character.

- **When you gain an item or a 'status', write it down on your character sheet.**
  'Statuses' track something you've done or that's happened to you, and may change your story or endings later.

Character skills
Your character's life so far has trained them in various skills, whether consciously or not—but only a few will be relevant in their journey into the tower. On your character sheet, you'll see:

Strength	Your ability to lift heavy objects, force doors or overpower a creature.
Agility	Your ability to dodge, slip through a crowd, move quickly or pick a pocket unnoticed.
Charisma	Your ability to persuade, charm, lie or act. *A low charisma might mean your character is quiet, unused to the social rules of the tower or unwilling to lie or change how they act to seem more appealing.*
Logic	Your ability to solve puzzles, calculate risks or recall and apply things you've read or been told. *A low logic might mean your character makes intuitive choices based on gut feeling or emotion or is used to a completely different background, culture or kind of magic to that of the tower.*

Stamina
Stamina is your character's ability to keep going or get back up after a hit (like health points in some games.) If your stamina reaches zero, you're unable to progress further and your journey ends.

CHEAT AT THIS BOOK

The story will tell you what to do and where to go, but it's also a book. It's not the boss of you. If it's your first time playing, you might want to start off playing as written—but there's no wrong way to play the game if you're enjoying it.

That said, changing your character's skill points or reading like a normal book will probably prevent you getting the full story in the order it makes sense. So below are the top recommended ways to adapt the way you're playing to suit you better:

STORY MODE: for exploring the story without having to start over

Take notes: You discover a **book of hints** another traveler has left. Taking lots of notes on one playthrough to use again with a different character or path is a good way to find the best endings or avoid a terrible fate.

Save your game: You have a magic device that lets you **rewind time**. Writing down each page number as you go means you can 'rewind' if something goes wrong and try another option.

Extra life: You begin the game with **health potions.** If you're enjoying playing and want your character to survive, add extra stamina points when your total drops to zero—or start the game with a potion that can be used at any time to give you +5 stamina.

HARD MODE: for a challenge

Make it harder: You have **magical foresight** and seek your true destiny. Check the *achievements* section at the back (**page 310**) to look for more objectives to aim for, such as dramatic deaths or ending the world. Try to complete them all.

Anything could happen: You are **haunted by chaos magic.**
• Before you start, roll a 6-sided dice to give yourself a fixed value for stamina.
• Instead of using fixed skills for your character, roll a 6-sided dice *every time* the book asks for a skill (strength, agility, charisma or logic) to give yourself a different number each time.
• If you reach instructions for a permanent increase or decrease, write it down and use it to modify your dice score each time.
E.g., 'your agility increases by 2': write down +2, and add 2 every time you roll for agility.

Off the beaten path: **Create your own character.** Once you've played most of the book's characters, you may want to read the section on **page 311** to create your own character and story. But if it's your first time playing, continue reading to begin.

IT BEGINS

The gates of the Locked Keep open only once every ten years. Tonight, on the night of the masquerade ball, it's your one and only chance to get inside and get what you need.

High above the city in the shadow of the mountains is a castle, with thick and seemingly impenetrable walls enclosing its outer and inner courtyards.

The doors through which the castle staff are allowed entry are heavily defended by armed guards and surveilled by masked royal inquisitors—ruthless agents of the crown rumored to have been given strange powers.

In the innermost courtyard, rising high into the sky out of the Locked Keep, is the tower of the spellbinder princess. It's said that even those who somehow make it inside find the tower guarded by generations of royal spellbinders' magical traps, dangers and barriers. There are many tales of those who tried to make their way in—and none of any who made it out.

There, at the top of the tower, is the famed 'requisition room': a huge store of supposedly-dangerous objects confiscated by the royal inquisitors.

The people in the town below whisper of the inquisitors' growing boldness. Once, they took only the most powerful magical artifacts to prevent dangerous uses. But since the mysterious princess stopped appearing in public over a decade ago, they've become more and more stringent. Almost nothing is known for sure about the princess, but many say the enchanted objects are taken to give her an endless supply to probe, analyze, and take apart to use in her own enchantments.

All you know is that the room holds magical trinkets and scholars' experiments gone awry, dangerous documents, secrets and ancient treasures—and among all of them, something you desperately want. You'll do anything to get it, and tonight is your one opportunity.

Only the exclusive guests of the ball and the hired servants helping prepare will be allowed entry by the guards at all—and only for tonight. But for once, the main gates of the castle will be open wide, its courtyards full of strangers and noise, bustle and confusion. The journey may be arduous, strange and full of perils—but if there's any chance at all to get into the tower, this is it, and you mean to seize it.

Turn to **page 6**.

CHOOSE A CHARACTER

To play, you'll need to use a **character sheet**—find them **on page 306-309,** or online at **hari-illustration.com/itt.**

THE THIEF revels in the idea of pulling off the most daring heist imaginable and getting revenge on the richest in the city, through any means necessary.

Best skills: Agility and stamina

Play style: The best prepared character, will find it easiest to get inside the castle, and fastest to reach the tower's mysteries.

Play for: Quick start

Challenging ————◆— Survivable
Quick play —◆———— More story

> To play THE THIEF, **turn to page 8.**

THE SAILOR is looking for purpose and answers: trying to recover a lost heirloom and information on a missing family member who left strange magic and an inquisitor cover-up in their wake.

Best skills: Strength and stamina

Play style: The strongest and most direct character, and the best in a fight.

Play for: Story & mystery

Challenging ———◆—Survivable
Quick play ————◆— More story

> To play THE SAILOR, **turn to page 12.**

THE LIBERTINE is a disgraced, dramatic courtier, in love with the wrong person and unwittingly caught up in something bigger.

Best skills: Charisma

Play style: The most used to navigating high society (if not physical danger.)

Play for: Drama! Intrigue! Romance?

Challenging —✧——————— Survivable
Quick play —————————✧ More story

> To play THE LIBERTINE, **turn to page 16**.

THE ACOLYTE was chosen first for the Great Library and now for a looming wider purpose. Compelled toward catastrophe by a terrible magic, the acolyte can change the course of destiny.

Best skills: Logic

Play style: The most knowledgeable character—can discover the most about the tower and its history.

Play for: Lore, and a challenge

Challenging ✧——————— Survivable
Quick play —————✧—— More story

> To play THE ACOLYTE, **turn to page 19**.

SEEKER OF GLORY

You came from nothing and wanted everything.

As a child, you learned the cold of winter and the feeling of hunger. You grew up in the rickety, crowded tenements of the lower city, where the roofs always leaked and the rats never stayed in the basement. And as you grew, you discovered that the rent everyone struggled and toiled for went to people who did not live here at all: they lived in their own lavish houses on quiet, well-lit streets in the upper part of the city. They hid in gleaming carriages and behind tall walls. One day, you thought, you would climb them.

You proved yourself resourceful. From doorways and ditches you watched and saw how things were done, listening for servants sent down on errands or bringing money home. You came to know how they spoke to each other, sounding out the noises in your mouth like a mockingbird.

You begged and scrounged yourself neat new clothes, washed your face carefully and cut your hair off at the jaw to give yourself a servant's looks as well as their voice. You asked and followed and learned and knocked on doors, and when you finally wriggled your way into a good position in a grand house in the upper city, you were full of hope. You were indoors and dry, with regular work and meals—you thought you had finally made it.

Your hope slowly rotted to venom.

You were made to rise before dawn and rest long after dusk, aching and exhausted. You washed underthings, scrubbed floors with soap that burnt your fingers raw and emptied stinking chamber pots—and were expected to be grateful for the chance. You saw other servants made sick and worn out and let go, and worse, you saw what waited if you succeeded: lifelong butlers and housekeepers bent and exhausted and worked to the bone, and for what? No relief and no reward; a life endured and not lived.

You worked and scraped and kept your face impassive. Your employers handed out small praise as if to a dog, and you learned how to stay smiling when you thanked them. You stood hungry beside laden tables while your masters ate from gleaming platters, meat tender on their tongues and wine hot in their cheeks. You were reprimanded if you did not stand still enough—they wanted no reminder of your existence. You saw what most people you grew up with never did: the soft sheets and easy abundance of the things denied you.

When you traveled with your masters out of the city, they passed by the rickety tenements you grew up in. Their noses would wrinkle, their talk turn sour, disdainful that you all had the gall to exist. You wanted to snatch the gems from their haughty necks, to furnish the cold children shivering in doorways with the fur from their cloaks. You wanted to wrap yourself in their silks and show them the only difference between them and you was that their cruelty to you made them soft and vulnerable, while it battered you sharp.

You watched and learned how they wanted things done and became exceptional. You worked your way upward and remembered your grievances. You learned how best to make yourself forgettable. You learned to bow, and remembered who made you do it. You learned to smile and speak to endear yourself to them, to lull them into a sense of ease. It made you charming, like the bright gleam of a knife.

You slipped through windows and up backstairs, gathered disguises and stories and invented invitations.

You wore different manners as easily as donning a cloak, planted evidence and muddied each circumstance. You began by selling unworn shoes and bolts of silk "lost in delivery," then moved on to their secrets and jewels and silverware. By the time they were missed, you had moved on to another position, reinventing yourself as you went.

You were nervous, at first—but nervous with a thrill of excitement, arrow-taut like a deer ready to spring and flee at the first sign of danger. You had always survived on scraps, and it had made you quick.

In a stolen dress, you made a calculated show of distress at having lost your purse and retinue until a passing gentleman let you calm down in a grand room in his nearby townhouse. If he realized something was amiss, it was too late—you'd left through a window wrapped in his fine dark cloak before he returned with assistance. Now in the guise of the gentleman, embarrassingly behind on some pressing payments, you handed over his stolen earrings and cufflinks to the pawnbrokers on the other side of the city. You told them you'd return as soon as your father sent you the money, and even take a lower payment if he could lend you a good horse, with which to reach your father faster. And so, with full pockets and no incriminating earrings, you were able to ride to the next town over and sell a good horse.

You were daring, and you could afford to be—you'd always had nothing to lose.

With each success or narrow escape, you learned and adapted and grew bolder. Often you worked by night, slipping over balconies and dosing guards' waterskins. Sometimes your guises did not work, but you were fast and learned never to be backed into a corner.

Like a vine that clings fiercely as it crawls up the brickwork, you weathered your defeats. You waited only long enough for your scars to heal before trying something bigger, better, more glorious. How could those in the upper parts of the city dare to try to lock you up or cut you down when it was them who *made* you. It was the starving and wanting that shaped you: perfect and coiled, ruthless and primed to strike.

You grew famous, and no less fearless. You gave out money to the families who raised you and the cooks who had tossed you scraps. You bought everyone drinks in the filthy, warm little inn where you used to beg. You paid for streets to be cleaned and doors fixed, for feasts on holidays and bacon for poorhouses and orphanages. You did it driven by love and bitterness, imagining the disdainful faces framed in carriage windows made to see what flourished in the gutters.

You stole ostentatiously. You wanted the denizens of the city above to know their sense of safety was an illusion, built like their high walls on the backs of the people below. You wanted them to feel as hunted as the families scraping together rent, hounded by debt collectors. You wanted them scared.

There was a price on your head and you reveled in it. You set your sights on higher risks, greater dangers and more daring capers. The more openly audacious the prize, the better—the swords of great duchesses and seals of court officials—an inquisitor's hat. One night in a dingy tavern, a traveler with a glint in their eye made a jest that you could even rob the princess herself of the famed opal crown.

You took this as a challenge.

Turn to <u>page 11.</u>

THE THIEF'S PREPARATIONS

The tower of the Locked Keep can be seen from everywhere in the city, even the narrow, winding streets where you grew up. The princess herself is said to be hidden away at the top, along with the black opal crown of the Lazurite Court and half the magic in the kingdoms. Imposing and impenetrable, the tower is said to be the hardest place to breach in the world. But you're the best—and all you'd ever needed was the narrowest chance.

As the day of the ball approaches, bets are being made—and few in your favor. Surely the odds were stacked insurmountably against you, people whisper, though few do it to your face. You pay it little mind—you've always thrived in the face of adversity.

You can imagine it—slipping into the midst of the enemy at their most hallowed event, the grand ball. The chance to move among the richest in the city, to take the black opal crown itself and show them all there is no safety for them, no superiority and no mercy: there is no other prize you have ever hungered after so keenly.

You don your simplest and least suspicious costume. Add to your inventory:
 + **Servant's clothing**

And you **choose** whether or not to add:
 + **A wicked knife (weapon, poisoned)**

You're ready.

Turn to <u>page 24.</u>

INHERITOR OF ASHES

The sea had always called to you, but answering it lost you everything.

You remember your father as broad-shouldered and well-built, and when you turned sixteen, you realized you'd inherited those shoulders, too. People who saw him in the steep, winding streets of the little harbor town might have thought him a soldier—but instead he trained his thick, broad fingers to cleverness and used them for whittling and enchanting, for crafting elegant little toys and neat little machines that he sold in the shop that made up the front part of the house.

You remember the tap of a tiny hammer as he built a wooden bird whose wings would flap when infused with the right magic, working away contentedly as he sat by the fire and your mother played the fiddle. But your attention had always been on her—on the bawdy songs and shanties she used to sing that made your father blush, on her wild hair as it blew in the salty wind as she stared out at the horizon. She had come from a land over the ocean, and even when you were young, you'd sat on her shoulders, watching the fishing boats coming in on the evening tide, and told her that one day you'd sail across and see it.

Your father had been strange for a while, before you went to sea.

The ordinary folk were only allowed to play with small magic, but you wondered if somehow too much of it had seeped into him. He seemed to grow thin and distracted, his broad frame dwindling as his mind wandered off more and more often. You would find him in his workshop, late at night—the shop had been doing less well, of late. You thought he'd been working hard to find new enchantments, new ideas for toys and gadgets. More and more you'd bring him tea and find him staring into space, tools still in his hands, unmoving.

Once, you heard him muttering about finding a key—but you could see the ring of keys for the shop door where they always were, swinging on his belt. When you asked if he wanted help looking for it, his eyes grew wild like a hunted animal, and he said he didn't know what you meant. You didn't ask again.

He'd always had a strict rule against reading at the dinner table, but now he did it himself, frowning his way through books of enchantments as he forgot to spoon potatoes into his mouth. Your mother drew her lips into a line of concern but never mentioned it, and you and your brother followed suit.

It's fine, your mother had said, her face painted with the wide smile ever-present through your childhood, without any of the mirth you remembered. And when you told her, hesitantly, you'd intended to go to sea when the frosts thawed in the spring— you'd found a place on a ship—she encouraged you to go, as you'd always dreamed. "We'll all be waiting for you when you get back," she said, and thinking about it now, you're not sure if she believed it.

Your work on the ship was hard and wonderful, everything you'd dreamed. You found it uncomplicated and uncompromising; easy to understand but a sweet, ongoing struggle to master. Your arms ached from the effort. You fell into your hammock exhausted at the end of each day and slept blissfully well, rocked by the waves. When the storms howled and the rain lashed the decks, you could only think of what was right ahead of you—the misery was predictable and soon over, one way or the other. When the waters were calmer, you could look out at the swells as they rose and fell, at the sun glittering on the water or the clouds rolling overhead. You learned to graciously lose at cards and dice and how to take a joke from the crew—you hoisted sails and watched your arms grow thick and corded with muscle.

It was a long time before you returned, weather-beaten and longing for home. You ached to see your friends and hug your mother and father, to see how your brother had grown and eat stew from the pot and hear your father's little hammer and mother's violin.

You stood in the street for a long time, stunned into stillness. You didn't need to go inside the house to see something was wrong.

Your eyes followed the warp to the tiles on the rooftop, now curving upward in the broken start of a spiral, as if made of putty. A white tree's skeletal fingers stretched through the broken windows. Your first thought was *how*—what kind of person could have done this?

Inside, you found the house empty and strange.

Most of the furniture was missing. In places, scraping marked the floors and walls, as if the heavy wooden tables had been thrown about by some great storm, or the room upended like a dollhouse turned upside-down. Your father's chair by the fire lay like a beached sailboat, smelling of lightning and covered in a strange white rot. The cracked tiles of the kitchen floor looked as if they'd begun to bubble like water and frozen halfway. In the cracks you could see a darkness—not the darkness of shadows or good soil beneath, but a fathomless void.

The feeling that someone was watching sang loud in your ears, prickling your skin, but each time you flung open a door you only found another room, empty and different from your memories.

All the things you'd left in your old bedroom were gone, and moss and fungi were growing in a jagged shape on the floor with perfectly neat edges. Your foot pushed down on the stone floor of your parents' bedroom as if it were fabric stretched over a frame, and you hurried warily back down the stairs.

Your father's workshop was the one room stripped entirely bare, all traces of him scrubbed away. There was only the trunk of the white tree, its bony boughs laden thick and heavy with something that looked like feathers but smelled of burning.

You dragged yourself out to gasp in the air outside, shaking out your head until reality felt more firm under your feet.

Everyone looked at you darkly when you asked, and told you only that your father is missing. You followed a trail of rumors and tracked down your mother, finding her pale and older than you remembered, sleeping on the floor of a family friend. She and your brother had been out in the market one ordinary day—she whispered it to you, as if recounting a dream. When she returned, the house had changed.

Guards had fenced off the house in the grief and confusion afterward. Then, agents from the spellbinder princess herself came, inquisitors all the way out in your little harbor town with their shining masks and strange lanterns. They cleared the house, gave orders that none may enter and left again. There was no word about your father.

They have taken the last possessions your family held dear: they have taken your father's tools and the dress your mother wore to her wedding. They have taken her precious violin, passed down from her mother before her, and the blanket your brother needs to sleep. You last saw him crying and crying. He hadn't stopped in days.

You felt helpless and restless, agitated and desperate to move. Nothing you said could warm or fill the emptiness in your family, but you would do anything to return any hint of their smiles to their tired faces. The little wooden bird you took to sea had grown cold in your pocket, the magic expended.

You didn't have the money for a new violin for your mother—but it wouldn't be the same anyway. You snatched at an idea like a person drowning and asked everyone in town where the inquisitors from the spellbinder princess have gone to—where they could have taken the violin and the rest of their secrets.

The answer came back, foreboding and simple: they have taken it into the tower.

Turn to page 15.

THE SAILOR'S PREPARATIONS

You've arrived in the lower reaches of the mountain settlement where the spellbinder princess has her tower. It looms up over the skyline of the upper city. The last of your money is gone now, spent on a dormitory bed in a crowded bunkhouse where the floors are never quite dry and muddy boots are hung up from a rafter over the smoky fireplace.

Evening has fallen, the last evening before the ball you've learned of, when the tower will be at its most vulnerable: the commotion of the party leaving space for someone careful to make their way inside unnoticed.

The bustle of the bunkhouse is dying down now, and you've finished the thin, greasy stew you were handed in a chipped bowl when you arrived. There are a couple of low voices from the other beds and the sound of quiet snoring. The light of the fire has almost died out by the time the room is quiet, and you think yourself safe enough to make your preparations.

Sitting on your bunk, you go methodically through the pack you brought with you in the light of the last spitting embers.

You pick your cleanest clothes with the least visible mending for tomorrow. You may still stand out at a ball of courtiers, but that can't be helped. At the bottom of your bag is a dirk—a long bladed dagger from your time at sea—which you can attempt to conceal in a special pocket along your thigh, or else leave stowed under the bed with your bulkier possessions.

Add to your inventory:
> + **A heavy, dark cloak**

And choose whether or not to add:
> + **A sturdy dirk (weapon)**

The next morning, you sleep in. You let the sounds of the bunkhouse clatter around you as you lie quietly in anticipation, until finally the owner rings a bell and bustles you out in the early afternoon.

You leave in your cloak and mended clothes with your hands strangely empty. It feels as if all there is left to you is the drive to restore something of your family's peace, to find your mother's violin in the room you have heard of in the top of the tower.

You make your way slowly and carefully through the narrow streets, now busy with merchants' carts bringing supplies to the keep and the first few ornate carriages of the guests beginning to arrive. Trying not to rush or draw attention to yourself, you move toward the upper part of the city, where the tower looms striking and ever-visible. **Turn to <u>page 24</u>.**

SPREADER OF SECRETS

You are a traitor to the crown, a disappointment to your family and a disgraceful excuse for a human being, they told you—and to be honest, you can't say that they're wrong.

You're hazy on the details of the charges against you—robed, masked inquisitors stormed in to read you the list before noon, so you were only half-awake and sure they couldn't be serious. Your family is far too well-known for them to march you to a jail cell, but when you dressed up in the fetching burgundy ensemble you favor on Tuesdays and tried to go out for the evening, you were stopped by guards at your front gates who insisted you were under house arrest. That was when you had the first stirrings of understanding that something really *was* the matter.

At first, you simply waited for it all to blow over, as things in your life were usually wont to do.

As an heir to a fiefdom in the mountains, you are destined to inherit a life of soft hands and soft beds, of scrutiny and stultifying small talk at state functions. No matter how outrageous your behavior, your tiresome parents still insist you must marry "well" and usually pay off whoever is making a fuss in an attempt to save the dregs of your reputation.

This time, however, they seemed strangely absent and even more cross than usual when you sent a note to try to summon them. You remained stroppily stoic in bed. Only after a fortifying drink or ten did you give in and start to write a few more letters about what was *sure* to be a simple misunderstanding. Your many noble and powerful friends would be greatly aggrieved by your absence already, and probably hadn't written to inquire after you out of shock.

The friends that *did* reply did so rather disdainfully, even going so far as to call your very reasonable letters "pleading" and "desperate." You told them you thought them all wretched bores all along, actually, and this only confirmed it—they were not worthy of your sparkling company. In their eagerness to offend, those who were especially cutting did at least provide some of the information you were after—the exact crime of which you were accused was, in fact, treason.

You thought perhaps the situation was starting to look less optimistic.

After persuading the servants into some careful blackmail, one rather shabby minor noble—whose first name you couldn't recall—grudgingly agreed to help smuggle you out of the house to avoid the court case. None of the gentry who'd be making up the jury were at *all* inclined toward you—you suspect that minor business last year of challenging the magistrate to a duel and sleeping with her husband may rather come back to haunt you. And where that leaves you is trapped in hiding in this dreadful little bedroom, half the size of your bathroom back at home.

The last friends who will speak to you pityingly informed you the *only* thing to be done is to leave the country—but the spellbinder princess's blasted inquisitors seized all your documents, along with that funny little red box Venny had asked you to look after.

And Venny—who had really become your closest confidante, favorite lover and honestly your best friend over the last few years—hadn't replied to your letters at all, not one of them.

You had always found Venny difficult to pin down, ever since their first arrival in the kingdoms. They would introduce themself as an aristocrat, merchant or ambassador from Estovar (depending on who they were speaking to) and, more truthfully, as a person who was both a man and woman at once. This made the courtiers squirm and blanch and seethe much more than the lying ever did. You had always found Venny's blithe confidence on the subject of gender admirable, but you wished they lived in a world that didn't require it of them.

It was not unlike Venny to disappear, but in the past they had always *re*appeared, unexpectedly showing up a few days later to shoot you a dazzling grin from across some party they surely couldn't have been invited to.

And so you'd found yourself stuck in your awful little hiding place *alone*—no money left and tragically down to the really filthy stuff pilfered from the back of your parents' wine cellar. It's only at that last desperate moment that you'd heard from Venny at all.

Somebody dressed head to toe in black—and who *knows* how they found you—quietly slipped into your room somehow. You were hit with a pang of disappointment when you noticed they were much too thin to be Venny, though they had the same little tattoo on their wrist. They told you Venny's message in hushed tones: that your only hope was to retrieve your documents and the little red box. At sunset the night after the ball, Venny will meet you at the city gates and take you over the border to safety in Estovar.

No amount of protest or pleading seemed to be able to persuade the cloaked figure to give any more details on Venny's whereabouts—it only seemed to make them rather uncomfortable—and all the guidance they would give is that the box and the documents were sure to be locked away at the top of the tower.

Turn to page 18.

THE LIBERTINE'S PREPARATIONS

After finishing your last bottle of horrible cheap wine and taking a well-earned restful daytime sleep to consider the matter, you wake feeling wretched. But now you feel wretched *and* reckless. Truly there is no way your situation could become more dire, which really means you have nothing to lose.

Besides, if anyone can get into the tower, *surely* it's you. You've always been able to get exactly what you wanted without much trouble, and this, you expect, will be no exception. What could go wrong?

You consider you probably ought to have some sort of plan of attack and rifle through the pathetic little sack of things your footman was able to smuggle out of your family home. There is one rather fine dagger you've always liked—though of course never had the chance to use—and you run your hands over your best set of clothes, rumpled from being hurried into a sack but still perfectly passable for a ball. You think there will likely be so many strangers you could probably slip in undetected with your (enormous) charm and wit.

Add to your inventory:
+ Fine court clothes

You also **choose** whether or not to add:
+ A jeweled dagger (weapon)

You call for a small, plain carriage—cleverly unobtrusive, though it *may* happen to be all you could afford with your last handful of coins anyway—and get it to drop you in the vicinity of the gates on the evening of the ball. Now all you have to do is find a way in.

Turn to <u>page 24.</u>

THE ACOLYTE OF THE GREAT LIBRARY

You were chosen.

The archivists came to your village and watched the children for a week, swathed in their robes of office and silence. On the final day, it was you they chose to become an apprentice.

Your father let you go reverently, honored to have a child who would rise to so lofty a position—but something in your mother's expression seemed afraid. She nodded quietly and raised no objections to the archivists—how could she?—but as they took you away, you could see that she was weeping.

The caravan trundled along the uneven road up into the mountains, and in the light of the rising sun you caught your first glimpse of the glinting domes of the Great Library. Over the years, you would come to know the library like your own hands and breath, like an unconscious extension of yourself. Back then, you could almost sense it already.

At first, you kept to the quiet corridors where all the apprentices slept, learning the library's architecture in abstract as you memorized the catalog in plain, austere classrooms. But as you began to learn your duties, the whole library slowly unfolded itself to you, piece by piece—its curving galleries, the high and winding stacks, the neat numbers inked on the shelves and enchanted ladders that stretched impossibly upward into the library's higher reaches.

You were a quick study, and through your careful diligence you rose swiftly through the ranks. Responsibilities were bestowed upon you, precious texts allowed into your care when you were not yet fully grown. Some of the other apprentices were sluggish and reluctant, robbed of their grand aspirations and former lives, chained to their new roles in the library. But you were like a fish that slipped into a river and found that they loved the current—you had been wishing for the water all your life.

Your fingers came to know the delicate papyrus of the ancient scrolls, the silk of thousand-year-old mathematical manuscripts, the clack of bamboo slips, the weight of vellum and the thick texture of paper in the bound volumes that stretch in great sweeps under the library's vaults and spires. Your feet tapped lightly in the warm corridors as if moving in a perfect dance, fetching and returning with beautiful efficiency. You went eagerly and finished early, leaving you long afternoons to leaf through penned folk tales, historical accounts, military reports, arcane instructions, agricultural advice—anything and everything you could find.

And so you came to know the books, too, over the solitary and blissful years—you became able to advise and summarize to the clerks, scholars, alchemists and enchanters who came to the Great Library, and it only propelled you higher. Distinguished researchers would sometimes come asking after controlled texts—knowledge only entrusted to a careful few, and available to only the most faithful and dedicated of the archivists—and eventually, you were granted access.

It was a thrill to be allowed behind the closed, hallowed door to walk among the restricted texts. The whole of the Great Library was open to you now, its oldest and most dangerous controversies and mysteries unshrouded and quietly waiting. So now, when you finished your daily tasks, you slipped into the quieter, plainer depths of the library, drifting away from the airy expanses of the upper floors and behind its locked doors. You read terrible accounts of violence that would destabilize the peace of the whole continent if they were widely known; ramblings by spellbinders playing with forces far beyond their reckoning whose minds had unraveled in the process; and one day, eagerly leafing through yet another shelf, you found the book about *the Key*.

The material of the binding looked modern, but the pages were ragged, torn and unreadable in places, as if it were very old. The cover was scuffed and pitted as if the carrier had been through some kind of struggle, and proclaimed no title or author. You frowned as you opened it—it was a book that would have been sent for repair or rebinding long ago if it had been in the main collection.

The writing seemed fragmented—truncated in places, and almost incomprehensible. You might well have given up on skimming the book and moved on, if it were not for stumbling over a strange mention of something the book only ever described as *the Key*.

The writer had penned the letters of the words in a violent, slanted hand wherever they appeared, and as you flicked, you found they appeared again and again. The pen had seemed to press harder into the page for this phrase than for the surrounding words, and the author spoke of it every time with a strange fervor—sometimes terrified, sometimes longing, often erratic, but always passionate.

They never described the appearance of the thing—only that in one mention, it seemed to be small enough to hold in one hand, and in another, that it may induce intense terror, pain or ecstasy in the holder. The clearest description was twelve pages before the end, where the book descended into jagged lines that were unable to be deciphered as text at all. Scribbled in the margins, it was explained this was not a key like one made to fit a conventional lock. It was simply an object destined, inexorably and terribly, to open the world.

As you scoured the pages, trying to piece together the information, you had to be jolted out of your reverie by an archivist clearing their throat—night had fallen, and this part of the library was to be sealed and locked. How much time had passed? Reluctantly, you put the book back in its place and returned to your chamber, where you turned the words of the book over and over in your mind, wide awake and impossibly focused.

The next day you went about your tasks at a pace, not dancing and honeyed but in a feverish rush. You finished them impeccably before the midday prayer and descended again to find the book about *the Key*.

In a week, you had memorized every legible word and most of the illegible parts too. You had checked the records extensively and found the book's origins were vague—marked donated a few years ago by someone with a common given name and no family name. None of the archivists knew much about it or why it had been preserved and kept on the restricted shelves. There were records of four separate individuals who'd come seeking it, and when you wrote to track their whereabouts, you found three had each turned up dead hundreds of miles away within a week of leaving the library. The fourth was missing.

The more you read over it, the further you became convinced that this book was a plea, a desperate warning. For one thing, at least, was clear from the frenzied jumble of the text—*the Key* was a grave threat, and it was not safe where it was. The book did not speak directly of its location, but you had pored over its every word and unraveled every hint. Once, there was a reference to an obscure piece of southern poetry that, from your reading, you knew spoke of a tower. Later, there was a mention of a famous jewel, and from your reading you knew which royal family was associated with it. So you knew: *The Key* was in a country far to the south in the mountain kingdoms, at the top of the tower of the Locked Keep, where they said a monster guarded every magical artifact their royal family had been able to steal.

And so one day, the order of archivists of the Great Library rose and went about their daily tasks to find their most dedicated and promising acolyte gone.

You had resolved to make your way into the tower to find *the Key*, and nothing could stop you.

As you rocked in the carriages and barges that gradually carried you closer, you went over the words of the book in your mind. You told yourself this *opening* had to be avoided above everything else, above your ties with friends and family, above your own life, above even your beloved duties at the library. The idea of *the Key* swirled and grew in your mind, reverberated into a frenetic shrill of alarm, your heart beating loud in your ears as you fixated on it, thrilled and awestruck over what it might be—what it might *do*. You had to find it to hide it away somewhere safe, you reminded yourself, somewhere no one could ever use it.

But the feeling had crept into you already, crawled inside you the moment you read the words for the first time, the second you noticed them out of the corner of your eye. Under the beating in your chest, the idea of *the Key* had already coiled itself around your veins, nestled in your synapses. Somewhere inside you, you know that above all, *the Key* clamors to be used: to fulfill its purpose, no matter the principles of its disciples.

Turn to page 23.

THE ACOLYTE'S PREPARATIONS

You arrive in a cold, wet town that calls itself a city. The cities where you're from are beautiful organic structures built up around rivers and rich arable plains, or fortresses laid out on hilltops, resplendent and proud. This town huddles cowering at the foot of a tall mountain range of black stone, rickety buildings built high and streets filthy underfoot. This is the furthest south you've ever been. Part of you tries to think of this as an interesting academic study—but it is colder and wetter than anywhere you've been before, and the truth is, you don't like it.

You don't speak the local language as well as you'd like, but it's enough to hold a conversation, to discuss politics and the weather with the woman who drives the mail cart, and to discover that you will find better rooms if you walk higher up through the city's winding streets, closer toward the tower. You learn about the ball and its history from people at market stalls. It's clear from the way people talk about the tower and what you see of it looming over the city that it will not be easy to get into. Waiting for the night of the ball seems your best chance of getting inside.

You find simple, clean rooms with a window that looks out on the tower. You spend two weeks shivering each night as you try to fall asleep, learning irregular verb conjugations from a small book you buy in the market, asking and reading about the names of local courtiers, and rumors about the princess. And as you read, you often find yourself staring out at the tower, looking at it through the mist in the morning and watching the occasional light flicker in its high windows when night falls in the evening. At some point, you stop drawing the curtains.

You wake on the morning of the ball with your head turned toward the window, so that when you first open your eyes, you see the tower.

You take stock of your possessions, laying them neatly on the table. There's not much left. It's almost as if you planned for the journey here, but not a journey back.

As you set off, you carry little with you. Add to your inventory:
+ **42 crowns**, in a small drawstring purse

Turn to page 24.

THE WAY IN

A storm is coming. The air is heavy with it.

Clouds have drifted in over the day as you made your preparations. As you approach the Locked Keep, the sky is now slate gray and slowly churning, rumbling softly with a threat of things to come.

The sky is darkest over the keep itself. Storm clouds stretching hundreds of feet up into the air circle the tower, as if it draws them in to shroud itself in the shadows.

You survey the castle in front of you, considering your best point of approach.

Ahead of you is the main grand gate, where serious-looking city guards line the streets and gleaming carriages of guests have just begun to arrive. The road here is cleaner than the rest of the city, neatly cobbled and wide enough for each polished carriage with its teams of horses to approach and wait for entry to the ball. The princess's inquisitors themselves seem to be inspecting each one thoroughly. When you see a carriage finally approved, you watch it travel straight through the main stone gate and a second set, right into the inner part of the keep.

Down the hill off to the left, you see a well-worn dirt track that leads to an opening at the side of the outer walls. You can make out a smaller door where a queue of cooks and servants are waiting to be let through. City guards are checking the foot traffic before each is allowed in, and beside them, carts stacked high with goods trundle through much more quickly.

Around to the right of the castle walls, the fast-flowing river that splits the city in two tumbles from the mountains above, sweeping downward before it winds more sedately through the houses. Here and there, the stones of the thick outer walls of the castle seem worn and loose where the water thunders by, rocks and branches scraping past in the fast current. If there were any way to get inside while avoiding the gates, it would be here.

> To **head toward the main gate, turn to** page 30.
> To **head toward the servants' entrance, turn to** page 25.
> To **head toward the river, turn to** page 41.

THE SERVANTS' ENTRANCE

As you approach closer, you see that the city guards in their worn uniforms look extremely tired—you wonder how much extra work the commotion of the ball must be for them.

The track is in a wide open field, so anything you do will be fairly easy to see, but everyone is plainly concerned with their own business.

The carts are mostly stacked high with sacks of rice and produce, crates of fruit and bolts of material. They trundle forward through the exposed field and barely stop as they approach the larger opening. There's no chance to jump aboard without finding a way to slow them down—but once at the opening, the guards seem to know the drivers, talking and waving them through with only a cursory glance at the contents of their wagons or trailers.

The people on foot each seem to be carrying papers that look like work permits or letters. They form a line along the muddy grass bank leading down to a smaller gate where the papers are obviously checked carefully.

> **Speak to the wagon drivers**, hoping for one who'll let you hide among their goods. Turn to page 26.

> Try to **take papers** off someone in the line without being noticed, so you can pass through the foot entrance. **Turn to page 28.**

- **If you have a weapon,** you can also try to **force your way past the guards at the gate.** Turn to page 29.

SPEAK TO THE DRIVERS

You catch up alongside the line of wagons and call out to some of the drivers.

- If your charisma is 4 or below:

Only one or two drivers slow to hear you. One young woman readjusting sacks of flour seems reluctant and eventually shakes her head and moves on. A thin, haggard figure with an unreadable face beckons you closer and asks in a low voice how you'll make it worth their while.

- **If you have enough money** in your inventory, you can offer them ten crowns. **Turn to page 27**

> **If you have no money,** they lose interest. The carts start up again, and you realize you will have to find another way in. **Turn back to page 25.**

- If your charisma is 5 or above:

You manage to strike up an easy conversation with a lively middle-aged woman who drives at a leisurely pace and slows further when you call out to her. You think she answers with the accent of a farmer from further north, so you ask where she's from, striking up a conversation about the countryside there and the weather on the journey, managing to slip in favorable implications about her fine muscled physique. You don't have much time before you reach the gate, so quickly get to the point. Coming a little closer, and speaking softly so she has to lean in, you admit in a frank and honest tone that you're embarrassed to say you've lost track of your little brother, who's only seven and so excited about the ball that he keeps speaking of sneaking into the castle to see what's going on. The woman softens at your story and agrees with a wink that she'll slow down a little and look the other way. If anyone *happened* to get into the space behind the crates on the left of her cargo, she tells you, she expects they'd be able to get into the courtyard easily enough.

You hop on, hide yourself in the gap behind the crates as instructed, and her easy chatter with the guards at the gate is uninterrupted as they take a good look at her papers and only a vague look over the produce. Safely through the gate, she quietly wishes you good luck with finding your wee brother as you wriggle out of the gap and off the cart, stepping out into the outer bailey.

Turn to page 38.

BRIBE THE DRIVER

The driver pauses for a moment and then gives you a sharp nod, face still impassive.

They pull off to the side of the queue and bring the wagon to a halt, calling out to someone ahead that they heard a keg slip and need to rearrange. As they hop down, expressionless, they hold out a hand. You slip the coins into their hand.

Remove 10 crowns from your inventory.

Opening the back doors of the wagon, they usher you briskly inside and behind a stack of crates where bottles clink. With a grunt, they drag some barrels in front so you're out of sight and close the doors on you. The wagon rolls on, and a moment later, an exhausted-looking guard opens the doors to give an offhand, perfunctory inspection that definitely does not involve moving heavy barrels. The doors close again and the wagon trundles on, opening onto the view of a plain stone wall a few minutes later.

The driver slowly unloads the barrels, then gestures for you to get up and leave with a raised eyebrow and a "come on, then." You nod in thanks as you step from the wagon, but they're busy moving crates, face still blank and unreadable. You emerge from around the side of the wagon into the outer bailey.

Turn to page 38.

STEAL PAPERS

- If your agility is 5 or above:

You walk along the line quickly, looking up at the gate as if hurrying toward it. You avoid the people in the line who are talking or laughing with each other—locals, you think, with friends who might notice—and quickly choose as your mark a man who stands with his arms folded confrontationally. He looks self-important to you, as if angry he's being made to wait in line at all, and his frowning attention is on the guards, not the letter slid into his belt. Your hands are fast, and the letter is out and tucked into the folds of your shirt without him even noticing. A guard at the front of the line calls out, telling you to join the back like everyone else, and you do so. You see the man taken to one side when he is unable to present his letter, blustering furiously as the line moves on. You present the letter yourself to a different guard and pass easily into the courtyard inside. **Turn to <u>page 38.</u>**

- If your agility is 3 or 4:

You hurry along the column, as if in a rush, trying to snatch a letter out of someone's hand as you bump into them "accidentally." But the person lets out a yell as you go for it, keeping the letter firmly in their grip. They accuse you of trying to steal it, and everyone in earshot in the line turns to look at you, murmuring and talking. Someone else agrees they saw you, and a guard at the gate yells out and starts toward you. You decide it's safest to try to make your exit, and hurry away in the other direction—the tired guard gives up after a few hundred yards, but you think it best to find another way in.

> Head to **the main gates**—turn to <u>page 30</u>.
> Head to **the river**—turn to <u>page 41.</u>

- If your agility is 2 or below:

You try to bump into someone and grab their papers in a way that looks accidental—but they hold on so tightly that you end up off-balance. They shove you hard in retaliation and you fall to the floor. Several people are looking at you now, muttering, and as your intended victim yells out that you tried to rob them, more heads turn, and a guard starts toward you, breaking into a run. You try to scramble up, but too slow—several guards are already upon you. Whether you struggle or not, you're completely outnumbered, and they overpower you easily, making no effort to hurt you, but searching you for valuables.

Lose any weapons or money in your inventory

You are marched roughly down a dingy staircase toward what you realize is the dungeon. **Turn to <u>page 85.</u>**

FORCE YOUR WAY PAST

You stride up to the guards who are quietly checking people over at the side entrance gates and try to muscle past. The first stumbles back in surprise but quickly regains her footing, standing her ground and calling out for help. Although you've pushed back this first guard, you see several more on the other side of the wall you couldn't previously, and tired or not, they hurry over in alarm as they see you trying to push through. There are four of them now, forming a wall—too many to push back, but the way behind you is crowded with civilians trying to see what's going on. There's no turning back now.

You draw your blade.

All four guards ahead start to pull out their own weapons, one of which looks like a nasty, heavy cudgel. You hear shouts as reinforcements clatter down unseen stairs, perhaps hurrying down from the battlements above—five or ten more, by the sounds of it.

"Put down your weapon!" one of them shouts, but you have time to neither resist nor comply. You feel hands grab you from behind. You watch, helpless, as the figure with the heavy cudgel swings for your head, and the world turns black.

Subtract 2 from your stamina score.
Lose any weapons or money in your inventory.

When you wake, you find you've been carried somewhere new.

Turn to page 85.

GUARDED GATES

A line of ornate carriages clogs the road ahead of the main guarded gates, inching forward at a painfully slow pace. A team of the princess's inquisitors checks over papers and carefully examines carriages' contents before guests are allowed entry, and each carriage seems to have its own set of personal guards. You will be under scrutiny here, but if you take the risk, this will surely be the fastest way into the ball.

The personal guards and thorough searching mean there is little chance of going undetected on foot, and you'd be very visible trying to catch a ride grabbing onto the outside of a carriage. But if you can move fast enough, you think there's a chance someone could hide underneath—if they could cling onto the bottom.

It seems as if the only other way in here would be to get *inside* a carriage, if a guest could be persuaded to help smuggle you in.

> **Hide under a carriage**—turn to <u>page 31.</u>
> **Speak to one of the nobles**—turn to <u>page 32.</u>

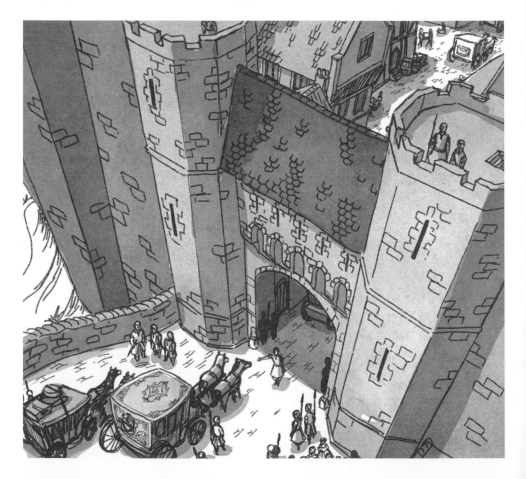

HIDE UNDERNEATH

You seek out a carriage with large boards that conceal the axles underneath. You realize you will only have the smallest of moments to get through the crowd and under the carriage before it starts moving again.

- If you have an agility of 5 or below:

You hurtle forward and make it to a crouch next to the wheels, but the gap has opened up ahead and already the carriage is moving onward before you can squeeze underneath. As you scramble forward trying to keep up, a group of guards shouts and seizes you, pulling you to your feet. **Turn to <u>page 33.</u>**

- If you have an agility of 6:

You're able to slip quickly through the crowds, duck onto the ground and roll between the wheels. In the commotion, nobody seems to have noticed you.

The carriage has large, decorative panels added to cover the wheel axles and show off its elegance. You manage to hook one hand underneath a wooden beam and another around a leather strap, lifting your feet off the ground just as the wheels begin to turn again. You carefully brace your legs against a wooden lip on the other side so you're splayed underneath the body of the vehicle, your neck and one arm contorted so the wheels can still spin freely without the axles rubbing up against you.

Your clothes are splattered with freezing water as you judder forward, and strange muscles begin to protest and burn the longer you remain contorted—but you grit your teeth and hold on. The carriage takes a mercifully short time to move to the front of the column and get checked over, and the guards seem to take little interest in the wheels. One glances down, sees nothing in the gap you wriggled through—since you're now poised above—and you feel the thing shudder into movement again, trundling through the open part of the keep and toward the gates beyond.

> **Slip out into the main courtyard,** beyond the main walls. Turn to <u>page 38.</u>

> **Wait until the carriage takes you deeper inside,** toward the great hall—the closer you can get to the tower, the better.
To do this, you must **subtract one point from your stamina** as the aches set into your shaking muscles, but you can manage to cling on under the carriage until you've passed the second gate and have a quiet moment to finally drop to the ground, where you roll out from underneath and crouch in the shadows of a courtyard. **Turn to <u>page 54.</u>**

APPEAL TO THE NOBLES

In the street, ordinary passersby are being hurried along by guards, but many have stopped to look from a distance. As you draw closer, you see that beyond the rows of guards, servants dressed in crisp uniforms that match the colors of their respective carriages move around, seeing to the needs and irritating whims of their employers. Each carries themself with the perfect posture and grace of a dancer, bowing and dipping to the disgruntled passengers within. You wonder if they enjoy their jobs—either way they seem to be doing them extremely well.

- If you are wearing **fine clothes** *and* have a **charisma of 4 or above:**
You cross the line of guards confidently, trying to look casual and unhurried as you scan the line of carriages for somewhere to make your approach. Most have curtains drawn, studiously avoiding you and everyone else in the street. Only a few of the finely-dressed people inside seem to be looking out to survey the scene—and you notice one further down the line seeming to watch you with interest. You think this is your opportunity. You call out to the figure, as if recognizing her, and make your way toward her. You're so convincingly assured she'll be pleased to speak to you that the guards—after a moment of hesitation—part to let you through, unwilling to cause trouble for someone important.

Turn to <u>page 34.</u>

- **Otherwise:**
The personal guards around each carriage eye you suspiciously as you approach. You manage to move through the train toward the front, but you stand out around the matching house uniforms of the grooms. When you try to speak, the guests in the carriages turn away awkwardly or don't reply at all—you don't seem to be an invited guest. Before you can leave, you hear a guard behind you call out in a tone that invites no argument, shouting for you to stop.

Turn to <u>page 33.</u>

SEARCHED

The guards make you hold out your arms and pat down your body, taking no care to be gentle.

- If you have no weapon:

Finding no invitation but nothing dangerous, they turn you away roughly, pushing you away from the carriages with more force than necessary so you stumble to the ground.

Subtract one point from your stamina.

Picking yourself up, you hurry back into the crowds as you hear a growl behind you—that this was your last warning. So much for that idea—you resolve to find another way in.

> **Head to the servants' entrance.** Turn to <u>page 25</u>.
> **Head toward the river.** Turn to <u>page 41</u>.

- If you have a weapon
concealed on your person:
The guards find it quickly. They take it from you, looking to each other in triumph, and there's some commotion as several more people grab you, pushing you to your knees roughly and asking questions. You think it best not to answer, now that it's clear you have no invitation.

You feel a blow to the side of your head.

Subtract two points from your stamina.

> **Continue to struggle and fight.** You won't be captured. **Turn to** <u>page 40</u>.

> **Go quietly.** Turn to <u>page 85</u>.

AN UNINVITED GUEST

"Do you have business with Lady Tamar?" asks a wary servant near the door—but they ask politely. You nod to the servant: barely an acknowledgment, as if you're so important this is only a formality. Now you have a name.

Leaning through the window, you drum up your best embarrassed, scatterbrained smile. You address her respectfully by name, and—using a family whose insignia you saw on a carriage at the back of the train—tell her that the Pauncefoots sent you to speak with her. "Apparently you made their acquaintance last time you were in town and made a wonderful impression."

Lady Tamar is dressed in the cutaway coat of a crisp military dress uniform—a sign of past service, you think, noting the medals and scars—but sprawls confidently across two seats in carefully matched accessories. A crisp collar frames her jaw, and her legs are wrapped in a softly iridescent silk. You're not sure whether she really believes you or perhaps recognizes you from somewhere—is she a little familiar?—but she looks restless and bored from the long wait, and seems to seize upon you as a distraction.

She asks a few shrewd questions and listens with a sharp smile as you launch into the start of a story, explaining how the Pauncefoots *assured* you they had your invitation but have let you down terribly at the last moment. You speak just quietly enough that she has trouble making out your words in the busy street— and as you hoped, she becomes impatient, calling imperiously to a footman to let you into the carriage. You thank her as you step inside, and the guards in the street move away, seeing nothing amiss.

Now you know you have a chance.

You tell the rest of your story, deciding you're a minor child of a family in general trade—to avoid unwelcome questions about specifics—who's mistakenly ended up without an invitation. You bend the story this way and that to keep it to her interest. You hone your character from scatterbrained toward impulsive. She seems to like any hint of danger or melodrama, so you add a scene where your carriage was overturned by highwaymen on the way here. She seems uninterested in the family hierarchies here, so you tell her you don't care about appearances either and are relieved to finally find a kindred spirit. She lets out a bark of laughter.

As you speak, the carriage you're sitting in inches forward. You will yourself to stay casual, but are extremely aware of the time ticking down. By the time you're almost to the gate, she seems as won over as possible, so you ask confidingly what you think you ought to do.

Of course, she tells you knowingly, she has no spare invitation—nobody does. Each is carefully addressed by name.

Ah. Your heart sinks.

But she gives you a wink, draws the curtains so the inside of the carriage is concealed, and announces to the straight-backed servant outside that her guest will be leaving and she will rest now, not to be disturbed. She opens and closes the door on the other side that's now out of view, facing the wall running up to the gate—for about the length of time it would take for a guest to get out and move away. With the door shut, she then kneels down to fiddle with the seat she was previously sitting on until it opens with a click, revealing a hollow inside the bench. She gestures down at it with a smile.

> You're impressed she would risk so much for a stranger just to liven up her day. To **hide inside the bench,** turn to page 36.

> Your dignity is above this. Insist that you remain sitting as normal in the carriage and **hope the guards will be just as charmed by your story.** Turn to page 45.

HIDE INSIDE THE BENCH

You quickly climb inside the hollow bench.

It's a large space—you wonder what it was originally built to hide—but you still have to curl up awkwardly, your back already aching as she swiftly closes the lid on top of you. You feel a creak above as she sits back down, and only seconds later, you hear the sound of the curtains being pulled back and the guards at the gate demanding her travel papers and invitation. You hear someone step inside and begin to move around, and realize they're searching the carriage.

You try to stay quiet in the dark, musty hole. You hear your own shallow breaths loud in your ears, and hope they're not audible to anyone else. You hear knocking along the wood, and the hollow sound turns to a soft thud when they reach the part where your legs press against the panel, cushioning it. The crack where the light leaks in goes dark for a moment as a heavily armored hand scrapes along it, checking the seams. You hear more footsteps, then the guard asking Lady Tamar questions you can't make out the answers to. You realize you're holding your breath.

After a very long moment, you hear the guard laugh at one of her replies—then doors slamming, and the carriage rattles to life again over the cobblestones. You're jostled in the movement, uncomfortable but relieved. After a long wait where all your muscles seem to be cramping at once, the carriage draws to a halt. You find yourself hoisted out of the bench and clapped on the back.

Gain the status: *Tamar's Ally.*

Tamar holds a finger to her lips, but her eyes are sparkling as you shakily emerge and sit on the seat opposite her, trying to compose yourself.

- **If you're playing the libertine**, turn straight to page 37.

Otherwise, you find yourself wondering whether she believed your story at all, or simply liked you. Perhaps she was interested in what sort of mischief or chaos you might cause if you were smuggled into the ball or holds no real loyalty to the spellbinder princess. But as she steps out of the carriage, the twinkle in her eyes vanishes, her bearing immediately straight and dignified.

On the other side, a slim girl with light brown skin and hair pulled back in a severe bun nods as she opens the carriage door, tells you Lady Tamar has made arrangements for you and leads you up a flight of empty stairs to a dressing room. The quick glance out of the window tells you that you are indeed inside the keep itself, smoothly helped inside by the Lady's daring.

The girl tells you she must leave to attend to Lady Tamar, nods knowingly, and leaves you there. **Turn to page 101.**

SEARCH PARTY

She watches you shrewdly, leaning back.

"If you needed a way into the ball, I'm surprised there wasn't someone you knew better who could help you," she says very neutrally, as if studying your reaction, reading you.

Does this woman know you? You think with relief that even if she does, her carriage is arriving from a long journey—she won't yet know you are wanted for treason. You scour your brain trying to remember where you might recognize her from.

"Someone good at organizing this sort of thing?" she says with a raised eyebrow, as if expecting something from you.

Venny, you realize. She doesn't live here and you've never spoken, but you think she might have been one of the many visitors to the city that Venny always seemed to entertain. You tell her carefully that the mutual friend the two of you have is missing.

For a tiny moment, her face falls and cracks and looks like thunder. "I wasn't informed," she says sharply, before correcting to a more studiously casual "I hadn't heard."

She grins at you convincingly, but you think you see the barest hint of a grimace in the smile. "I was hoping to see them. I shall have to seek them out," she says, measuredly.

Gain the status: Birdsong.

She says no more, plainly unsure whether to trust you—that makes two of you.

As she steps out of the carriage, her straight-backed bravado is fully back in place, standing every inch the experienced general.

On the other side, a slim girl with light brown skin and hair pulled back in a severe bun nods as she opens the carriage door, leading you to an empty part of a quiet courtyard and telling you Lady Tamar has made arrangements for you. She leads you up a flight of empty stairs and through several corridors to a dressing room. A quick glance out of the window tells you that you are indeed inside the keep below the tower itself, helped smoothly inside.

The girl tells you she must leave to attend to Lady Tamar, nods warily, and leaves you there to wonder what exactly just happened.

Turn to page 101.

THE OUTER BAILEY

The courtyard inside the first set of walls is all bustle. People dart in and out of the stores and barns that line the walls; geese and pigs are driven through pens and archways; carts trundle by piled with cloth or fruit or seafood. Merchants bringing deliveries shout to be heard over the commotion, checking their expensive goods off a list.

Small buildings line the walls that must be stables and barns, grain stores and bakehouses. The smell of the pigs and the city below is now overlaid with fresh bread and spices, onions and garlic frying in fat.

You seem to pass mostly unnoticed now that you're through the main walls, but you see the gate to the inner castle beyond is crowded with guards and several figures in the robes of the princess's inquisitors, ornate metal masks covering their faces below broad-brimmed hats.

The inquisitors swing contraptions that look like lanterns attached to long chains, which glow unnervingly with a pale fire, scanning for magical objects and intruders. Though favored upper-class guests and the most powerful and well-liked in the court usually find leniency, the inquisitors' reputation is for brutal and uncompromising punishment that no one has the power to check. It's well-known that the inquisitors answer only to the absent spellbinder princess, who rarely troubles herself to intervene.

Looking hastily away from the inquisitors at the gate, you cast around for some other way into the buildings toward the tower and see one door in the inner wall that servants move in and out of. It looks like the only way leading into the inner parts of the castle.

Your only other choice would be to approach someone for help—but looking around at the hubbub, it's hard to make out who might aid you and who'd report you.

- - **If your logic is 5 or above:**
You look over the figures in the courtyard, searching for small clues about their business, inclinations and loyalties. **Turn to page 48.**

- - **If your logic is 4 or below:**
You find it hard to get any sense of who to trust or even what all these people's jobs and purposes are. As you try to peer at them, you notice the glint of an inquisitor's mask turned toward you, watching. Realizing you'll have to make a move, you head for the only corridor that leads to the inner castle, trying to follow a group of servants.

> **If you are wearing servant's clothes,** you blend in easily with a group of workers carrying empty crates, falling into step at the back of their trail. **Turn to page 47.**
> **Otherwise, turn to page 46.**

TAKING THEM DOWN WITH YOU

You kick and flail with as much strength and venom as you can muster. People are running in your direction and you take another blow on your side—there must be twenty or thirty guards surrounding you now.

At least you'll go out fighting, you think—but you're panting now, and the guards around seem to simply be toying with you, unsure of what to do. You swipe out with a final blow, determined to take some of them down—and it's just the justification they need to run you through.

You bleed out on the cobblestones, failing to even get inside the main gate. It makes a wonderful talking point at the ball.

Your journey ends here.

THE RIVER

The thick walls of the keep are smooth and flawless most of the way around, but here by the river, debris carried by the fast-flowing water has worn grooves and indentations into the surface, where plants and moss have forced their way between the huge stones.

Although there are places where you may have to jump or swing your way up, you can see indents that may serve as footholds—gaps where someone nimble or strong enough may be able to pull themselves up onto the battlements high above.

You'd have to climb out to the stretch of wall above the water to have the best chance. Below, the river crashes by, effortlessly tossing rocks and hurtling down in a white spray.

> **Attempt to climb the walls**—turn to <u>page 42.</u>

> **Search around the walls** to try to find any other hint of a way in—**turn to** <u>page 43.</u>

Make your way back, and head to
> The servant's entrance—**turn to** <u>page 25.</u>
> The main gates—**turn to** <u>page 30.</u>

CLIMB THE WALLS

- If your agility is 5 or above:

You climb the walls deftly. You quickly feel out each foothold, testing every plant you attempt to pull yourself up by. Where the walls are weak and crumbling and vines pull away from the stone, you're careful enough to swing yourself to the next or skitter away, leaping and digging your fingertips into the smallest of cracks until you can work up the momentum to swing your legs upward and roll, panting, over the top of the battlements and out of sight. **Turn to <u>page 56.</u>**

- If your strength is 4 or above:

You're not able to make some of the hand holds, cursing as you find you're a little too slow for your momentum to carry you upward. You manage to dig in and avoid slipping down into the river, the muscles of your arms straining with effort as you keep moving along the wall sideway. Further along, you reach a place where you can eventually climb upward. Your hands are scraped raw where your hold slipped, and you're exhausted from the effort of clinging on, but you manage to heave your way up to the top and over the edge.

Subtract 1 from your stamina score.

Turn to <u>page 56.</u>

- Otherwise:

You make the first few holds but the stone is slick with spray, the jumps better suited to someone more experienced. Your arms shake with the effort of holding on, and the next handhold is a little too far. As you swing toward it, you tumble spectacularly, finding your hands clawing at thin air as you fall with a belly-flop down into the rushing river.

Winded and choking, you're pulled down into the roar of the fast-flowing current, white water and foam filling your vision as you're swept downstream away from the keep. Your hands scrabble uselessly, failing to find purchase as the current knocks you against the rocks and turns you over so you lose all sense of which way is up. You try to scream and gasp in freezing water, head hitting hard against stone. The world turns to darkness. **Your journey ends here.**

INSPECTING THE WALLS

Taking your time to check along the smooth, thick walls of the keep, you realize you can't see an outlet for wastewater. You are sure that even if the sewage was carted away or dealt with by some expensive magical technology, in this wet city at the bottom of the mountains, there will have to be a drain for rain water somewhere.

Sure enough, as you peer into the river, you're able to make out a rusted metal grate below the surface of the water of the fast-flowing river, blocking a tunnel that must lead from the castle.

For someone who had the strength to swim down, it would probably be a good way to get inside the keep unnoticed.

But the river is wide and deep, tumbling downward and turning to white spray where the force of the water hits the rocks. It thunders past the keep walls down to where it winds through the city below with a roar.

> **Attempt to swim down to the grate**. Turn to page 44.

Make your way back, and head to
> The servant's entrance—turn to page 25.
> The main gates—turn to page 30.

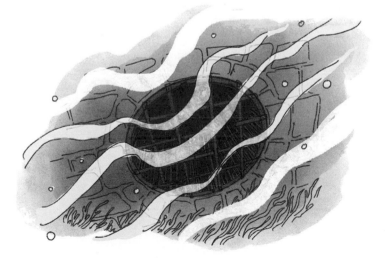

THE GRATE

- If your strength is 2 or below:

As soon as you plunge into the roar of the fast-flowing river, white water and foam fill your vision, soaking you through and pulling you under the surface. Unused to the exertion, you're swept downstream away from the keep. Your hands scrabble uselessly trying to find purchase as the current knocks you against the rocks and turns you over so you lose all sense of which way is up. You try to scream and gasp in freezing water, head hitting hard against stone, and the world turns to darkness. **Your journey ends here.**

- If your strength is 3 or 4

You struggle down beneath the surface, battered by the force of the water, body flailing wildly behind you in the current. As you feel your hand close on the rusted metal of the grate, parts break off in your hands and you wriggle through the gap left to avoid being swept away. As you squeeze past the ragged metal, it cuts your hands and tears your clothes and sides.

Subtract 3 from your stamina score.
(If it drops to zero, the current overcomes you, and you do not make your way out.)

You have just enough breath to scramble up the pipe, heart pounding, and find a pocket of air above the oily water to gulp into your burning lungs. You slowly drag your way upward—freezing, bloody fingers slipping on the seams of the pipe.

Eventually you emerge, coughing and retching, into a wide stone tunnel in almost total darkness, crawling through ankle-deep water. You feel exhausted—but you've done what was important: you've made it inside. **Turn to <u>page 68.</u>**

- If your strength is 5 or above

You take a deep breath and swim down to the grate in a few confident strokes, your body holding fast against the strong current.

The rusted grate looks eaten away, as if some chemical has hastened its demise. You apply force around the edge where bolts are missing and slowly pry the entire grate free, leaving a wide entrance to a pipe you can swim up. The water is unpleasant, but you're able to move through quickly and reach a pocket of air before your lungs start to burn.

You climb out into a wide stone tunnel, where you stand in ankle-deep water in almost total darkness. **Turn to <u>page 68.</u>**

I'M SURE THE GUARDS WILL LOVE THIS

At your refusal, Lady Tamar raises an eyebrow, as if to say, "Your funeral." She closes the bench and sits back down on it heavily, watching you.

You're almost level with the gate guards now, and you wipe your hands on your thighs, realizing you're sweating.

The gate guard examines her papers and begins to make a thorough search of the carriage. When they check your invitations, you're suddenly being looked at with suspicion by rows of well-armed inquisitors, agents of the spellbinder princess herself in shining, unreadable silver masks, armed no doubt with all kinds of magic. Lady Tamar gestures at you lazily, and you realize she's watching with interest because she's ready to see a show.

You swallow, and tell the guards the story, this time much less embellished, adopting almost a humble, straightforward approach. Lady Tamar is smiling.

The guards ask you to step out of the carriage.

Turn to page 33.

FOLLOW THE SERVANTS INSIDE

A woman who seems to be issuing instructions calls out to you sharply as you get closer to the group you try to join, asking what you're doing.

You try to pretend not to hear and make it through the door—but the person in front of you has stopped at the commotion. They turn with a frown, their tall, broad figure and the crates they're carrying completely blocking the narrow passageway ahead.

The woman who seems to be in charge has caught up with you, marching toward you, demanding to know where you think you're going. You find yourself trapped between the two. She seems to be organizing a great deal of people and to want everything to stay in its right place—and you are in the wrong place.

- If you are wearing fine clothes:

The woman is immediately suspicious, looking you up and down with an immediate dislike. As you try to smile and explain yourself, saying you've been sent on some errand for a guest who urgently needs you inside, her expression hardens. She clearly does not believe you.

She grabs your arm with a grip you're unable to shake, and as the servant in front of you moves to help, several more people now block the narrow corridor where you're trapped. Someone is sent to fetch a group of guards from the gate who outnumber and overpower you easily. Satisfied you've been dealt with, the woman returns to her work.

When you are unable to produce an invitation, two guards take your arms and march you roughly down a dingy staircase, toward what you realize with a sinking feeling is the dungeon. **Turn to <u>page 85.</u>**

- Otherwise:

You manage to tell her that you were sent to meet someone, though when she asks what for, you draw a blank and say that you're not sure—only that you were to report to the steps going into the keep. You come across so inept that she doesn't seem to think you any sort of threat, only someone in the way of her getting efficiently back to her work. She shoos you away down the corridor with the servants, one of whom apologetically opens a side door for you on their way down to the kitchens. He tells you it's this way to the keep and sympathetically wishes you luck with whatever difficult employer gave you such vague instructions.

With relief, you emerge from the side door into a small courtyard. **Turn to <u>page 54.</u>**

THE SERVANTS' CORRIDORS

You find yourself following a group of neatly-dressed servants through tight, winding passageways that seem to run through the walls separating the inner and outer courtyards.

You reach a large room thick with steam and the smell of food and spices, where a fire burns in a huge brick hearth and twenty or thirty people all bustle around, shouting and clanging as the food is prepared. The group you were following all put down their crates and boxes where they're directed, and you try to copy them. The room is full and busy, so when the others turn to go back the way they came, you easily split off and survey the rest of the room without drawing attention.

You see people coming in and out of storerooms, chefs overseeing the stirring of huge pots and rolling of pastry dough and turning of meat over the fire. You see people washing pots and pans, chopping great piles of long tubers, colorful leaves, shallots and bright red pickled roots from a jar. Not too far from you, you see a woman draped in a bright fabric overseeing the presentation of canapes, drizzling them with a sauce that seems to make them fizz and sparkle with magic. They are laid out on a silver platter, and when she finishes, she gives a curt nod to a group of three or four people dressed in plain but impeccable clothing who take the trays and head up a set of stairs on the far side of the room toward the keep.

You think this sorcerer is unlikely to be part of the usual kitchen retinue and won't notice she hasn't seen you before. Sure enough, when you join the group and follow their lead, picking up a silver tray, she gives you the same nod. You follow the person in front of you as they head up several narrow sets of stairs, and finally you emerge into a large, crowded room, slip the tray onto the nearest table, and turn to look around you.

Turn to page 102.

IDENTIFYING AN ALLY

You think back on everything you have read and heard on how castles in this part of the world operate, the many small chores and works necessary to keep a large building running as efficiently as it seems to be. Even if the princess herself never appears, there must be people doing that upkeep: fixing leaks and broken tiles on the roof after a storm, feeding goats, churning butter, bringing in hay and bringing out waste.

You keep an eye out for the workers who seem familiar with the place—permanent staff or regular traders and cooks—and notice most are in good clean clothes, better quality than many in the lower city. These people have a safe, stable, long-term income and a place to sleep at night—no amount of bribery would be worth them risking that.

You try to look for more promising candidates to help you, systematically eliminating groups from consideration: gate guards who move as if frightened of the inquisitors; too-loud musicians and players who draw attention; children whose loyalties and silence may be unpredictable; anyone who seems to take enjoyment in the power they have over those in their employ and may relish turning a suspicious figure in.

What you have left are a few stragglers you can't identify and two caravans with the unusual cargo that marks them out as specialist merchants. No ordinary carts of food or supplies move through to this part of the castle—watching them carefully, you think both must be here to provide some peculiar curio to add interest and spectacle to the ball. Might they risk helping you, if they never plan to do business here again?

Driving one of the carts is a small woman in plain traveling clothes and an ocean-blue headscarf who eyes the inquisitors' contraptions warily, with what looks like distaste. You recognize the unusual sight of a wristwatch just visible under her sleeve from its faint arcane glow and decide she must be carrying magical goods.
> **To approach her, turn to** page 49.

Standing leaning against the other vehicle—a wooden wagon with beautifully painted sides—is a man with sharp features and very inadequate clothes for the mountain climate. He watches the inquisitors coolly as he waits to pass through. The open door of the wagon reveals what looks like vases and vases of glittering glass flowers.
> **To approach him, turn to** page 52.

THE MAGICAL GOODS DEALER

The woman gives you a nod as you approach, flicking her eyes back to the inquisitors at the inner gate as she speaks. "Are they going to search you, too?"

You tell her carefully that you're not sure if they'll let you in, and she cocks an eyebrow in surprise, asking only half-jokingly whether you carry a dangerous magical artifact. You explain you simply have no invitation or work permit.

She lets out a long, considering hum and looks you over. She's waiting for you to continue, but doesn't seem opposed to the idea of helping you.

> This woman is interested in magic, so perhaps you can tell her some of the truth—that you want to get in to retreive something magical that was taken into the tower. **Turn to <u>page 50.</u>**

> It may be too dangerous to be so explicit. **Tell her you were supposed to have an invitation for the ball but have lost it. Turn to <u>page 51.</u>**

SPEAK THE TRUTH

You tell her about the spellbinder princess's requisition room, and there's a glimmer of recognition in her eye. She agrees slowly that she's heard of it, and then leans closer to tell you quietly that though she may live and trade here, she never thought much of places where magic was controlled only by the richest and most powerful.

Thinking this a good sign, you continue on, and tell her in the vaguest terms that there is something the princess's inquisitors have confiscated that you need.

She looks back over at the waiting inquisitors as if considering.

"My assistant was ill, couldn't make it," she tells you. "So there are two admission passes on my paperwork. *If* someone were to sit in the seat at the back of the cart without my knowledge, I expect they may be able to pass through the gates."

She gives you another nod and turns away from you, beginning to inch the horse forward toward the inquisitors, who have finally let through the last group they were searching. She's moving slowly enough that you can easily get a hold of the handrail and pull yourself up onto a raised seat, probably designed for a servant or child, that faces backward off the back of the cart.

You try to sit still and calm, hearing your own breathing as the cart pulls up to the gate.

The inquisitors take a long time examining her goods, swinging lanterns filled with pale blue fire that illuminates the shadows between boxes and seems to shimmer where the light touches spellbound objects. One inquisitor sweeps a lantern over you, but moves on quickly when nothing seems to light up. You let your breath hiss out as they move away.

After a lot of moving boxes around, the cart is given leave to move through the gate. It swings left and pulls to a halt beside a wall, and without looking back at you, the driver goes to speak to an official-looking man with a list, talking about timings and unloading. You're able to drop down from the seat unnoticed and look around at the inner bailey.

Turn to <ins>page 54.</ins>

TELL HER YOU LOST YOUR BALL INVITATION

Her face hardens as you explain you lost your invitation. She definitely doesn't believe you. What would you be doing at the servant's entrance if you were the kind of person who'd legitimately have an invitation for this ball?

Although you continue your appeal, she's lost interest and does not seem inclined to listen. After a while, she tells you she needs to leave and nudges her cart toward the inquisitors.

> **Speak to the glass flower merchant. Turn to <u>page 52.</u>**

> Head for the only corridor that leads to the inner castle, trying to **follow a group of servants inside. Turn to <u>page 46.</u>**

THE GLASS FLOWER MERCHANT

The man's level gaze breaks as he sees you approach and smiles widely. "You want to see inside, eh?" he says, not waiting for an answer. He opens the door to show his wagon's interior, sparkling with reflected light in all colors from the delicate glass flowers that sit gathered like huge bouquets, wrapped with wide ribbons or standing in sumptuous glass vases.

"These will decorate the tables of lords and ladies, generals, princets and spellbinders," he says, leaning in close, with a wink—"but *you* can see them for free. And only five crowns for a stem, if you wish to take one with you—the nobles will not miss only one. Are you attending the ball yourself?"

You judge it will be safe to tell him that you want to go but don't have an invitation. At this, he clucks his tongue and waves his hand aside, as if the whole thing is trivial.

"The ball is like any other, an amusement for the fine people of the city and the lands beyond. And you," he flashes you a smile, glancing down at the money in your hands, "seem like a very fine person indeed. In fact, allow me to show you our special stock."

He gestures you inside the wagon to a corner where you can't be seen from outside, then unlocks a large cabinet where huge paper flowers sit on each shelf. He takes one from toward the back and gives it to you with a flourish, so you can clearly see the piece of thick, creamy paper nestled in the middle—it's an invitation to the ball.

"You can have the glass stem for five or, for a person of distinguished taste, you can have this beautiful bloom for thirty."

- **If you have 30 crowns**, you can choose to buy an invitation. **Turn to <u>page 53.</u>**

- **Otherwise,** you can:

> **Speak to the magical goods dealer.** Turn to <u>page 49.</u>

> Head for the only corridor that leads to the inner castle, trying to **follow a group of servants inside.** Turn to <u>page 46.</u>

BUY AN INVITATION

You hand over thirty crowns as the flower seller thanks you profusely and praises your taste.

You slip the invitation into a pocket and emerge from the wagon carrying a paper flower the size of a cabbage—to any onlooker, it'll be clear what you were buying inside.

One of the inquisitors flanking the gate to the inner courtyard accepts the invitation from your slightly shaky hands, the metal mask covering their face angled down as they inspect it. You try to stay calm as you wonder whether it was forged, stolen or simply sold to the flower merchant—but after a moment, the inquisitor hands it back without a word. Their blue lantern seems to illuminate nothing suspicious on your person, and you're allowed to continue beyond the tall, thick walls into a smaller, quieter courtyard.

You're standing in the inner bailey, an open space ringed by the huge, ancient, weather-worn walls that enclose the oldest and grandest part of the castle. In the center looms the Locked Keep, where lights flicker in the high windows and the whirl of dark clouds that encircle the great tower above rumble ominously.

It's quieter here—none of the shouts of guards or squeals of animals in the outer courtyard or city below, only servants moving around efficiently and helping guests down from their extravagant carriages. You remember that this must be the busiest day this courtyard has seen in some time—you can only imagine the deathly silence that accompanies the spellbinder princess's usual isolation.

You walk up the steps to the keep, where nobody seems to check your invitation. When, unsure where to go, you hand it nervously to a watchful servant in a neat, expensive uniform, you're led up through the winding corridors. The servant gestures to an open door, bows and leaves you at an entranceway where you can hear the music of the ball beyond.

Turn to <u>page 101.</u>

THE INNER BAILEY

You are standing in a small courtyard at the heart of the surrounding castle, beyond the tall, thick walls that close off this area to commoners—the inner bailey. This is the oldest and grandest part of the castle, huge and ancient and weather-worn. Servants, workers and cooks in fine uniforms move efficiently around, and figures in extravagant gowns and robes step from their carriages to be led into the guest rooms, all in the shadow of the great Locked Keep that looms up ahead of you, dominating the courtyard. Lights flicker in the high windows of the keep, and above, the whirl of dark clouds that encircle the great tower rumble ominously.

It's quieter here—none of the shouts of guards or squeals of animals in the outer courtyard or city below. You hear only the faint sounds of music and murmur of voices. You remember that this must be the busiest day this courtyard has seen in some time—you can only imagine the deathly silence that accompanies the spellbinder princess's usual isolation.

Now that you've made it to the inner part of the castle, everyone here hurries around efficiently and quietly, attending to their tasks. You don't seem to be attracting much suspicion, and the guards are fewer and more polite, dressed in uniforms that look more elaborate and ceremonial. You see an inquisitor, masked and wrapped in their robe of office, standing near the main stairway where the guests disappear up into the keep. They seem to be slowly sweeping a lantern of blue flame over each, looking for magical objects—but not searching them otherwise or checking invitations. They must have already been searched more thoroughly at an earlier gate.

> **Blend in.** Follow the guests up the stairs into the corridors of the keep. Turn to <u>page 67.</u>

> **Sneak around the side** to find a quieter entrance. Turn to <u>page 55.</u>

A QUIETER ENTRANCE

Moving around to the side of the keep, you spot a small door in what seems like an isolated area and head toward it.

To your surprise, you find the door opens easily when you turn the handle—but as you cross the threshold, a wave of pale blue fire shoots from the lock. Pain shoots up your arm from the doorknob, and the hand that was in contact with it seems to crackle alarmingly even when you draw back, as if it were bursting aflame. Your head swims, and you can't tell whether the effect is an illusion or real.

Subtract 2 points from your stamina.

___

- If this reduces your stamina to zero:

You fall back, collapsing to your knees, reeling from the wave of enchantment. You hear footsteps running your way, and the last thing you see is the cold metal gleam of an inquisitor's mask before the world turns black.

___

- If you're still standing:

You continue forward, stumbling as the pain in your arm refuses to relent, even with the blue glow dissipated. You find you're in an almost-empty storeroom, with two sets of steps leading off to your left and right. On the otherwise-empty shelves, an unlit inquisitor's lantern is propped up on one side. The spellwork on the door was obviously to prevent anyone getting a hold of it—but you can't even see how the thing works. Hearing footsteps away to your right, you head quickly up the left-hand stairs, still cradling your arm, which is still half-numb and painful to move.

You run up the stairs as fast as you can manage with your head still swimming, turn a corner and keep moving. You've made it to the carpeted corridors of the keep and see a guest disappearing into a room a little way along. Seeing a guard standing at the foot of a narrow stairway, you head away from them, down a corridor where you turn to follow the faint sound of music. It's coming from an open door, an entranceway leading through to the ballroom—in the direction of the base of the tower. Hearing footsteps behind you again, you duck quickly inside.

Turn to <u>page 101.</u>

THE BATTLEMENTS

You are standing on the top of the castle's outer walls.

There seems to be nobody directly near you. The few guards you can see are far away on the other side of the battlements, near the servants' gate. They seem focused on the people you can hear crowded down below, and the tall parapet mostly hides you from their view. Through the gaps, you can see down to the river churning below to your right and a busy courtyard on your left—the outer bailey—where wagons roll in and workers rush from door to door.

Ahead, the path along the battlements stretches out, winding along the walls where it climbs upward to ring the inner courtyard. There, the keep nestles in the steep rock of the bottom of the mountains and the tower stretches upward into the dark clouds above.

With the noise of your footsteps covered by the bustle and commotion in the courtyard below, you make your way quietly along the walls toward the keep.

You make it to the end of the walkway, where two sets of narrow stone stairs lead up and down. One heads up to the higher walls of the inner bailey, where you can now make out the murmur of guards waiting above. It sounds like two voices, and as you listen, you hear one set of footsteps heading away, and then quiet. Perhaps there's only one left on the other side. The other stairs head downward, leading into the huge, thick walls below your feet.

> **Head down the stairs**, hoping to find a less-exposed passage through to the keep. Turn to <u>page 57.</u>

> The walls are completely exposed but the most direct way forward to the tower. Perhaps you could slip past the guard while their back is turned. **Try to sneak past— turn to <u>page 63.</u>**

> You can take one guard, as long as they don't raise the alarm. Make a noise to try to **draw them down the stairs, then attack. Turn to <u>page 64.</u>**

DOWN THE STAIRS

You head down narrow, winding stairs that open out into a stone corridor.

Before you have much time to get your bearings, you hear voices approaching just around the bend ahead of you, accompanied by the telltale clank of metal. You realize you are in the guard corridors inside the walls but are very clearly not a guard—something you can not easily explain away.

You glance around quickly, but there's nowhere to hide in the bare corridor—only a window on your left and a heavy wooden door on your right.

The window is some way off the ground, and the fall may hurt—but perhaps that's better than the guards reaching you, and it looks out onto a quiet nook of a larger courtyard. The door has a large, battered-looking padlock that's orange with rust—you think it may give way with the right amount of force applied.

> To **try to smash the lock and open the door,** turn to page 58.

- **If you have a weapon,** you can stand your ground to fight the guards, drawing your weapon to strike as they come in view. **Turn to page 60.**

> **If you *do not* have a weapon,** you can still put up a fight, and ready yourself to strike one of the guards as they round a corner. Turn to page 59.

> You can **choose to climb out of the window** but must **subtract two from your stamina score** to do so as you endure the force of the fall and hurry away into the courtyard. **Turn to page 38.**

SMASH THE LOCK

- If your strength is 6 or above AND you're carrying a weapon:

You smash the hilt directly into the metal panel of the lock with enough force that the corroded iron immediately splits with a crunch. You manage to wrench the heavy door shut behind you before the guards round the corner—but you definitely hear something in the mangled lock thunk into position as you do so.

Breathing heavily in the dark corridor, you hear their murmurs pass by on the other side of the door, followed by footsteps up the stairs to the battlements. When things have fallen quiet, you tug experimentally at the door, but sure enough, some internal piece of the mechanism has wedged itself more permanently closed, and no amount of fiddling or force seems to free it. At least the guards definitely cannot follow you.

Turning behind you, you now see a faint glow as your eyes have adjusted. The dark passage seems to descend a long way, but at the bottom, you can make out a faint light. You head onward and drop down to emerge out into a tunnel. **Turn to <u>page 68.</u>**

- Otherwise:

Your first blow clangs loudly against the metal plate. Though the lock is damaged, it holds fast when you pull at the handle, and you realize too late it would need more time to be properly broken open.

You hear the guards round the corner and let out a shout, and you hear them hurry forward. They have seen you pulling at the closed door. It's too late to talk your way out, but you could still fight.

- **If you have a weapon,** you move to draw your blade to fight. **Turn to <u>page 60.</u>**

> **If you *do not* have a weapon,** you can still put up a fight. **Turn to <u>page 59.</u>**

> **Surrender**—You don't fancy your odds against two. Let them seize you without resistance and march you away down below. **Turn to <u>page 85.</u>**

PUT UP A FIGHT, UNARMED

- If your strength is 5 or above:

As he moves into range, you slam your elbow down to strike the first guard in the head. The force of the blow knocks him to the ground, where he moans, struggling to get up, and begins to crawl back along the corridor for help.

Now one-on-one, your odds are better, and the remaining guard draws her sword nervously. "I don't want any trouble," she says in a low voice, and you realize she's edging carefully back toward the way she came, after the other figure.

> **Let both guards escape**. You're here for the tower, not to end lives. **Turn to <u>page 61.</u>**
> Tough luck. Trouble has found her anyway—to **go in for the kill, turn to <u>page 62.</u>**

- Otherwise:

You hit out at the first guard, but he recovers quickly, wrestling hold of your arms. You struggle and kick and hear a grunt as your elbow hits true—but you're unable to break free. As you try to twist, you see his face has contorted into a gratified sneer, pleased at the excuse to use force.

You feel a sharp blow as the edge of the metal shield on his arm slams into your jaw. You try to wriggle backward as he hits you again and again, and the world spins and flickers around you. The other guard looks uneasy, giving him a warning look, but she does not intervene. When you fall to the floor on the next hit, she stands silent, and he only kicks you again. There will be no punishment or consequences if a prisoner is killed "accidentally" while trying to escape.

Reeling on the floor, you realize your arms are at least free now, and you're close to the open window behind you. Seeing only one way out, you throw yourself backward and tumble through it.

Subtract 4 points from your stamina from the guard's blows and the heavy landing below. (If your stamina drops to zero, the guards' blows have exhausted you. The fall is the last thing you do—you land awkwardly, your head hits stone, and the world turns black.)

If you're still alive, you find you've fallen behind a stack of boxes in a quiet nook and can hear the guards arguing above, obscured from view—they do not think you've survived the fall. Battered and bruised, you drag yourself to your feet and stagger around a corner and emerge into a crowded courtyard. **Turn to <u>page 38.</u>**

PUT UP A FIGHT

- If your agility is 4 or below:

You draw your blade too slowly. The first guard moves toward you in a rush, eagerly slamming into your arm to knock it out of your hand, and it goes skidding away down the corridor where the other guard quickly picks it up.

Remove your weapon from your inventory.

Turn to page 59.

- If your agility is 5 or above:

You can draw your blade lightning-quick and strike at the first guard through his open faceplate as he runs toward you. He shouts in alarm and staggers back, blood dripping through the hands he draws to his face. You lunge sideway around the other guard before she can fully draw her sword, and you're close and quick enough to see every gap in her armor, each place where the chainmail does not cover.

You strike fast and duck her swings, which grow increasingly wild in the face of your single-minded viciousness.

You press forward. Up close, you can see the fear in her eyes, the frightened-rabbit pulse in her throat. You slice at the wrist of her sword-hand and her blade clatters to the floor. As she scrambles backward, you realize the other guard is already making his way back around the bend, still dripping blood.

> **Show mercy—let this guard escape**, too. You'll be long gone by the time they fetch help. **Turn to page 61.**

> **Cut her down. Turn to page 62.**

LET THE GUARD ESCAPE

The remaining guard scrambles away in the direction she came, fear and relief and resentment mingled together in her features as she turns and quickly helps the other guard away from you.

You follow them down the corridor another twenty or so paces, where they disappear behind a large door.

You need to move quickly—you hurry down steps close to the door, trying to put as much distance between you and the alarm that will surely sound soon behind you.

Moving swiftly and decisively, you try to make your way through the corridors in what you think is the direction of the tower. Each time the passage splits, you turn away from any noise that could be guards. You carefully avoid a train of neatly dressed servants carrying trays and check each window you pass to reorient yourself. The height of the tower makes it visible from most places in the city, and you find yourself able to move quickly in the right direction until you find a window not far off the ground. It looks out onto a quieter courtyard beyond, where you're shielded from view by a parked carriage.

You quietly open the casement and lower yourself down, then walk out around a corner into the inner courtyard.

Turn to page 54.

GO IN FOR THE KILL

You press forward and strike the final blow. Guards know this job comes with risks.

The remaining figure stumbles back against the wall.

Time seems to slow for a moment as you realize you can see her eyes through the helmet, which widen as her head lolls forward. She moves like a horrible parody of a puppet whose strings have been cut, limbs suddenly loose and clumsy. But when she thumps to the floor, it's nothing like a doll—it's wet and heavy, meat and mortal. Blood is pooling beneath her where something inside the armor has broken, now unmendable, unthinking. You look down on the ruin of a person, a once-intricate machine of joints and nerves, of thoughts and dreams—something living and breathing unmade into nothing.

Gain the status: *unmaker*.

Distantly, you hear a noise of a bell ringing out an alarm. You don't know how long you've been standing here. You move swiftly down the now-empty corridor, taking a turn that seems to lead away from the ringing and deeper into the castle. Behind you, the body lies slumped where it fell. The nerves twitch and still, and then it does not move.

You choose a split in the corridor at random once, and then again, head full of noise. Where you find a dead end or a procession of neatly dressed servants, you turn back in a buzzing daze, adrenaline forcing you forward and forward until the shouts behind you fade to nothing. You hope they have given up.

You look out of windows to reorient yourself, descending stairways until you find a window not far off the ground. It looks out onto a quieter courtyard beyond, where you're shielded from view by a parked carriage. You realize you're panting, and you slow your breathing, willing your heartbeat under control.

Forcing yourself calm, you quietly open the casement and lower yourself down, then walk out around a corner into the inner courtyard.

Turn to **page 54.**

SNEAK PAST THE GUARD

You try to move as quietly as possible up the stairs. When a guard comes in sight around the corner, you wait until he seems to be looking away and then hurry forward as quietly as you can.

But the battlements of the inner walls are completely exposed, and he starts suddenly, perhaps seeing movement in the corner of his eye.

- If your agility is 5 or above:

You're able to move quickly enough to throw yourself back down the stairs and around the corner before the guard sees you. You quietly hurry down the stairs and are gone before he comes to investigate. **Turn to <u>page 57.</u>**

- If your agility is 4 or below:

Before you can draw back, the guard turns the corner, grabbing your arm and giving a panicked shout for help.

You raise your hands, trying to speak to him, but he's immediately suspicious and gives you little chance to explain yourself. Several others hurry out of the stairway below, leaving you cut off with nowhere to go. When you can't produce an invitation or provide a reason for your presence they find adequate, they search you.

As you try to wriggle free, you feel a blow as you're thrown to the ground, and for a while, the world turns black.

Remove any weapons from your inventory as they take them from you.

Subtract 2 from your stamina score.
(If it drops to zero, you do not get up again.)

Turn to <u>page 85.</u>

FIGHT ON THE BATTLEMENTS

You stand next to the stairs, crouching flattened against the wall, and give the stones beside you a hard thump. It's not loud enough to carry, but enough that a few seconds later you see the guard emerge, frowning and starting to descend the stairs.

Seeing nobody, he passes your hiding place and goes to look out over the parapet.

He's close enough for you to see the gaps in his armor where you could strike, and to see that under his helmet, he is very young.

> **If you have a weapon, you can choose** to slip it through the gap in his armor at the shoulder. He'd be gone before he could cry out. **Turn to <u>page 66.</u>**

> Whether you have a **weapon or not**, you can **hit him on the back of the head** to try to knock him out instead. **Turn to <u>page 65.</u>**

KNOCK HIM OUT

- If your strength is 4 or below:

You hit him as hard as you can on the back of the head and he goes down with a grunt, crumpling to the floor where his head slumps against the wall in front. As you make your way up the stairs, you see that he's reeling but still conscious, and he lets out a little moan as he tries unsteadily to get up on all fours. Without him, the inner walls seem empty. You sprint as fast as you can to a stairway on the far side and make it before he is able to stand and shout for help, disappearing down into the keep. **Turn to page 67.**

- If your strength is 5 or above:

You hit him hard on the back of the head and he falls forward to the stone floor, out cold. It'll leave a nasty bruise, but you can hear him breathing.

You realize you could easily take a moment to put on his helmet and loose tunic over your clothes, and from a distance, look like any other guard.

+ If you want to, you can choose to put on **a guard's uniform.**

You make your way up the narrow stairs to the inner walls. Below, in the inner bailey, you can see guests' carriages arriving and people in elaborate outfits stepping out, smartly-dressed servants helping them inside, and several looming inquisitors, masked and wrapped in their robes of office, slowly sweeping lanterns of blue flame over the courtyard, looking for magical objects. The walls above are empty, though—the guards stretched thin around the usually-abandoned castle. You can make your way without issue along the inner wall to a stairway leading down toward the keep.

Turn to page 67.

A QUICK KILL

Your blade slides quickly through the gap where his breastplate meets his pauldrons. He has no time to cry out—only burble as his eyes widen in shock.

You lower him to the ground as he spasms so his fall won't make a noise. He moves like a horrible parody of a puppet whose strings have been cut, limbs suddenly loose and clumsy. You think, absurdly, that your hold feels like an embrace, a last comfort to a scared child. His head lolls back and you see his big eyes are dark brown and horrified. Thoughts come unbidden into your mind—you wonder if he's still a teenager, if he's ever had a sweetheart, if he lives with his parents. Who will miss him—who will have to clean his empty body?

As you roll his torso to the floor, it no longer feels like an embrace or a doll—his body is heavy and wet with blood, meat and mortal. You look down on the ruin of a person, face still close to his as you let go of him, quietly. On the ground is a once-intricate machine of joints and nerves, of thoughts and dreams—something living and breathing, unmade into nothing.

Gain the status: *unmaker*.

You clean your blade and walk along the battlements of the inner bailey, thankfully empty as you make your way across. You walk toward a stairway on the far side, and follow it down into the building, trying not to think of his scared brown eyes.

Turn to page 67.

THE KEEP

You find yourself in a winding corridor and fall into step behind a group of guests who seem to be heading deeper into the keep. Everyone seems too busy to pay you much attention, hurrying past with plates of food or carrying trunks and luggage full of fresh clothes for guests to change into.

A few of the guests you're following seem as if they've been drinking already, shrieking with laughter as they totter forward in elaborate costumes. They draw the full exasperated attention of the few servants or personal guards you do come across. Now that you're inside, it's assumed you have a reason for being there, and you seem to fade into the background or fall beneath the notice of the busy attendants in comparison to the demanding visitors.

Around a corner, the guests peel unsteadily away into private rooms where they seem to be preparing their hair or stowing coats, so you continue onward, trying to look as if you know where you're going. You wander through the corridors of the keep, occasionally having to double back when you hit a dead end.

Hearing the sound of music at a junction, you follow it and notice an open door leading into an entrance chamber full of cloaks and hats. It seems to lead to the ball— and in the direction of the base of the tower.

- If you're *not* wearing a guard's uniform:
or to change out of it in the dressing room, **turn to page 101.**

- If you're wearing a guard's uniform:
With so little scrutiny, you realize you may be able to bypass the ball altogether. Trying another corner, you find you can make your way up a guarded set of backstairs unchallenged. The guards at the door are busy speaking to a worried-looking servant and actually give you a nod as you pass by. You're able to follow the passage ahead that seems to come out beyond the ballroom, closer to the tower itself. **Turn to page 129.**

THE UNDERTUNNELS

The water around your feet is dank and musty, but not foul-smelling. To your relief, you seem to be surrounded by rainwater and muddy runoff from taps, gutters and drains, rather than a sewer. You can barely see ahead of you in the near-darkness, but you follow the slight movement of the water, heading upstream.

After a while, there is a very faint light from a shaft in the ceiling—the opening is far above your head and the sides are sheer, slippery and unclimbable, but it lets you see a short way ahead.

The tunnel itself is mostly featureless, extending into darkness ahead and behind you, smooth stone walls unchanging. The only movement is the water, where you now see a slight oily residue coating the surface, opalescent and shimmering. It reminds you of something enchanted—and when you see a narrow ledge, you step up to avoid sloshing through it.

You walk on into the lightless space ahead, shivering in the cool air as you slowly dry off. Occasionally, you hear rushing water and follow the noise to look for another tunnel—but each time your hands reach out, you feel the bars of sturdy metal grates over each one, unrusted and immovable when you try to shift them.

Eventually, you hear faint sounds of movement up ahead. In the gloom, you can make out a small, irregular opening up on your left, about the size a person could easily crawl through.

Drawing closer, you see it's a passage that looks hewn out of the rock. You can make out a flickering light coming from cracks or chinks in the stone of its ceiling, as if from torches some distance away. You hear a clink of metal and distant footsteps. It seems the gaps look up through the floor of a shadowy room, and the passage continues horizontally under the floor.

Back in the main tunnel, the oily water continues to flow, shimmering and strange. Ahead, you think you see another shaft of light where there might be a shape—but it's too far away to see clearly. Trying to listen instead, you hear what you think might be a squelch, and then nothing—only the quiet and the water.

> Pull yourself up to **crawl along the side passage.** Turn to <u>page 69.</u>
> **Continue up the main tunnel.** Turn to <u>page 73.</u>

A CLINK OF CHAINS

You crawl along the passage on your hands and knees. It seems to be cut more roughly into the rock than the stone architecture of the main tunnel. Once or twice, your hands slip on the damp stone as your now-tired muscles give way and you thud to the ground.

Further ahead, you see a few more spots where light shines through the stone slabs that make up the floor of the room above. You're moving to look up through them and see if you can discern any more, when out of nowhere, something slams down heavily on the floor over your head, causing you to start and let out a small, involuntary noise.

One of the spots of lights darkens as someone moves over it.

"I knew it," you hear in smooth, accented voice, spoken very quietly. "Did the nightjars send you?" Their voice is so low that you can only just hear it, even when your head must only be about a foot below theirs through the stone.

You don't know if you should respond, or even how—you've never heard of the nightjars. Could this be a guard, in the darkened room above? What would anyone be doing so deep under the castle?

You hear them sigh when you don't reply and a shifting of weight. They must be lying right down on the floor, and when they move, you think you hear metal on the stone.

"Too much to hope for, I suppose . . .

"I know where that passage comes out, you know," they say casually. They're still whispering, but it's as if they're whispering an offhand comment during a play and not speaking to someone unknown in a concealed passage under a castle. "Whoever you are, I could help you, if you tell me where you're going—or else I could raise the alarm and make sure an inquisitor is there to greet you when you step out."

It's hard to know how much help or harm this person could be from the other side of the stone.

> You might as well tell them, if there's any chance they can help you. **Speak to the person through the floor—turn to <u>page 71.</u>**

> Ignore the voice and **continue crawling down the passage. Turn to <u>page 70.</u>**

CRAWLING DOWN THE PASSAGE

You continue moving down the passage and hear an intake of breath from the person behind you.

"Wait," they hiss, "or I'll summon an inquisitor!" And then, when you don't stop moving: "You'll get lost down there. It's no skin off my back, but you'll regret it-"

You crawl onward until their quiet voice fades out of earshot. You noticed they were still speaking quietly, as if they didn't want to attract the attention of someone up there at all.

You crawl down the passage for a long time in the quiet and darkness. No more cracks illuminate your way forward, and you feel your way onward in the lightless dark. You are very aware that you're a long way under the earth, down in the rock itself—you imagine the press and weight of all the castle over the top of you, all the heavy footfalls and clattering carriages far above.

After about twenty minutes of slow progress, the surface of the passage seems to grow rougher, more jagged underneath, tearing at your clothes and hurting your hands.

> - **If you are wearing** anything described as '**fine clothes**', they are ruined. Replace them with '**ruined clothes**' in your inventory.

The passage also seems to be growing gradually narrower, forcing you to move along on your belly at some points, stone pressing in on all sides in the pitch black.

> The passage must go somewhere—**push forward, squeezing ahead.** Turn to <u>page 72.</u>

> **Wriggle your way out, reversing until you can turn around** and head back, crawling along until you drop out back in the main tunnel, where you're able to continue on. **Turn to <u>page 73.</u>**

SPEAKING THROUGH THE FLOOR

You ask, as quietly as possible, where the passage comes out.

You can hear them smiling as they reply, pleased to have hooked you. "I must know what you're doing down there before I can trust you—I'm sure you understand."

Their voice is smooth and inviting, and you doubt they can really stop you from there. So you tell them quietly that you were trying to break into the tower to retrieve something from the requisition room.

They become suddenly quiet at the mention of the room, and you hear movement as if they're shifting closer to the crack as you speak. As soon as you've described the object you're looking for, they cut in, voice dropping any smoothness as they scramble to tell you something.

They tell you their name is Venny and describe a small red box that was confiscated from them. They seem to have dropped all pretense of politeness and are speaking to you with some urgency now. "It has the potential to be extremely dangerous and cannot be left in the hands of the spellbinder princess," they tell you with what sounds like real, raw emotion. "But . . . I am currently indisposed, and I fear my stay here has left me too weak to retrieve it myself."

In the darkness, still crouched on your hands and knees, you listen to the person in the room above as they insist you swear on your life you'll get the red box. When you ask what it is, they darkly reply with the word "magic" and nothing more. They tell you a time and place they will try to meet you the next day to exchange the box for a reward—but warn you it is likely they will not make it.

"If nobody is there to meet you, you must leave the city. You *must* take the box with you," they hiss, sounding genuine and a little desperate. "Keep it hidden, and throw it into the ocean at the deepest place you can, so that no-one can ever find it again. Please."

Feeling you have no other choice, you agree to help them. They tell you what to look out for to find the right passage up to the keep, then urge you to continue upward.

Gain the status: *Venny's mission—the nightjars.*

You crawl on, feeling out on your right hand side for an opening they mentioned. Sure enough, as the passage widens out about ten minutes later, you feel the wood of a door in the pitch darkness that would be all too easy to miss. Nudging it open, you ease yourself down to the floor below, where you feel around and find you're in a new passage, tall enough to stand in. Moving your feet, you find it's just as they said—you're on a stairway, which you begin to follow upward through the dark. **Turn to page 81.**

SECRET TUNNEL

The secret passage you've found yourself in deep, deep under the castle narrows to a squeeze.

You're alone in the darkness. The rough, cold stone presses against your limbs as you try to wriggle forward. It will widen out again soon, you think, calmly at first, and then increasingly wildly. You try to force the panic down as you move forward and become, in small increments, unable to move. The stone scrapes the flesh of your arm, catching as you try to inch it onward in the absolute blackness.

You let your body slump, panting in the tiny space you've contorted yourself into. You want to thrash and scream and stretch, but you're held tight, pinned by the stone in all directions. You try experimentally to see if you can wriggle back in the direction you came, but you can't get the traction, limbs trapped at awkward angles where you can't get a good hold to force yourself back.

The only way to go is forward.

It takes five long hours to wrench yourself through, rock tearing through your clothes and the soft flesh of your thighs and shoulders to make it, scoring deep gashes where you drag yourself forward. With some effort, you pull yourself up onto your elbows and manage to extend your shaking hands ahead of you in the slightly wider crawl space you've emerged into. You start to sob as they hit solid rock out ahead of you.

In front, you run your hands over the surface where the passage narrows to a crack smaller than your head. You are crouched in a dead end barely big enough to sit up in, bleeding and shaking and exhausted. The world starts to swim and contract, and your heavy head falls forward again onto the stone, down in the utter darkness under the Locked Keep.

You will never make it up into the tower, and never escape.

Your journey ends here.

SQUELCHING IN THE DARKNESS

You move carefully forward down the main tunnel. As you move closer to the next shaft of pale light from far above, you begin to make out a shape in the gloom beyond.

At first, what you see is only a huge shadow that looks like a beached whale, taking up most of the tunnel's width. The skin of the creature is pale and anemic like a cave animal, slimy and amphibious, with the oil-slick shimmer of enchantment from the water all over it.

As you edge toward it, pressed up against the wall, you can see it's long like a fish or an eel, grown almost the size and shape of the whole tunnel—and it's still alive. A wide face is pressed down in the shallow, shimmering water at the far end, snuffling like a bottom feeder, sucking something out with the occasional squelch.

Long whiskery barbels protrude around the mouth in all directions, the ones above the water snaking through the air as if sniffing.

Closer up, the pale and almost translucent skin of the creature ripples with shimmering fronds in lines along its back, and you think you can see shapes in its long body, things it has swallowed glinting and glimmering inside.

You're perhaps twenty paces away from it now, and there's a narrow, shadowy way along the edge of the tunnel where the huge creature's body does not extend.

> **Try to sneak past**—turn to <u>page 74.</u>

> **Try to run past the creature**—turn to <u>page 75.</u>

> **If you have a weapon,** you can also choose to **attack the creature**—turn to <u>page 76.</u> (Otherwise, you can't figure out how to damage something so large without a blade.)

SNEAK PAST THE CREATURE

- If you are *not* wearing a **dark cloak:**
You try to creep forward as carefully as possible, but one of its barbels quests out toward you, and suddenly the whole creature twitches and begins to move. **Turn to page 75.**

- **If you are wearing a dark cloak:**
You pull the hood up over your face and make sure it covers as much of you as possible as you creep forward past the creature.

One of its barbels twitches toward you as you inch along the wall, and you stop, trying to control your breathing as the long tendril sways through the air, questing toward you. But whatever sense it uses can't make you out against the dark wall, and after a while, the tendril wanders back. The creature resumes its squelching filtering of the water.

You move forward and away, blending unnoticed into the shadows.

Not far ahead, the tunnel turns a corner to a large chamber where countless smaller pipes pour water down onto the stone floor. At least one is conspicuously shimmering with what you think now must be magical residue, water tinged with spellwork poured unthinkingly away that feeds and alters the things down in the tunnels. You wonder if there are more or if the creature you saw has eaten its competition.

On the other side of the chamber, stone steps lead upward to a door with a damp and almost unrecognizable lock. Dripped on by opalescent water from a pipe above, the lock is crystallized in places and pulsing and alive-looking in others. The lock hangs loose and completely useless, the door actually open a crack where the lock's jeweled tendrils have forced it open.

You climb the stairway, taking a moment to sit down and shake out your shoes and squeeze the last of the water out of your socks before you go on. Most of the rest of your body has dried, leaving only a faint dampness that shouldn't be too visible.

Easing the door open, you see more steps, which you follow up into a quiet courtyard. **Turn to page 54.**

RUN PAST THE CREATURE

As you try to hurry forward through the gap, the creature turns, its huge head of quivering barbels raising up toward you, blocking the tunnel ahead.

- If your agility is 2 or below:

The creature's wide, fleshy mouth opens to reveal a cavernous pink interior, glowing with strange trails of lights. You try to move away from the thing's head but slip down into the oily water, where you find you're suddenly being sucked in a fast-moving current toward its mouth.

As you try to scramble away, a glow expands out from its fringed mouth, lighting the room up an eerie green and sending an unfamiliar sensation tingling through your body. Your head swims and your limbs slow to a stop. You feel bright lights and dazed, fragmented memories, hearing laughter and impossible birdsong as a wave of enchantment washes over you. You're almost completely unconscious, blissfully uncomprehending, by the time you disappear into the creature's huge mouth. **Your journey ends here.**

- If your agility is 3 or above:

You move fast enough to dodge to the right and clamber up over the thing's slimy body, hands grasping at fronds to haul and slide your way over and come skidding down on the other side. You hear it sucking and blubbering as it tries to maneuver around to face you, but you're far away down the tunnel by the time its huge head swings around.

You splash away until the squelching sounds behind you grow distant. Around a corner, you find a large chamber where smaller pipes empty water onto the floor—at least one conspicuously shimmering with what you think now must be magical residue. Could the thing behind have grown from something ordinary, fed by water tinged with spellwork poured unthinkingly away? You wonder whether there are more—or if the thing has eaten its competition. Better not to linger and find out.

On the other side of the chamber, stone steps lead upward to a door whose damp lock is being dripped on by some of the opalescent water. The lock is almost unrecognizable, crystallized in places and pulsing and alive-looking in others. The lock hangs loose and useless, the door actually open a crack where the lock's jeweled tendrils have forced it open, and you splash up the steps out of the water, closing the door behind you.

You find yourself at the bottom of a set of stairs that lead upward, where you can see the dark clouds that ring the tower up above. You try to quietly shake the water off your shoes—the rest of you is almost dry now and not too conspicuous.

Trying to slow your breathing and look like you weren't just running for your life, you climb the long set of steps, coming out into a quiet courtyard. **Turn to page 54.**

ATTACK THE CREATURE

You step into the water and move carefully along the tunnel toward the creature. You draw your blade as quietly as you can and try to move toward its long belly, where you think you see shapes inside through the semi-translucent skin between two large, softly-rippling fins.

As you draw within a few paces, you hear the squelching of its face cease as the huge head begins to rise. You run the last few steps toward it.

Throwing your body forward, you plunge your blade into what you hope is the creature's stomach or organs, trying to cut a long stripe along its side to have any hope of damaging it.

You hear a blubbering keening from the creature's head as the whole huge body begins to thrash, twinkling lights along its sides flashing an eerie green. You step back out of reach of the wriggling tail, but the green light seems to crackle out in arcs like lightning toward you—and as one hits the water near your feet, a tingling flash seems to run up your body.

Your head swims and your limbs slow to a stop, as if moving through treacle. You feel bright lights and dazed, fragmented memories, hearing laughter and impossible birdsong as a wave of enchantment washes over you.

Subtract 1 point from your stamina.
(If this drops your stamina to zero, you fall into the water and the sensation takes hold of you completely. You're almost completely unconscious, blissfully uncomprehending, by the time you're sucked into the creature's wide, fleshy mouth.)

If you're still standing, you shake your head to try to get rid of the feeling and push through it to stab again and again at the creature's slimy side, slashing through the translucent skin like jelly until viscous organs start to drip through the gashes, spilling out around you. The creature's mouth is trying to twist around toward you, but the green light fizzing along its pale sides is fading, and by the time its wet barbels are close enough to reach you, the creature has slowed to a stop.

Seeping out from a wet, transparent sac in a pale yellow fluid you step back to try to avoid are a collection of bones—little rat skeletons and human skulls and others, huge and irregularly spined and warped, which you can't imagine belonging to any creature you've ever seen before. In among them, as the sac's contents ooze slowly out into the water at your feet, you see scraps of clothing, pieces of battered metal that look like they were once a ladle and a pot, and here and there, small things that glitter and catch the light.

If you search through the ooze and ruined objects, you find
+ **A huge lilac gemstone**
which you can wash off and add to your inventory.

Something seems to give way in the huge corpse, and something bright blue and steaming starts to leak from somewhere else inside—you hurry to the opposite side of the tunnel to get away from it. Stepping around the edge of the slippery head with as little contact as possible, you're able to finally slide over the creature into the tunnel beyond.

A little way ahead, the tunnel turns a corner, and you follow it around to a large chamber where countless smaller pipes pour water down onto the stone floor. You hope the flow will eventually wash the sloppy remains of the creature away.

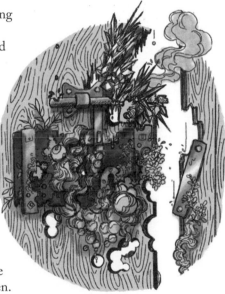

At least one pipe is conspicuously shimmering with what you now think must be magical residue—water tinged with spellwork poured unthinkingly away that feeds and alters the things down in the tunnels. Thinking of the strange bones, you think there must have been many, once, before this last creature won out over its competitors.

On the other side of the chamber, stone steps lead upward to a door whose damp lock is almost unrecognizable. Dripped on by the opalescent water, it has crystallized in some places and grown pulsing and alive-looking in others. The lock hangs loose and completely useless, the door actually open a crack where the lock's jeweled tendrils have forced it open.

You climb the stairway out of the water and take a moment to sit down, taking off your shoes and socks to wash any last traces of ooze off your hands and feet, finally pouring the water out of your shoes and squeezing your socks until at least they won't drip behind you ask you walk. Most of the rest of your body has dried, leaving only a faint dampness that shouldn't be too visible.

Easing the door open, you see more steps, which you follow up into a quiet courtyard.

Turn to page 54.

EXAMINE THE LOCK

You crouch by the door in the dim light, and see that there are a series of cylinders holding the door closed, each engaged with a different type of magic.

You think you understand the mechanisms well enough that with the right tool and plenty of time, you could probably trick the spellbound mechanism into thinking the right key had been used.

Then, as you peer at the lock more closely, you see that the two larger cylinders have already been quietly, carefully disengaged—including one with a nasty piece of ignition spellwork, which if mishandled, would have covered the person trying to defuse it in a horrible, fast-burning fire.

You look back at the other figure in the cell and are surprised to see they've stood up and have made their way to within a few paces of you in almost complete silence. They slowly draw a short piece of wire from where it was hidden in their curly black hair, holding it out for you in a shaking hand.

But their expression is perfectly calm. They look at you almost wryly, and then down to their shaking arm meaningfully. You see now there's a neat slice in the once-fine fabric, the print of boots and bruises blooming on the brown skin at their wrist.

They lean very close to you so their smooth, accented voice is too low for the inquisitor outside to hear. "In the last few days, I have found my hands less steady than I am used to. But perhaps yours are more so."

You nod, looking up into their dark eyes. Their round face looks almost mischievous.

"There is only one inquisitor posted permanently down here tonight—the rest are up at the ball. He is a young man, of a low rank: you can tell by the mask," they tell you quietly. "Every few hours he leaves to use the good, clean bathroom two floors above, and for at least three or four minutes, the corridor is empty. If there were any noise then, nobody would be here to hear it."

No other plan of escape seems obvious to you, so you take the proffered wire, slipping it into your sleeve and settling down to wait. The prisoner nods at you approvingly, moving silently back to their shadowy corner to take up exactly the same position as before.

You both sit still for a long time. Your back begins to ache, and you feel the cold stone of the floor through your clothes.

After what feels like at least an hour, you finally hear the chair in the corridor creak. You close your eyes, and hear footsteps as the inquisitor approaches. He pauses for a moment to look in at your cell and then moves quickly off down the corridor, the sound of him heading up stairs receding into the distance above.

You move to the lock, bending the stiff wire into a hook and feeding it into the opening where the key is supposed to go. You understand what you should do, in theory. The prisoner has come to stand nearby, but not *too* close, probably in case something goes awry. You don't recognize the spellbinding exactly—something to do with cold, but you're not sure what.

You feel the metal give as the first part of the mechanism slides smoothly out of the way—but you know there are five more, and it's taking too long. The prisoner is not speaking, but you see them watching, looking carefully through the bars.

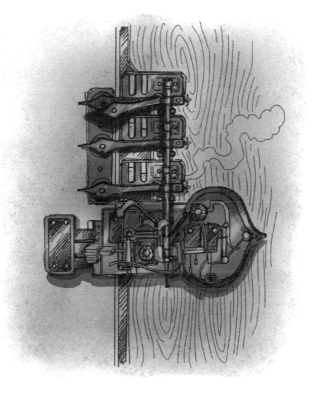

> **Take your time.** You don't know what the lock might do if you make a mistake. Turn to <u>page 82.</u>

> **Go quickly.** If you don't do it now, your next opportunity may be too late to get into the ball and tower at all—it's worth the risk. Turn to <u>page 80.</u>

BREAK THE LOCK QUICKLY

You start to move more quickly, trying each part of the mechanism only briefly before deciding to move on. You click the next three parts into place, and on the last, slide the wire to a metal plate that you *think* has too little resistance to have spellwork on it, pressing and expecting the lock to click open.

Instead, there's a loud noise like the chime of a bell. You pull back with a cry as a shock of cold spreads through the hand holding the wire.

Subtract 2 from your stamina score.
(If your stamina drops to zero, the cold is the last thing you feel.)

Your fingers have turned shriveled and blue where they were touching the wire, the flesh all around is withered like a mummified corpse. You dread to think what would have happened if you'd made a mistake on the larger cylinders.

Everything is quiet—you hear no footsteps approaching at the noise. The other prisoner is watching you warily.

Tentatively, you reach out and find the wire where you dropped it on the floor. Your hands sting, but you're still able to hold it. One end is now clustered with sharp blue crystals. Taking a deep breath, you fold the other end into a hook, and try again—the lock has not reset, and you take the last remaining part more slowly this time.

There's a clunk as the cylinder disengages. You let out a long breath you didn't realize you were holding as you slide the cylinder away freely and pull open the door with a scrape.

Out in the corridor, the other prisoner thanks you as you both make your way down the passage away from the cell. In the light of the torches, you can see how exhausted they look—skin sickly pale where it should be a rich brown, gait lopsided where they move with a limp. They wince with each step, spots of blood leaking through the fabric at their side from an unseen wound, and at the end of the corridor, they tell you they have no choice but to leave, bitterness seeping into their smooth voice.

They point off to your left where a stone stairway leads upward, describing a passage that leads to the keep and the ball—". . . if you've misplaced your invitation," they say knowingly. "And a piece of advice: an old friend of mine, Lady Tamar, shall be up at the party. You'll recognize her from her scars. Be careful of having a drink with her," they tell you with a wink, as if it's a punchline.

Gain the status: *Tamar's Ally.*

They wish you good luck and limp down the corridor away from you. **Turn to page 81.**

THE WAY TO THE KEEP

As you climb, you find the stone stairways deep under the castle completely empty, the only noise and movement further up.

Following your instructions, you search for an opening off to the side of a small landing area—rather than continuing up toward a dim light leaking from the edges of a door. The opening leads into a narrower passage, cool and still and completely dark after just a few steps. Feeling your way, you ascend rough-cut stone stairs in the darkness that go up and up, past what sounds like a break room for guards and a kitchen where the stone grows warmer—you think you must be in the inner walls of the keep itself.

Finally, you see slivers of light ahead where the passage ends. Your hands touch smooth wood, and when you listen, the room on the other side sounds empty. You emerge from a door that comes out a couple of feet above the ground, hidden behind a tapestry. You drop down as quietly as you can, closing the door behind you, and find yourself in what must be a guest bedroom. The bed is made up, but the room has no evidence of guests having arrived yet.

You can hear the echoes of laughter and music from somewhere not too far away. Brushing yourself off, you carefully step out into the corridor, trying to look as if you belong. A few servants are walking around, but they seem too busy to pay you any notice. You're able to follow the sound of voices around a corner into a sort of entrance chamber.

Turn to page 101.

BREAK THE LOCK SLOWLY

You take your time slowly finding the right place to slide your improvised wire hook, narrowly avoiding pressing a plate inside the cylinder you're sure would have set off the spell. Your hands start to sweat, and as you eliminate each *wrong* option for the last catch, you hear distant footsteps starting to approach again. Cursing under your breath, you find the last metal catch gives a little more than the others as the wire pushes on it—and you know it's because no spellbinding presses back against it. Sliding it home, there's a clunk as the cylinder disengages, and you're able to slide it away from the doorframe.

The steps have reached this floor now and you hold your breath as you hear them pass by, going back to sit in the chair at the far end of the corridor.

You try to calculate what to do, whether you could sprint without being caught in the narrow corridor—but before you can reach a conclusion, the prisoner is pulling the door open with a loud scrape. They move quickly to crouch in the shadows behind the open door and gesture for you to join them.

> **Join the prisoner** behind the door. **Turn to <u>page 83.</u>**

> **Sprint for the way out,** leaving the prisoner to their fate. **Turn to <u>page 84.</u>**

BEHIND THE DOOR

You dart behind the door to join them as you hear the inquisitor stand and start hurrying this way. Your heart races as you try to stay silent and unmoving, hoping the prisoner has some sort of plan.

You glance back at the corner where the prisoner was sitting before, and start as you see what looks like a figure. You realize they must have arranged and shaped the straw over the top of the bucket while you worked on the lock. In the stark shadows, far from the rectangle of light cast by the door, it really looks as if a person could be lying there.

From your place behind the door, you hear rather than see the inquisitor burst into the room and then stop, breathing hard. He moves quickly toward the far corner, and as soon as he passes you, the prisoner steps silently out, looping their shackled hands over the inquisitor's head and pulling the chain taut against his neck.

For a moment you're frozen, unable to move as the inquisitor gasps for air against the bruising force. His hands scrabble for something in the folds of his robe, and he pulls out a lantern lit with blue fire—but his arms grow weak before he can use it, slumping limp against the figure behind him.

The other prisoner relents, easing the still-breathing body down to the ground. They look tired, but they appear completely unruffled. You wonder if they would have killed the inquisitor if you weren't here.

Turn to page 94.

RUN FOR IT

You sprint out of the open door as fast as you can, heading down to your left, away from the dead end. You hear a shout behind you as the inquisitor notices and, as you glance behind you, see a flash of blue fire.

- If your agility is 4 or above:

You whip around the edge of the corner as the blue blaze blasts the wall where you just stood. *(Continue reading from 'either way' below).*

- If your agility is 3 or below:

The edge of the blue light engulfs you before you reach the corner. For a moment you're unable to see and a screaming, searing pain hits your back and spreads through your body like plunging into ice water.

> **Subtract 2 points from your stamina score.** (If your stamina reaches zero, you collapse to the ground, unable to continue—the last thing you see is the metal mask of the inquisitor as your body withers and judders to a stop.)

If you survive the blast, you stumble around the corner.

- Either way:

You find yourself at the foot of a long stone stairway and take the stairs two at a time, hearing the inquisitor behind you send another jet of blue fire and then start to follow you up.

> If you have the status *Venny's mission—rendezvous*, change it to *Venny's mission—the nightjars*.

You run wildly up stairs and more stairs, around winding corridors, picking doors at random that sometimes open on store cupboards and dead ends. You're a long way down, and it all seems very empty—a castle kept with a skeleton staff, you suppose, apart from the parts closer to the ball.

You reach a ground-floor corridor with a window looking out onto a courtyard, where a large carriage shields you from the sight of anyone outside. Hearing people talking up ahead, you climb quickly out of the window, then press yourself against the wall behind the carriage. You try to calm yourself, slowing your breathing, before emerging into the open space.

Turn to <u>page 54.</u>

TRAPPED IN THE DUNGEON

You have been taken to a room deep under the castle.

You're aware of a heavy door clanging shut behind you as you're thrown to the ground, and a gruff voice tells you'll be dealt with after the ball is over. You're left in the quiet, listening to the guards' footsteps receding along the corridor outside.

The room has thick stone walls and no windows. The only light spills in from a square opening in the door, and you stand to peer out of it through the bars.

All you can see is a long stone corridor to your left lit with torches and a dead end to your right, where one person sits unmoving on a chair at the end. They wear the robes and metal mask you recognize as the uniform of an inquisitor. If you try to speak to them, they do not reply.

Turning your attention to the inside of the cell, your eyes slowly adjust to the gloom. It's large and mostly empty, with a bucket and some straw on the ground over one side. With a start, you realize you are not alone in here—a large, quiet figure sits in the deepest shadows in the far corner. In the darkness, you can't tell whether their stillness is sleep or if they are watching you.

- **If you're the libertine,** the shoe stretched out toward you is familiar—this is the one person you could recognize almost anywhere. Turn **straight to page 88.**

- **Otherwise:**
> Try to **speak to the prisoner.** Turn to page 86.

> **With a logic of 5 or above,** you can also choose to examine the lock and to try to understand its mechanisms. Turn to page 78.

TALK TO THE PRISONER

The prisoner stirs when you speak to them, as if waking from sleep—or pretending to. They stand quietly and move a few steps closer to you. In the flicker of light from the door, you see they have hair that falls in black curls around their face, and their jacket—now torn and dirty from the cell or their capture—was once fine silk brocade.

"Don't worry," they tell you smoothly, in a voice with a hint of an accent, "I'm no danger to you. I'm a *political* prisoner." They say it like they're making a joke.

The prisoner tells you they have been spuriously accused of plotting against the government and locked up unjustly. They say it in a way that sounds practiced, as if they've had to answer this question many times before. They lean toward you conspiratorially in the darkness. "To tell the truth, I think some of the nobles of this country simply wanted me out of the way. I have too good a memory for who's bribing the inquisitors or cheating on their spouses."

Their voice has a hint of wry humor—as if you're taking a stroll in the park, not locked in a dungeon—and they sound very casual when they ask you why you were trying to get into the ball.

> **Tell them the truth:** you were trying to get to the requisition room. Turn to page 90.

> **Keep the information to yourself.** Turn to page 89.

THE PRISONER'S PLAN

The prisoner tells you quickly they'll attract the inquisitor's attention by pretending to fall ill.

"I have been treated surprisingly gently so far—I suspect they need me alive for a show trial. All you must do is subdue the inquisitor once he comes inside to investigate. The masks are there to intimidate you, but the one outside is a young man, really very junior—you can tell from the markings on the mask. They keep the strongest above tonight."

They give you no time to ask questions or disagree—immediately falling backward and letting out an alarming strangled yell so convincing that you're not sure if something has gone wrong. They slam their manacles against the wall in a horrible jangle and collapse to the ground.

You hear hurried footsteps, and the masked face of the inquisitor appears in the door, demanding to know what happened in a voice that sounds young and slightly panicked. You tell him the prisoner just collapsed on their own, seeming to hit their head.

The low-ranked inquisitor hurries to open the cell to check on the prisoner, muttering something nervously to himself—it sounds as if he has indeed been told it's important to keep them alive, and you wonder exactly how important their 'political' imprisonment is.

The inquisitor hurries over to the figure on the ground, leaving the door open a crack behind him. Pulling a lantern of blue fire out of the folds of his cloak and making it whir into life with a gesture, he seems to scan the light carefully over the prisoner's body.

You need to move quickly.

> **Abandon the plan and run for it,** leaving the prisoner behind to fend for themself. **Turn to page 84.**

> **Abandon the plan and remain quiet,** making no move to strike or run. **Turn to page 91.**

> **Try to knock the inquisitor out** from behind, to down him for long enough to escape. **Turn to page 92.**

> You notice the inquisitor wears a dagger at his belt that has come a little loose, the handle pointed toward you. You could easily draw the blade and **stab the inquisitor** while his back is turned—but it will have to be a lethal blow. **Turn to page 93.**

VENNY, THE SPY

"Venny!!" you yell, in what might have been a shriek if you weren't so very dignified.

Venny grins back at you from the floor, looking bizarrely disheveled. Their brown skin looks strangely ashen in the dim light, and a few dark curls have come loose to frame their round, worn face. It feels surreal to see Venny at any sort of disadvantage, though somehow even shackled in a dungeon they give off the air of being in complete control of the situation.

At first, you are furious—how could they *possibly* have got themself captured? Who in the world is going to save *you* if *they're* already cooped up in here? But as you try to reprimand them, you start to get hoarse, and worse, tearful—so you decide to stop and belatedly pretend you're very calm in the face of danger.

Venny tells you very sincerely that they were captured trying to clear your name. This can't possibly be true, but you find it very sweet they made the effort to say so. One of their hands brushes your ankle in an attempt to win you over, and you're irritated to find it's working.

Venny tells you how pleased they are that you took their advice to try to recover your documents from the requisition room. And the red box—they add, as if this is an afterthought, not the thing consuming their mind entirely, their crucial secret box. "Even if you *were* captured right away," Venny continues, with a smile that seems so genuinely fond that you feel as if your heart might burst.

You never asked what was inside the box the inquisitors confiscated and arrested you over. Venny has never volunteered the information, and you care so much about them that you've made a point to never even bring it up. Just because Venny is probably a spy and has perhaps been getting you to take on a lot of risk and hold on to incriminating things, that doesn't mean Venny doesn't *respect* you. But you're very tired and it's very dark and horrible down here, and before you know what you're saying, you've blurted out a question about the secret box.

Venny winces at the question. "I can't tell you exactly," they say carefully, "but I can tell you it's very dangerous. It's very important it's kept out of the hands of the princess."

You open your mouth to speak but Venny has knelt up to take your hands, gripping them tightly, with an expression on their face you've never seen before—almost scared. "Please, if you've ever cared for me,—" this is a ridiculous thing to say and Venny knows it, as if there was any moment you *hadn't* cared for them—"you *have* to get it back. I'm too weak to make it, but *you*—"

You hear a screech as the door of the cell opens. Two masked figures block the light, leaving you deep in shadow. Hearing your hushed discussion, the inquisitors have come to question you. **Turn to <u>page 95.</u>**

KEEP THE INFORMATION TO YOURSELF

Something about this person leaves you feeling off-balance, as if they have the upper hand somehow. You realize you never told them you were trying to get into the ball, and they must be trying to confirm a guess.

You explain warily that the guards did catch you trying to break in but reveal no more information. The prisoner nods at you, eyeing you up. They look like they're planning something, turning it over in their head.

Eyeing the barred door where the inquisitor sits on the other side, they move closer to you and tell you in a low voice that they have an idea of how to get out.

Turn to page 87.

TELL THE PRISONER THE TRUTH

You tell the prisoner that you were trying to get into the tower to retrieve something from the requisition room.

They become suddenly still at the mention of the room but motion for you to go on.

You begin to explain the situation in more detail, but as soon as you've described the object you're looking for, they seem to have stopped listening.

They drop any smoothness, telling you hurriedly that their name is Venny and describing a small red box that was confiscated from them. They seem to have dropped all pretense of politeness and are speaking to you with some urgency. "It has the potential to be extremely dangerous and *cannot* be left in the hands of the spellbinder princess," they tell you with what sounds like real, raw emotion. "But I fear my treatment here has left me too weak to retrieve it myself." They say it bitterly, like being captured and beaten was a personal failing.

The prisoner tells you they have a plan that will let you both escape but insist they'll only help you if you swear to take the box if you get to the requisition room. When you ask what the box is, they reply "magic" and nothing more, sounding grim in the darkness. They insist they'll reward you handsomely if you can make it out of the tower, arranging a rendezvous where you can give them back the box.

"Even if you can't," they say, dark eyes shining in the faint torchlight with something that might be fear, "or if you cannot find me, if I do not meet you at our agreed place, you *must* destroy the box. Keep it hidden, and throw it into the ocean, at the deepest place you can—somewhere no-one could find it again, not even you. *Please.*"

Feeling you have no other choice in the face of their fervor, you agree to help them.

   Gain the status: *Venny's mission—rendezvous.*

Turn to page 87.

ABANDON THE PLAN.

You make no move to strike.

The inquisitor examines the other prisoner for a moment, but warily, at some distance, and seeing little wrong, starts to move away. Realizing you won't make a move, the prisoner lunges frantically from the floor, trying to slam their manacled hands against their captor's head. But their movement is too slow, too desperate and exhausted, and the inquisitor, still on his guard, dodges deftly, twisting the hand holding the blue-fire lantern. The thing flares into life, tongues of light leaping at the prisoner on the floor, who lets out a hoarse, strangled cry and then falls silent.

The inquisitor moves to the door, giving you a wide berth, and locks it behind him.

The other prisoner has no visible burn marks, but they do not stir when you approach. They're still breathing, but their breaths come shallow and labored. Up close, you can see the curl of hair at the nape of their neck, the shimmering thread of their once-fine jacket.

The prisoner does not wake. After a while, a group of guards comes to drag the other prisoner away to another cell, head still lolling as the guards lift them by the shoulders, legs trailing heavily through the straw.

And then you are alone in the cell.

There are two inquisitors stationed outside now, and neither will reply when you try to speak to them, not even about getting you some water. Hours pass. Eventually you fall asleep on the hard, dirty floor. When you wake, the light out in the corridor is steady, and you are not sure if morning has come.

You're let out, filthy and miserable, three days later. The guards hired for the ball have dispersed, and the inquisitors don't care to hunt down the ones you encountered.

You emerge stumbling back out onto the street, bitterly disappointed. Your window of opportunity has passed—**your journey into the tower ends here.**

ATTACK WHILE HIS BACK IS TURNED

With as much force as you can muster, you hit the inquisitor over the back of the head with an elbow.

- If your strength is 5 or above:

He topples to the ground and hits the floor where the mask hits the stone with a heavy clack. He seems to be out cold. The prisoner gives you an approving nod, completely unperturbed at this show of violence. **Turn to <u>page 94.</u>**

- If your strength is 4 or below:

The inquisitor stumbles forward, dazed and reeling as if unused to fighting. The prisoner quickly steps behind, loops their shackled hands over the inquisitor's head, and pulls the chain taught against his neck.

For a moment you're frozen, unable to move as the inquisitor gasps for air against the bruising force, hands scrabbling at his neck, before slumping limp against the prisoner behind him.

The prisoner relents, easing the still-breathing body down to the ground. Their breathing is heavy, but they appear completely unruffled. You wonder if they're only leaving him alive to save energy. **Turn to <u>page 94.</u>**

A LETHAL BLOW

You slide the blade from the sheath and, as the young inquisitor turns at the sound, punch it into his back. You feel it tear through his robes and judder messily between ribs. There's no cry—only a soft, low sound of the air going out of him, almost like a sob.

You have to twist to get the blade back out and it feels horribly like carving meat in a way that makes you want to retch, hitting muscle and sinew as you struggle to get it free.

+ Add **a long knife (weapon)** to your inventory.

There's an awful, guttural noise as he tries to draw breath into his ruined lung, then sinks lopsided downward to his knees. His eyes are wide and horrified as his hands move uselessly to his chest, and he looks up at you with a face that's completely open, like a shocked child. You look on, unable to move, as he slowly drops to the ground.

The metal of the mask clangs against the stone floor, but the body falls wet and heavy, meat and mortal. He dies slowly. Glancing up, you see the prisoner looks calm and largely unmoved at this show of violence—though their face is momentarily grim, jaw set at the soft animal noises coming from the dying boy.

You look down on the ruin of a person, a once-intricate machine of joints and nerves, of thoughts and dreams—something living and breathing unmade into nothing.

Gain the status: *unmaker*.

Turn to **page 94.**

ESCAPE WITH THE PRISONER

The prisoner moves determinedly to the fallen inquisitor's keys, quickly managing to find the one for their shackles and—impressively—getting it into the keyhole and turning it themself with their teeth before you can wonder if you should offer to help.

Manacles off, they ask if you'd mind waiting a moment as they efficiently strip the inquisitor of his mask, outer robe and hat, revealing a tall youth whose cheeks and arms are tattooed with winding marks of spellbinding.

The prisoner pulls the loose robe over their clothes, keys in hand as they straighten. They flash you a slightly wild grin before moving the hat and gleaming metal mask into place, their costume complete.

Outside in the corridor, the prisoner pulls the door closed, locking the fallen inquisitor inside. Out in the light, you can now see they're limping a little, and their now-masked form moves along the torchlit corridor with a lopsided gait.

By the time you reach a junction, they've slowed to a crawl behind you, the exhaustion of whatever they've endured down here starting to set in. Cursing, they tell you they have no choice but to leave—but point off to your left where a stone stairway leads upward. They tell you a secret way up to the keep, "... for those who may have *misplaced* their invitation to the ball."

Before turning and moving in the other direction, they thank you, voice sounding serious for a moment.

"Some advice: I've heard of a winter painting, up in the keep. I have it on good authority it's best avoided.

"And secondly, there's an old friend of mine up at the party, Lady Tamar—a military sort. Lively. You'll recognize her from her scars." And then, their smooth voice turns playful, and it sounds like they're smiling behind the mask. "Be careful of having a drink with her!" they tell you, as if it's a punchline.

Gain the status: *Tamar's Ally.*

They wish you good luck and limp away down the corridor away from you, inquisitors' robes swirling convincingly behind them.

Turn to page 81.

QUESTIONED

Circles of metal that glow faintly with some kind of markings snap shut around your arms, making you dizzy and your arms fall weak at your sides. You're unable to resist as the inquisitors march you slowly to an empty chamber lit with a lantern of blue fire that seems to dull the sounds in the room. You are sat on a hard wooden chair, and the inquisitors begin to question you.

The inquisitors keep asking you the same things over and over: where Venny was when—as if you had any idea—and things about some group that goes by the "nightjars." You've never heard of them, and say so, but quietly begin to suspect Venny may be one of them.

As the questions go on, you realize they don't seem to know much more than you do and must not have the evidence they need to keep Venny locked up. What they want from you is something they can use—they want you to say that Venny's been asking for secrets or forced you to hold onto the red box.

> You may have been doing it willingly, but Venny *has* been asking for secrets—it would be so very easy to tell the inquisitors what they want. You could hand Venny over, try to forget about the whole thing, and go and have the quiet, stifling life your parents want for you. You'd have comfortable things all around you, at least. And you weren't made for prisons or hard work. Just give in—**inform on Venny. Turn to page 96.**

> You're outnumbered and outmatched, and think the best course of actions is to **execute a cunning plan.** *Pretend* you're about to inform on Venny to get closer to one of the guards, then use the moment to seduce them and steal the keys or something equally ingenious. **Turn to page 100.**

> You think of Venny, locked up and rotting away in this horrible dark place, and then of Venny, executed in front of a jeering crowd, and the thought makes your chest shrink and spasm and sends you into a panic. **Tell them you'd rather die than inform on Venny. Turn to page 97.**

INFORM ON VENNY

The inquisitors take your statement. You'll have to appear later in court, too—they clearly have their own political motives for keeping Venny alive, rather than making them one of the many disappearances for which the inquisitors are so notorious. They talk seriously about the necessity of a public trial: to send a message to foreign powers and make a show of "rooting out corruption." You manage to stifle a bubble of hysterical laughter at hearing this from the mouth of an inquisitor.

You do not see Venny at the trial. You only appear obediently to deliver your monologue when required, wearing the drab, somber clothing they provide. When it's over, you're told you won't have your travel documents restored but your record will be wiped clean—you can return to your family house, to the life your family wanted for you. You do not manage to force a smile.

One gray, rainy morning weeks later, you're summoned by your parents. They tell you Venny has been executed. You watch raindrops slip helplessly downward on the other side of the glass. Now, everything can return to normal, your father says in a warning tone. You can't reply. You force the sob to stay in your throat until you've made it out of the room.

You try desperately to ignore what's happened, to squash it down, wipe it out of your memories and go about your life. Your drinking gets worse. Once, someone mentions Venny at a dinner party and you have to excuse yourself to go and retch in the bathroom. And then, the topic never comes up again. Everyone forgets but you.

You marry the woman your parents choose for you and inherit your seat. They tell you sternly how much lower her standing is than what your match might have been *before*. You can't find it in yourself to pretend to care.

Your new wife looks at you with disgust, and you can't blame her. You don't make her share your bed.

The spellbinder princess's power grows and grows. You hear of terrible magic weapons employed in the war against Estovar, flattening entire villages. You wonder if any of those villages are where Venny was from, and what sort of life you would have had if you'd both been able to go there. You wonder if the weapons would have been possible if you'd managed to make it into the tower and taken back that little red box.

But instead, the war goes on. So do you, somehow.

Your journey ends.

LOYAL TO THE END

The inquisitors do not take well to this. You realize that the questions they were asking mean they definitely already know who you are, which is someone rather unpopular with the court at the moment and already an accused traitor. Someone, you realize as the first blow strikes, who will not be missed.

You call them a colorful and, you think, rather inventive and poetic series of insulting names before you're knocked clean off your chair and your head hits the floor. Pale blue fire flows from the lanterns and dances in the inquisitors' hands, glinting off the unreadable facade of their cold metal masks.

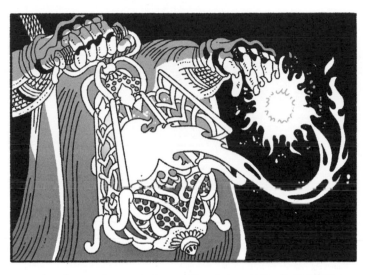

Things become very slow and very dark, and the sharp magical cracks that seem to split the air and make everything smell of some sort of chemical are not letting up. Something slices into your back and you are relieved to find yourself already too numb to fully feel it.

You may not have got into the tower, but compared to rotting away in your room, you think there are certainly worse ways to go. At least this was dramatic—rather heroic, really.

The world turns black mercifully fast—you were never one for taking a hit. A lover, not a fighter, you think blearily as the cold, comforting arms of oblivion welcome you into the nothingness.

In your last thoughts, you think of the crease Venny would get on the left side of their mouth when they were smiling, and wonder if Venny will still be there when the inquisitors return to the cell.

Your journey ends here.

FREE VENNY

You use the keys to fumble out of your cuffs and out of the room into a blessedly empty corridor. Venny is at the cell door in the dark of the window, watching. Your hands are shaking so badly that, after a minute, you simply pass the keys through the bars into their waiting, reliable hands. They open their own shackles much more smoothly than you did, immediately turning the matching key using their teeth, then starting efficiently on the cell door.

"I heard you calling for paper," they tell you, finding the key and flashing you a dazzling, unreadable grin. "For a moment, I thought I was done for."

You tell them earnestly that you'd *never* turn them in. You're not sure they believe you.

Out in the light, Venny looks bruised and rumpled, a strange unkempt shadow of the person you know. Their usual grace is thrown off in a limp as they move forward, and they hold a hand to their side, wincing at an unseen injury.

With the keys, Venny determinedly opens another door, seeming to expect the storeroom that lies on the other side. They take a canteen and a long knife and stow them in their clothes, movements heavy with exhaustion.

> - **If you do not have a weapon,** add **a small dagger** to your inventory as they thrust it into your hands and you stow it away.

Staggering back into the corridor, Venny makes no move to lock it again, leaning heavily on the wall as they edge increasingly slowly down the hallway. You watch with alarm, but think they would not take an offer of help kindly. You follow and worry

quietly, as if nothing is amiss. As the two of you approach a junction, they reach out a hand to stop you, listening. There are footsteps approaching.

Venny is panting. "I can't do it," they tell you suddenly, voice almost a sob, which catches you off-guard—defeat is not a mood you've seen on them before. "You have to get the box. *You-*" and they laugh slightly hysterically, though you don't see what's so funny, "are still the only person who might be able to do it, the only one left standing between us and destruction."

They speak through gritted teeth. Spots of blood have started to appear on the tattered silk of their tunic, seeping through from a wound below. With dawning horror, you realize Venny is telling you they can't come with you. And you can't stay here to get arrested or escape back to live in your little hideout forever—the only way forward is up into the tower, alone.

Venny's thumb strokes your jaw as they quickly tell you a secret way up to the ball. They whisper hurried advice you find difficult to make sense of: avoid a "winter painting" and not to take a drink from a general covered in scars called Lady Tamar. You nod in response, unsure what to say with their face so close.

Gain the status: *Tamar's Ally.*

"Be at the city gates at dusk. I'll meet you. Blend in—for god's sake, don't let anyone recognize you. *Get the box.*"

The footsteps are very close now. Venny says your name, gently, like it's something precious, and tells you they know you can make it. The last thing you hear them say is choked out as they clutch their side, and it sounds like "run."

You turn and sprint to stairs you take two at a time. Behind, you hear an inquisitor start to shout before a muffled thud cuts them off. Venny will be alright, you tell yourself, heart constricting horribly. You wonder if you should have kissed them.

You run wildly up stairs and more stairs, trying to remember Venny's instructions.

Turn to page 81.

A CUNNING PLAN

"Alright!!" you cry, and you're thrilled to be able to produce a single tear for the moment as required.

You tell the inquisitor sitting opposite you how Venny has always mistreated you and underestimated you, and you're quite ready to throw them under the coach and horses to get the revenge you've always wanted.

Frankly, this inquisitor seems exhausted by you and very ready to believe you would betray Venny at the drop of a hat—which stings.

You tell them in carrying tones to fetch you paper and a good ink pen to write the statement down, as you do not want your words to be misrepresented. Grudgingly, one of them agrees and leaves the room, keen to make you cooperate. The other sits back, regarding you—it's now or never. The ring of keys sits at their belt.

You lean forward toward the tired inquisitor, face hidden behind their mask of office. You tell them, in a voice that you try to lilt a little as if thick with drink, that you've always had a *thing* for masks. They stiffen as you lean close, going into quite a lot of detail about the things you like to imagine inquisitors doing to you, and you reach out a shackled hand, as if unsteady, to land at their hip.

They either find you so dangerously tempting or are so deeply uncomfortable that they spring upward to get away. They seem to be in a state of such agitation that they don't notice the jangle of keys as they slide from the belt loop at their hip and into the folds of your clothes.

As they slam the door and walk off, muttering about looking for paper as well, the mechanism locks behind them.

But you have the keys.

Turn to <u>page 98.</u>

THE DRESSING ROOM

You're standing in a small chamber full of coats and hats. At the end of the room on your left, you see a door that leads to the ball itself. On the other side of the doorway, guests mill around, almost all wearing masks. Most must have greatcoats left in carriages or rooms to stay overnight, as the dressing room is mostly unused. Casting around, you see a couple of cloaks, and in the corner, a small table with a few masks placed on top.

If you want, you can **choose to take:**

> **+ A green velvet cloak (fine clothes)** with embroidery in golden thread. It covers enough of you that no matter what you were wearing underneath, you seem to be wearing fine clothes. (Replaces any cloak you're currently wearing).

Looking at the masks, you find several that seem like they'll fit. You can **also choose to take one** and add it to your inventory, or else continue into the ball unmasked.

> **+ A plain white mask**, round and smooth, that almost looks like the face of a white porcelain doll. You think it looks like it will attract very little attention—but something about it is unsettling, the round hollows of its eyes seeming to stare back at you.
> **+ A copper mask**, which looks like lace—but when you look closer, you see it's made of a lightweight metal, thin wires woven into a perfect shape.
> **+ An ornate fox mask** that covers your whole face, with golden filigree that swirls around the eyes and curls up into golden ears.
> **+ A bird mask** with a long beak painted in dark, elegant colors.

Gathering yourself, you turn to your left and the only way toward the tower—out into the ball. **Turn to page 102.**

THE BALL

You emerge into a space so large and crowded that it's difficult to get your bearings. You seem to be in a very long room, packed with a mass of people laughing and chattering in many-colored robes, capes and dresses. Candles suspended in delicate lanterns meander slowly over the tops of feathered hats and elaborate hairpieces, their reflected light glimmering off thousands of tiny tiles set into mosaics in the ceilings. You can hear the beat of rippling music coming from a door off to your left, through which more people seem to be lining up to dance.

Formally-dressed servants weave through the crowd with drinks and plates of curious food designed to amuse the guests—fizzing canapes topped with sweets that look like jewels, or orbited by shadows of illusory butterflies.

- **If you're wearing the *plain white mask*,** turn straight to **page 111.**
- **If you're NOT wearing a mask** and you're the **libertine,** turn to **page 104.**

- **Otherwise:**

Glancing around, you see a glimpse of a doorway at the other end of the long hall leading right toward the base of the tower. The crowd is so thick that you'd have to push through to get there—most likely it would be easier to blend in if you joined in conversations as you worked your way toward the door. The room is busy, and the guests are varied enough that even if you're wearing the plain clothes of a servant or worker, you could perhaps go unnoticed if you seemed to be part of the party.

The only other door you can see leads into a side room where people are dancing. Beside this door is the only person you see standing alone—a woman who's facing in your direction with a wide smile on her face.

> **Try to blend in** and speak to people as you move toward the door. **Turn to page 103.**
> **Try to push through** the crowds to the door. **Turn to page 107.**
> **Approach the smiling woman**. Turn to **page 112.**

INTO THE CROWD

You move into the thrum of bodies as if heading purposefully to speak to someone. Close by, several groups of nobles are huddled tight, speaking in low giggles or with arms slung around each others' shoulders in companionable conversations you doubt you'd be able to join, blocking most of the way forward.

Further away, there's a clear path to a few other groups that seem more approachable, and would get you much closer to the far door.

On one side of the ballroom, several people are joking and laughing in booming voices. It seems like the most varied and rowdiest group in the room, and they stand next to a table where a servant with a severe bun pours more of a pale blue wine for each of them. Each is dressed completely differently, some in sashes and medals—you think they might be dignitaries or ambassadors from neighboring countries—and you suspect it would be easy to sneak into the fringes unnoticed.

Close to the far door in a gap in the crowd, two elegant figures are speaking to someone wearing the robes of a minor spellbinder—a rare curiosity at a party, or anywhere outside their usual reclusive circles of magical learning. The two figures listen with interest as she speaks to them, and you think she must be answering their questions about magic.

Finally, on the other side from the dignitaries, a small man leans close to a woman with big, dark eyes and tight coily hair that extends in a glittering silver halo around her head. As you watch, their animated conversation is cut short by someone from the crowd calling him toward the dancing. As he leaves, reluctantly, she glances around looking for someone else to talk to.

> **Approach the raucous dignitaries' table. Turn to <u>page 121.</u>**

> **Approach the group with the spellbinder. Turn to <u>page 124.</u>**

- **If you're wearing a mask,** the woman with silver hair seems to recognize you as another guest as she looks around. Shes gives you a little wave as she meets your eye, inviting you to come and talk—though not in the way most people might greet each other at a formal ball. To **approach the woman with the silver hair, turn to <u>page 116.</u>**

A SHOCKING GUEST

As you try to head nonchalantly into the crowd, smiling at the people you pass by, someone lets out a shriek from the other side of the room. To your dismay, you see it's a man who looks vaguely familiar, staring straight at you, pointing an accusatory finger at your unmasked face and talking animatedly to the people around him.

You can't even remember who the blasted man *is*, but he seems to remember you well enough. You consider that turning up to the biggest social event of the year without a disguise when you're wanted for treason may have been somewhat of a misjudgment.

> You're sure the situation is salvageable. **Make a dramatic speech, explaining how the treason was all accidental** and Venny misled you terribly, and you really miss all your friends and repent. **Turn to <u>page 105.</u>**

> You're probably already doomed. **Make a dramatic speech, explaining how the treason was all very deliberate**, and you hate the pack of them. **Turn to <u>page 106.</u>**

THERE'S BEEN A MISUNDERSTANDING, YOUR HONOR

You start to spin a long (and you think, rather convincing) tale about how Venny led you astray, and you had no idea you'd done *anything* wrong, right up until they captured you.

You realize several people you've seriously wronged are in the crowd, and your past outrageous behavior is unlikely to have endeared many of them to you, so you go further back and get into more detail about how your father's expectations for you were so high that you were miserable and had no chance but to become a disaster.

You're pleased to notice some sympathy stirring in the crowd, along with some pity and disgust—although as your mouth keeps on moving and you continue talking, you're uncomfortably aware of how much you're saying is true.

You finish with how sorry you are and appeal to a few people who might previously have considered you friends, saying how wonderful they are and how much you miss them.

The crowd mostly looks uncomfortable now, unsure what to do. A woman who'd actually drawn a sword from under her dress has paused, unwilling to move toward you. You realize guards had been filing in around the edges of the room, ready to seize you, but they haven't done it yet. An inquisitor in a large red sash calls out to you, and asks you if you'd be willing to say this all in court—to testify in full against Venny and bring them to justice. Ah. Your heart sinks.

> **Agree to testify against Venny.** Your shoulders sag in defeat as you nod. You feel sick all of a sudden, but it's so easy to let the inquisitor march you through the corridors into a bare, empty room where they take your statement. What else could you really have done? **Turn to <u>page 96.</u>**

> **Refuse to testify against Venny.** For a moment you saw a way out, an easy path back to your old life. But thinking about your old life makes you feel slightly nauseous anyway, and here in the face of your certain doom thanks to your own lack of forward planning, you think this is your one dramatic chance to do something brave at the last moment. They have left you alive and let you speak and make a spectacle of yourself, so they must *really* need the evidence—and you'll be damned if you'll be the one to give it to them. You decide to give up on trying to sound innocent and take on the role instead of a treasonous master collaborator. **Turn to <u>page 106.</u>**

GUILTY, AS CHARGED

You always *did* think Venny was wrong to put any faith in you. But if you're going to be captured or killed, you might as well do it with style.

You clamber up onto a nearby table and launch into a gripping (and, you think, quite persuasive) speech about how the country has gone to the dogs, and actually you were right to want to tear it all down. The princess confiscating magical artifacts this way and that—why, there was a time when people were free to do the magic they liked! And if they blew themselves up in the process that was their own fault and responsibility, and they were damn proud to do it.

You get a lot of horrified silence—and one or two drunken cries of "hear hear," quickly shushed. Worse, you see the guards that have filed in to line the edges of the room moving forward, no doubt waiting to seize you.

So you change tack a little and start talking about how none of them had the guts to stop you—in a rather provocative way that leaves a nice convenient gap for one of them to try to stop you *now*. Sure enough, at this point, a woman—in an extremely tasteful dress that spills over her shoulders and swirls around her beautifully—steps forward and challenges you to a duel, to a satisfying gasp from the crowd. You can't quite remember who she is until she starts talking about how you slept with her husband. *Alvertos*, that was his name—now he *was* memorable.

Someone thrusts a rapier into your hand as she draws her own and leaps toward you. You manage to parry with a clang—but only after she's already drawn a bloody line across your chest. She seems unlikely to stop there. You grin back at her, tossing your hair out of your face defiantly, as if you are not very aware of your imminent demise.

You never put a great deal of effort into learning to fence, but it's good enough to put on a decent show. You leap to the side as she tries to strike you, and yell in pain as she scores a hit along your other arm that bleeds horribly. You wonder how people will describe it when they tell each other the story.

Even as she cuts you down bit by bit, you're in your element here. You slip in one-liners about how much Alvertos enjoyed his time with you, and how you think you're beginning to see her "point" (this is very funny). The crowd gasps and boos with each development. You're getting tired, now, the room growing dark, and your feet skid in the blood pooling in front of the scandalized guests. You think wretchedly of Venny as you pant on the ground. When did things all begin to go so wrong? But then you think of how appalled your father will be when he hears what's happened to you, and you let out a last manic laugh as the woman runs you through. Really, as dying goes, you're rather pleased with how it's turned out. You manage to croak out that you regret nothing before collapsing to the ground as the crowd watches, horrified and enraptured. You fall to the floor with a gratifyingly theatrical scream, and in your last moments, you're pleased to see all eyes are on you. **Your journey ends here.**

SLIP AWAY

Your movement attracts some attention as you try to squeeze your way through the crowd. You notice a servant wearing a uniform in the princess's colors frowning at you as you bump past them, as well as a few figures who were about to go and dance, who turn to look at you.

- If your agility is 5 or below, Turn straight to <u>page 110.</u>

- If your agility is 6 or above, you elicit some curious looks, but you manage to slip through a brief opening in the crowd ahead before anyone stops you. You're able to move toward the door at the end of the room so quickly that the frowning servant behind loses sight of you. You hear a shout from behind, but you're fast enough that you've ducked under an elbow and through the door into the corridor beyond before anyone can reach you. **Turn to <u>page 129.</u>**

SHOVING AHEAD

You have to push roughly past the tall woman to squeeze through in the tight crowd, who lets out a yell as you hit her arm and her drink is knocked from her hand. It falls to the floor and shatters, making people nearby leap back, rendering the way ahead even more impassable.

Before you can wriggle any further forward, you feel a gloved hand on your shoulder, heavy with metal.

Turning, you see the formally-dressed inquisitor has caught up with you, leaving a wide gap and eerie silence in the crowd where people have moved to get away from them. They are no bigger than you, but their presence is icy cold, dampening the mood instantly. You hear the muffled laughter and music carrying on from the next room.

"A clumsy mistake," the tall woman says formally. Her sleeveless robe exposes intimidatingly muscled arms and she stands taller than the inquisitor, but facing them, her face has blanched pale. She bows as she steps back apologetically from the smashed glass. "My apologies, inquisitor."

The inquisitor gives her a slow nod. Before you can move, you feel something sharp in your arm, though the inquisitor didn't seem to touch you. Your body goes slack, and when the inquisitor walks away, hand on your shoulder, you find your feet are moving in step, powerless to resist.

As you're steered away, you turn back to see the servant with the silver filigree instrument sweeping into half a curtsey in front of the tall woman, telling her sympathetically not to worry, as two more servants efficiently clear the broken glass and place a new drink in the woman's hands. Before you're led through a doorway, the crowd has begun to talk again, even if the sound is more nervous and subdued.

The inquisitor takes you to a bare stone room in the keep with a lone chair that you sit heavily down upon against your will. Your arms will not lift to strike or move as they search you.

- If you do not have a weapon:
You are questioned. They ask after the names of of things that you do not recognize— guests at the ball, a group of unlicensed spellbinders, a bird that must be a code word for something.

And then you are left alone in the room.

Your limbs are still too heavy to be under your control, and you find yourself unable to cry out. A long time passes, and eventually you are brought water and a bucket, and you're asked the same questions again. You can't answer them.

You're let out, filthy and miserable, three days later. The guests and workers of the ball have dispersed, whatever plots the inquisitor was asking you about must have gone ahead or not. They don't seem to have the evidence to hold you or do anything further.

You emerge stumbling back out onto the street, bitterly disappointed. Your window of opportunity has passed—**your journey into the tower has ended.**

- If you have a weapon:

The inquisitor straightens up when they find it. The gleaming metal mask covers their face, but they move briskly as if angry or triumphant.

Another inquisitor is fetched into the room. You turn cold as you hear snatches of their conversation, discussion about "evidence" and "treason" and "inquisitorial authority." When they speak to you directly, it's to ask questions you cannot answer about spellbinders and "nightjars" and other names you've never heard of. You see one of them nod, and with a creeping horror, realize you're not being sent to the dungeons or thrown out of the ball—you're an intruder, an armed threat, and nobody that will be missed as far as they're concerned.

One of them pulls out a lantern glowing with pale blue fire. The last thing you see is the strange fire starting to swell and expand, then shooting toward you in a blinding, screaming blaze.

Your journey ends here.

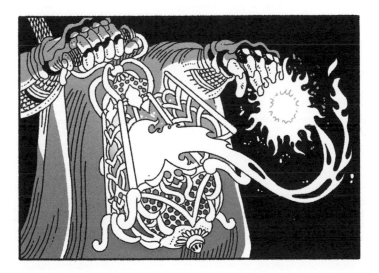

YOU ATTRACT ATTENTION

You try to slip through the crowd, but eyes have turned toward you: a strange, solitary figure trying to hurry against the flow of slowly meandering people.

A servant in a smart uniform at the edge of the room has caught sight of you, and you see them speaking quietly into an elaborate metal device whose silver filigree twists and moves as they talk. They look up to nod at someone at the edge of the room. With a start, you turn to see a figure in the formal robes of an inquisitor has appeared in the shadows of a doorway. They begin to walk along the edge of the ballroom, not right toward you, but watching in your direction. People in the crowd look slightly alarmed, and move out of the way to accommodate the robed figure.

Ahead of you, a tall woman has moved slightly to whisper something to a friend, blocking the way to the far door. You slow as you approach her, and the inquisitor halts too, watching to see where you're going.

> **Keep trying to push through** to the door on the far side, shoving past her. **Turn to page 108.**

> **Continue moving more slowly, finding someone to talk to in the crowd** as if you were only hurrying on your way to talk to them. **Turn to page 103.**

ALWAYS A STRANGER

Nobody in the crowd catches your eye. You move forward nervously—the crowd is so dense, surely one of them will notice someone so out of place. But as you move toward a mass of crowd and see no way forward, people suddenly begin parting for you.

As you move between two figures in dresses with great wide hoops, one is jostled and spills their drink. You breathe in, sharply, waiting for them to whirl on you and complain, but they only exclaim at the stain, glancing around past you as you continue on through the crowd.

As you walk, nobody looks at you. Eventually you tap on the shoulder of someone serving drinks to see if you can catch their attention, but they only frown at the tap and move on, their eyes sliding away from your face.

Gain the status:
unknowable.

You move easily toward the door at the back of the room, but reach up to take off the mask before you leave, unnerved.

Your hands brush the skin of your face and find it cold and smooth. You realize the mask is gone. You move to a silver serving platter set down on a table and see your own face staring back at you, with a change you can't put your finger on—as if your eyes are strangely hollow.

Remove the plain white mask from your inventory.

The figures in the room continue to mill around, looking right through you, no matter whether you want them to or not.

With nothing else you can do, you continue through the far doorway out of the ballroom. **Turn to page 129.**

THE SMILING WOMAN

By every standard of this age, this woman is beautiful.

There is a gleam in her eye that you cannot place. Is it that she is an intruder, too? Does she recognize you? Or does she simply like the look of you? "I've been waiting for someone to ask me to dance," she says sweetly. She's so beautiful—you wonder why nobody is talking to her. "And the dancing is just about to begin."

You find yourself already speaking, asking her to dance.

In the room with the music, she moves carefully and elegantly, her feet exactly where they should be, her dress fanning out as she spins. Your eyes are on the teeth of her lovely smile.

Moving close into a stance where her hand rests at your hip, she guides you through the steps. As the dance ends, she leans toward you. In a low voice, she asks to speak with you privately, nodding toward a small door that heads off the main room. She is still smiling, placid.

This may not be the way up toward the tower, but you have a strong feeling that it would be good to talk to her. And don't you need all the help you can get?

As you follow her into the side chamber, her shadow seems to ripple strangely, stretching and pulling as if growing and distorting out of the corner of your eye.

"Are you alright?" she asks, gentle and warm, and you assure her you are. When you glance back at her long shadow, flickering in the candlelight on the far wall, nothing seems amiss. "I don't know that I've seen you before, out in society," she says sweetly. "I wonder what you're doing at the ball?"

You're not sure what she means by this but think it would be best to keep quiet. Her smile stretches wider at your lack of reply. "I can give you a gift," she says, stepping closer. You find yourself unable to move or look away. "Whatever it is you want here, this gift can help you."

You feel the warmth of her as she leans into your arms and watch her eyelashes flutter closed. She seems perfectly human, and lovely. She draws closer, as if to kiss you. This woman has been nothing but kind, you think—and even if something were wrong, playing along *could* be to your benefit.

> Try to **step away** and politely excuse yourself. Turn to <u>page 113.</u>
> **Let the smiling woman kiss you**. Turn to <u>page 115.</u>

- **If your logic is 3 or below and you have a weapon,** you can also **choose** to **draw your weapon.** Turn to <u>page 114.</u>

STEP AWAY FROM THE SMILING WOMAN

The woman seems confused and a little crestfallen as you pull away. You think perhaps she is not used to anyone turning her down. She looks down at the floor, shyly.

You wonder if what you saw of her shadow—what you *thought* you saw of her shadow—was the magic of the tower affecting the room itself. There's so much magic here—it would make sense if things like shadows could be affected. Besides, perhaps *she* would be a valuable ally if the shadows turn on you.

"Oh," she breathes quietly. "I thought—I'm sorry if I was mistaken?" She still hovers close to you, her cheeks a little flushed, her eyes bright and interested, locked on yours.

"If you *do* like me, I promise I can give you a gift that will help you, if you just trust me."

Her eyes are *very* bright, her interest in you unwavering. She seems unwilling to elaborate on the gift without some confirmation of your affection.

> Make your excuses and leave the room, returning to move through the crowd. **Turn to page 103.**

> **Let the smiling woman kiss you.** Turn to page 115.

STRIKE THE SMILING WOMAN

Some deep impulse makes you step back, drawing your blade. The distant music sounds distorted in your ears—and you notice the door behind you is closed.

The smiling woman does not flinch or move away at the sight of a weapon. Her smile only widens and widens, stretching and extending as she opens her mouth. For a moment you're frozen as her jaw seems to gape, unhinging as her face unfurls, peeling back to reveal a great maw within. Fleshy protrusions twist sinewy along rows upon rows of teeth that descend in a wet, alien spiral into the pulsing throat.

And then the huge mouth lunges toward you like a snake. The human arms and body hang limp like a doll the creature is wearing around as a costume. Blind instinct kicks in as you sweep your weapon toward it. Your blade catches on flesh, but the thing still pushes forward toward you, cavernous mouth hanging open as if to envelop your face.

- If your strength is 5 or above:

You can shove the thing back roughly enough that it stumbles and falls backward, giving you just enough time to wrench the door open and run back into the main room, stowing your weapon as you go. **Turn to page 110.**

- If your strength is 4 or below:

The thing overpowers you. Your blade cuts into the gummy flesh of the mouth, but the creature seems hardly to notice as the human arms spring back to life and push you with impossible force up against the wall.

Subtract 2 from your stamina as you feel her fingers clench and bruise. (If your stamina drops to zero, her hands move to your throat, crushing it swiftly.)

Mandibles extend from the strange flesh to crawl over your cheeks and sink your face into the churning mouth. You try to scream into the darkness of the throat, but hear and remember nothing as the creature takes you, twisting your organs to its shape.

When you emerge from the room, you feel warm and contented, as if waking from a good dream. There is a beautiful woman on your arm, face split in a wide smile. None of the guests in the room give you a second glance. They cannot see the way she has changed you—and when you try to think about it, the things you remember are a dance and a beautiful darkness. The woman is still smiling as she leads you to a place where you can easily continue upward and bids you farewell. But although your reflection is the same, something now slumbers within you—a gift.

Gain the status: *bearer of gifts*.
Your **strength and agility** both **increase by two.**

Turn to page 146.

A KISS FROM THE GIFTED ONE

With a sweet, calm smile, her face unfurls. Wet, alien protrusions line rows of teeth sunk into pulsing gums and sinews, an architecture of fleshy fractals that seem to spiral down into her throat. All you can think is how beautiful she is inside.

The creature kisses you, mandibles crawling over your cheeks to sink your face into the churning mouth.

You sigh into the darkness as the thing twists your organs to its shape.

When you emerge from the room, you feel warm and contented, as if waking from a good dream. There is a beautiful woman on your arm, looking contentedly back at you, face split in a wide smile.

None of the guests in the room give you a second glance. They cannot see the way she has changed you—and you find it difficult to remember what's different anyway. When you try to think about it, the things you remember are a dance and a beautiful darkness.

You resolve to continue toward the top of the tower, and the woman is still smiling as she leads you to a place where you can easily continue upward and bids you farewell. But although your reflection is the same, something now slumbers within you—a gift.

> **Gain the status:** *bearer of gifts*.
> Your **strength and agility** both **increase by two**.

Turn to **page 146.**

THE WOMAN WITH THE SILVER HAIR

"I don't know *anyone* here, do you?" the woman asks brightly as you approach within earshot, her cheeks round as she grins at you. She wears a finely-woven silver shirt that matches the unnatural metallic sheen to her hair, with fine lines like writing seeming to sew themselves slowly across its folds in a pattern of leaves. As you watch, the pattern grows incrementally as the lines continue in pulses like heartbeats. As you come closer you can see her long eyelashes are also painted silver, bright against her dark skin.

You smile and agree you don't know many people here, and she launches into two witty anecdotes. The first involves a faux pas in a country where nodding turned out to be a terrible insult, and the second is about being caught in the rain, having packed completely the wrong clothes for the weather in this city. The stories are well-rehearsed, amusing without being outrageous, and pitched perfectly to be light and forgettable at a party.

Stories out of the way, she leans forward to ask, "Are you invited to this sort of thing often?"

You try to tell her you're not used to this sort of party in a way that avoids prompting more questions, but she watches curiously as you reply. Her eyes crinkle as her grin seems to become more genuine, and she turns to talking about the spellbinder princess.

Her tone is inviting, almost gossipy—"*I* heard she stops people getting hold of dangerous magical objects. But then some people say she only confiscates things she wants to get her hands on herself! I've no idea if it's true. What do you think of her?"

She watches expectantly for your reply—you find it hard to tell whether she approves of the inquisitors' strict rule and confiscations or not.

> **Tell her you approve of the princess**—you think her inquisitors' rule is tough but fair, since uncontrolled magic can be dangerous in the wrong hands. **Turn to page 117.**

> **Tell her you disapprove of the princess**—that her inquisitors seem to keep magic from ordinary people as a way of maintaining control. **Turn to page 118.**

> **Deflect the question and compliment her eyes instead**. Parties are meant for flirting, right? **Turn to page 119.**

> **If your logic is 5 or above,** you notice her hair glistens with unusually strong magic and can **choose** to ask her about it instead. **Turn to page 120.**

TELL HER YOU APPROVE OF THE PRINCESS

"Of *course*," she says, eyes wide and serious.

She goes on to tell you a story about a magical ring. Once a fairly harmless protection charm, its power grew when the wearer moved to a new and more magical city, and anyone with even the slightest annoyance with him would suddenly show up with gruesome injuries. Finally, the wearer was killed and the ring thrown into the ocean by the frightened townspeople. She ends the story saying somberly that much worse could have happened—and if the spellbinder princess had been around back then, the whole thing would have been avoided.

Turning and seeing the minor spellbinder now standing alone, she excuses herself graciously, telling you they've conversed by letter and she must speak to them for propriety's sake. She whirls away in a cloud of shimmering dust from her shirt before you realize she never gave you her name.

Watching the threads weaving spellbound lines across the back of her shirt, you spend a moment wondering whether she's really so disapproving about magic—before moving through the now-thinning crowd to the far door.

Turn to page 129.

TELL HER YOU DISAPPROVE OF THE PRINCESS

As you express your disapproval for the spellbinder princess, she listens with a new eagerness.

"Hmm," she muses, eyes bright. "Makes you wonder what might happen if all these objects were back in the hands of the common people. But I hear the tower is full of dangerous magic to prevent anyone reaching her . . ."

You watch the woman carefully but think it safe to nod in reply, and you ask carefully what sort of dangers people say there might be.

The woman with the silver hair—you realize she's been careful not to tell you her name—leads you toward the doorway to lean casually on the wall. She tells you in a voice too quiet for anyone else to hear that the spellbinder princess doesn't even want people to *know* about the sort of magic she has access to, to ward them off climbing the tower. "She wants the barriers to seem so strange, they may be impenetrable—but the truth is that if *she* can traverse it, so could most people, if they keep their heads."

She glances down at the strange markings making neat little patterns across her shirt, and tells you she has to go—but first she shakes your hand in farewell, letting a little golden plum drop from one of her sleeves into your hand with a wink.

　　　+ Add a **small golden plum** to your inventory.

"I have heard people say to avoid any sign of falling snow—and to stay away from the caves," she says in a low voice, before she moves, shimmering, through the crowd. You're not sure what insight she has but file the information away carefully in your mind.

You're close enough to the far doorway now to step easily through.

Turn to <u>page 129.</u>

SPARKLING CONVERSATION

- If your charisma is 4 or above:

You manage to compliment her smoothly in a way that makes her slightly roll her eyes. She politely talks to you for a little while longer about the weather, telling you a story about being recommended completely the wrong shoes for wet cobblestoned streets, but she's a little shorter with you, as if slightly tense or bored. At the first opportunity, she excuses herself graciously to speak to somebody else. She's whirled away in a cloud of shimmering dust from her shirt before you realize she never gave you her name or can wonder why she asked about the princess. At least from here you can easily make it through the far door. **Turn to <u>page 129.</u>**

- If your charisma is 3 or below:

You deliver a clumsy compliment about her eyes that makes you cringe as soon as it's out of your mouth, but she laughs good-naturedly at the clearly unpracticed line, saying you really were telling the truth—you don't seem used to this sort of society.

She asks whether you are from the city below rather than the court, then, and if so, how you came by an invitation? She says it in a casual voice but with keen eyes, and you swallow, mouth turning dry as you wonder how to reply. You tell her you are from the city below, thinking that's safest, but can't think of anything further to say to explain your presence.

Sensing your discomfort, she changes tack but seems to continue to push forward, saying how interested she'd be to hear the opinion of someone from the region but not the court on the reign of the spellbinder princess and her confiscations. You get the feeling she wants you to express your distaste for the policy but can't get a clear read on why.

> **Tell her you approve of the spellbinder princess**—that you think the inquisitors' rule is tough but fair, since uncontrolled magic can be so dangerous in the wrong hands. **Turn to <u>page 117.</u>**

> **Tell her you disapprove of the spellbinder princess**—that you think the inquisitors go too far, deliberately keeping magic from the common people as a way of maintaining control. **Turn to <u>page 118.</u>**

SILVER HAIR

The bright metallic silver of her hair is certainly magic, and difficult magic—a curious and unusual sight here in the kingdoms, where spellbinding is largely restricted. You also wonder why she was invited if she doesn't know anyone.

You mention that her hair is a fascinating piece of spellbinding and must be very difficult to maintain. Her eyes light up at the acknowledgment, and she begins to tell you the method she's been developing to keep the spell active for as long as possible.

As you discuss the magic, she seems satisfied by your reactions, perhaps assured you will not report her, and her guard relaxes. From the way she talks, you begin to suspect she's from a group practicing magic outside the official registered college of spellbinders—not explicitly outlawed but often eliminated by inquisitors on invented or spurious charges. You wonder how she got her hands on an invitation.

When she expresses earnestly how many people want to get hold of some of the magical artifacts in the requisition room, you think it's safe to hint that you may be one of them. She nods fervently, steering you away from people nearby to murmur more quietly. "Some say there's a reason the tower—and then the whole *city*—was built here: a *fracture* up in the air above, a split in reality that leads to the space Between worlds. Reality bends more easily the closer you get to one. That's why you get miles of magical dead zones in some places, whereas in others—" she leaves the sentence unfinished, gesturing around at the lanterns floating overhead and the sheen of her hair.

"*Some* people have gathered measurements consistent with the gate being inside the tower itself." She says this meaningfully, glancing down at the threads making their slow winding way across her shirt—you realize with awe they must be coded readings of some kind, recording data in thread faster and slower as the magic waxes and wanes when she moves around the keep.

She tells you anyone trying to get to the top of the tower might have to go *through* the space Between worlds. She herself has been inside a fracture, but only once. "Even for the few who know most about it, the Between is a strange and difficult place to navigate. Anyone who *did* find themself there ought to stay away from any hint of falling snow and caves. And above all, keep a hold of themself."

Glancing down at her shirt again, she looks up with a smile, grasping your shoulder warmly. "I have to move. Good luck." She shakes your hand in farewell, smoothly letting a little golden plum drop from one of her sleeves into your hand with a wink.

+ Add a **small golden plum** to your inventory.

You watch her move effortlessly through the crowd to another corner of the room to strike up another conversation and make your way through the now-thinning crowd out of the room. **Turn to <u>page 129.</u>**

THE DIGNITARIES' TABLE

A man with pale skin and a bushy red beard welcomes you into the group as you approach and hands you a glass of the blue wine that's just been opened, with a gesture that slops a little onto the very fine brocade on his chest. He cries out something that sounds like "the more the merrier," if it was said a little slurred and in an accent that sounds like you have a mouthful of marbles.

Looking around, you see most of the group has some kind of military insignia and seems as if they may have already had a lot to drink—another broad white man in a similar vest has a face flushed entirely red, two thin figures in matching uniforms giggle against a wall in *extremely* relaxed poses, and one woman is leaning so far over the table you suspect she might be propping herself up to keep herself standing. "A toast!" she yells, as everyone in the circle raises their blue glasses high, and you quickly try to mirror their movement.

You glance to your left to watch when the person next to you will raise their glass to their lips, so you can copy them, and notice a tall woman with light brown skin and a broad smile who stands a little more upright than the others.

> **If you have the status** *Tamar's Ally,* you realize it's Lady Tamar. **Turn to page 122.**
> **Otherwise,** turn to page 123.

LADY TAMAR'S TOAST

Lady Tamar is wearing a smile that you think doesn't quite meet her bright, shrewd eyes. She turns toward you and nods, raising her glass along with the others and revealing the edge of a small tattoo at her wrist where the cuff slides back.

The woman at the table is giving a long speech about a new treaty that will be signed the next day—she mentions the spellbinder princess selling them magical technology that will mean great advances in warfare. As she does it, you see Tamar's grin twitch a little wider, in a way you think holds no mirth whatsoever. Her grip on the glass is tight. Everyone else in the circle looks delighted as the speech-giver alludes to how wide a scale of destruction and massacre may now easily be inflicted.

Lady Tamar is still smiling brightly as the speech ends, but as you begin to raise the glass to your lips with the others, she glances at you, catching your eye. You think you see her shake her head ever so slightly as the others drain their glasses. Pausing, you watch as she tips her own glass back—you notice her lips stay firmly closed against the liquid. You do the same, making sure not to let any of the wine into your mouth.

She excuses herself, clapping you on the back as she leaves. You notice the girl pouring the wine has vanished, too.

There's a cry as the woman at the table knocks her empty glass off the edge, and some of the others in the group fall about laughing. You notice one of the thin figures seems to reel as they place the glass back on the table, slumping against the wall and beginning to slide down it.

You put your still-full glass down, slipping back through the crowd to the far door that's now in reach. As you go, you look back at the group—they were all so drunk that people don't seem to notice much of a change. One more staggers to the floor, sitting down heavily. The howls of laughter around him only get louder, but the red in his face seems to have drained right out into a pale, blotchy mess, and he topples over to tug ineffectually at the legs of the woman at the table. Someone else in the group who tried to sit in a chair has missed, breathless laughter wheezing out of them as their legs give out. Next to the table, another now lies unmoving on the floor.

Lady Tamar is nowhere to be seen.

As heads in the crowd turn, you take advantage of the distraction, winding forward toward the far door. Behind, you hear another crash. You suspect the treaty may not be signed tomorrow, after all. **Turn to <u>page 129.</u>**

THE NEW AGE OF WARFARE

The woman at the table begins a long speech about something you can't quite follow—some new treaty which they're here to sign. It seems as if the spellbinder princess is selling some kind of new magical technology to them. It will mean great military advances, she says, and a new age of warfare.

Everyone in the circle raises their glass high and drinks. For a moment, you're frozen, trying to decipher what they were talking about from the fragments you heard. A look from a particularly loud man on the other side of the circle makes you hurry to smile and copy them, raising your glass to drink a small sip—you want to avoid anyone drunkenly drawing attention to you.

But your stomach turns as you piece together what's being said around you—a magic weapon that could wipe entire villages off the map and scour the land. The people in front of you laugh uproariously, thoroughly drunk and happy, apparently thrilled at the prospect of such easy massacres. You notice the tall woman beside you has made her excuses and is now walking away—you don't know the politics of what's going on in any of these nations, but you wonder if she feels as bitterly about it as you do.

You put your glass down without drinking the rest, and excuse yourself before you say something that gives you away. There's a gap in the crowd now, but as you try to move in the direction of the door you're aiming for, you're surprised to find yourself unsteady on your feet. You notice an empty chair at the side of the room and head for it, sitting down heavily.

You rest for a moment, but the feeling does not fade—you wonder what was in the wine and find yourself extremely glad you had only a tiny sip.

+ Lower your strength score by 2.

Glancing back toward the table of dignitaries, you see one or two of them also seem to be reeling, one of the men staggering to sit down heavily on the floor as the others shriek with laughter around him. Their glasses are empty. It doesn't look that different from the drunken spectacle they were presenting before—and now you think about it, you wonder who got them so drunk in the first place. The tall woman is nowhere to be seen now. You wonder if they'll last long enough to sign the treaty in the morning, after all.

As you watch another member of the group slide down the wall, head lolling unnervingly, you decide it would be best not to linger at the ball.

You find you're able to control your legs enough to stand, but you feel weak and wrung out. The howls of laughter have turned a few heads in the crowd, and you take advantage of the distraction to walk, slow and shaky, out of the far door. **Turn to page 129.**

THE MINOR SPELLBINDER

As you approach, you see the figures with the spellbinder are wearing exceptionally delicate tunics with the most elaborate decoration you've ever seen. The cut looks like men's formal dress, but from one of the distant northern kingdoms—with carefully matched colors you think must indicate they are a couple.

The sight of two men together publicly is much rarer here at the ball than in the lower city, and you realize the gap in the crowd is due to courtiers in local fashions giving them a wide berth. All seem unwilling to show anything but deference to powerful foreigners, whatever their customs—but in a few, you suspect a schooled politeness in their expressions, overlaying a sinister venom that flows beneath and behind closed doors. Most of the visiting guests seem to pay the couple little mind, however, and the spellbinder speaks to them eagerly.

- If you're wearing fine clothes or a mask:
The minor spellbinder steps back graciously at your approach to allow you into the circle. You gather she must be used to people—especially travelers—asking her questions about magic. **Turn to page 126.**

- Otherwise:
As you approach, the taller of the two men scowls at you in distaste, turning away and trying to block you out of the group before you even arrive.

> **If your charisma is 3 or below,** it takes you a moment to think of how to introduce yourself without giving too much away. By the time you step forward, the man has gone back to asking the spellbinder absorbing questions, pointedly ignoring you in a way that would now be difficult to interrupt. One or two people notice you hovering, and you're still some way from the door—you decide it would be safest to wander back into the crowd. **Turn to page 103.**

> **If your charisma is 4 or above,** you move forward and quickly introduce yourself by a fake name, addressing the spellbinder rather than the people she's standing with. You tell her how interested you would *also* be to hear about her work, and her face lights up in a smile at the prospect. It's a little abrupt, but you've inserted yourself into the circle in a way that would be difficult to dismiss. **Turn to page 126.**

ASK ABOUT WHAT HAPPENED TO YOUR HOUSE

You carefully describe some of the things that happened to your house—the white feathered tree, the bubbling tiles, the cracks through to a great void—without being too specific about where you saw them. You heard a story, you say, a friend came across a place like it.

The spellbinder replies excitedly that this is exactly the kind of thing she's been talking about—marks of reality growing weaker in the places close to the Between. "These are just the sort of thing that happen near a gate—or near an artifact that draws on the Between and bends reality around it," she tells you.

You explain that the things you described are new, and ask, in a voice you struggle to keep level, what could have caused it. It was a house, you blurt out—a house in a town your friend passed through.

The spellbinder pauses—noticing your distress, you think—and tells you someone must have done a great piece of magic there or brought a very powerful artifact.

Someone went missing, you tell her in a whisper, unable to stem the flow of questions. Someone in the house, you say. But there was no body. Where did they go?

The spellbinder is gentle when she tells you she doesn't know. She says that she's sorry. Her hand strokes along yours, something that might have been a comfort or a thrill in another situation—another life, one where you weren't consumed with guilt over what happened to your father because you were gone. You could have stopped it, you think. You're sure you could.

"Most likely, your friend is gone," the spellbinder is telling you. "But there's a chance that they could be . . . *in* the Between."

Her eyes are bright now. She's still holding onto your hand but seems not to notice. "I've never been," she tells you in a low voice that turns conspiratorial. "Most people who go in never come out. But I've always wanted to. And according to rumors. . . ." She tips her head up in the direction of the tower. "We're not far from a gate, now."

You barely remember to thank her as you pull your hand away and stride toward the far doorway, determined to make your way into the tower.

Turn to <u>page 129.</u>
Turn to page 129.

THE PRINCE AND THE SPELLBINDER

As you move into the circle, the smaller man gives you a little bow. He has long hair, a fine-boned face, and introduces himself as Prince Mihai. You can't quite place his accent or read his face, but there seems to be genuine friendliness under his impeccable court manners.

When you try to ask politely about which kingdom he's from, the scowling man on the prince's arm introduces himself as the prince consort but without giving his name—you think this must be meant as a snub. Ignoring you, he then returns his attention to the minor spellbinder, prompting her to continue what she was saying about something he calls "the Between."

"It's the space *between* the worlds, you see," she's saying, "and there are places in the world—some people call them gates, ruptures, fractures—where you can actually *get* to the Between."

The scowling man continues to question her and interrogate her replies, asking about how the gates are made. Prince Mihai is too well-mannered to look truly bored, but you see him trying to catch the eye of someone carrying trays of drinks, and wonder how long this discussion has been going on.

As the spellbinder expands on theories about gates to the Between being a natural phenomenon, the scowling man still seems unsatisfied. "The closer you get to the gates," she says excitedly, "the more reality bends and warps, and the easier it is to do magic. Some think the places where magic is more difficult may simply be too *far* from any gate to draw on the energies of the Between."

The Prince is draining a glass of peach wine as the scowling man impatiently lets go of his arm to address the spellbinder more directly, almost frantic. "But *could* one open a gate, theoretically? *Can* it be done? Does it have to be done by a spellbinder, or could there be some sort of object that would let anyone do it, some sort of *key-*"

- **If you're playing the acolyte, turn straight to <u>page 128.</u>**

- **Otherwise:**

The spellbinder tips her head to one side and replies that it's *such* an interesting question, but all theoretical. If it *were* possible, it would be so dangerous that the person making the gate may well not survive. She continues on about expeditions that have been made into the Between—some say the spellbinder princess has been there herself—but the scowling man seems to have lost interest. He tugs at Prince Mihai's sleeve, who gives you an apologetic bow as he's steered away into the crowd. You wonder how long this man will last as the current prince consort.

> **If you're playing the sailor, you can choose** to ask about what happened to your house. **Turn to <u>page 125.</u>**
> **Otherwise,** you thank the spellbinder—the movement of people means you now have a clear path to walk easily through the far door. Turn to <u>page 129.</u>

THE PRINCE CONSORT'S QUESTIONS

As the scowling man's mouth shapes the word in his language that translates to 'key,' the world slows around you. Unbidden, your head snaps fully toward him.

The spellbinder's voice has dulled to a drone, merely background noise against the roar in your ears: *The Key. The Key, the Key.*

Now that you're looking for it, you recognize the frantic note in the man's eyes. At his side, Prince Mihai seems to watch his partner with resigned disappointment—you wonder if he used to scowl all the time. Thinking of the style of their clothes, from a country much closer to your own, you consider how far they must have traveled to come to this ball. You wonder if the scowling man arranged it, using the prince's connections and dragging his partner with him.

The spellbinder has gone off on a tangent about expeditions that have been made into the Between—but the scowling man seems to have lost interest. He tugs at Prince Mihai's sleeve, making a motion to try to and leave.

"Have you ever been to the Great Library?" you think, and then the three have stopped to stare at you. You realize you said it aloud, clear and calm in a language they can understand, cutting right into the flow of speech. Your voice rang like a bell and sounded unfamiliar in your throat.

The scowl has left the man's face for the first time, his eyes widening as he looks at you. You wrench your gaze away from his to speak to the spellbinder, trying to return to the normal world. You explain you're an archivist there and how few books there are about the Between. The spellbinder princess is so secretive about her knowledge, you say—but as the minor spellbinder replies to you with interest, you can feel the Prince Consort's eyes upon you.

You know the answer is yes: He has been to the Great Library. Four people read the book on the restricted shelves below the main halls. Only three were found dead, one left unaccounted for. This man has read about *the Key.* Whether he was consumed with a desire to know about it and his search led him to the library, or whether he happened upon the book in idle curiosity and sparked a madness, he *knows.* As the spellbinder continues on, his eyes stay fixed on you. He knows why you're here. He knows you've read it, too.

The prince consort does not move as you calmly thank the spellbinder, hands shaking a little, and cross the rest of the distance through the crowd to the far door. But you are sure his eyes are on you as you slip from the room.

Gain the status: *followed.*

You head into the corridor beyond. **Turn to page 129.**

THE CORRIDOR BEYOND THE BALLROOM

Ahead of you, a corridor curves around in what you estimate must be the direction of the tower, and you think you can see stairs beyond.

On the wall is a long line of faded portraits, depicting each of the royal spellbinders. It ends in a painting of the current spellbinder princess: a pale girl with dark hair, much younger than her predecessors. She is not wearing the robes of office or surrounded by books or equipment like the others—as if the painting were originally made for some other purpose. She looks sullenly out of the frame, as if watching the hallway.

Down a corridor to your left, you see one door is slightly ajar, and you can see an empty room with something shimmering on the far wall.

> **Investigate the room. Turn to <u>page 131.</u>**

To your right is an open doorway, where you can see a room with long tables of food laid out for the guests after the dancing. It has a ribbon over the door to mark it off-limits, but it seems to be empty. Huge tapestries cover the walls, and food and silver lay unguarded on the tables.

> **Duck into the room with the tapestries. Turn to <u>page 130.</u>**

> **Ascend the stairs. Turn to <u>page 146.</u>**

THE TAPESTRY ROOM

Your footsteps echo on the stone as you enter the long hall. A fire crackles in the hearth, and you hear the distant clink of glasses and laughter from the ball in the next room. Otherwise, all is silent.

On the tables, dishes and cutlery have been laid ready. The dishes are empty, but bottles of all shapes and sizes and jugs of water sit nestled between table decorations and huge bowls of fruit, waiting for the guests to filter in at the dinner hour.

Take any of the following, which you slip into your pockets to add to your inventory:

> + **A golden peach** from a fruit bowl on the high table.
> + **A carving knife (weapon)** next to a space left clear for a platter of meat.

A huge tapestry covers most of the wall on one side, faded with age. It depicts some kind of parade or procession.

The figures carry flags and instruments and march toward an archway picked out in silver thread, giving an impression of unreality: a glowing white landscape within. Though the images seem mostly symbolic, the scenery reminds you of the steep climb up to the city, mountains rising from the rocky heath below. You frown as you look over the whole tapestry—the arch stands alone, with nothing on the other side. It's almost as if the figures are joyfully marching into somewhere and never coming out.

To its right, a smaller tapestry shows a coterie of minor spellbinders gathered near the base of the castle you're standing in. Another bright white light is picked out in silver in the same way: a window high in the tower.

> **If you have a logic of 4 or above,** you piece this together with what you've heard of the tower. **Turn to <u>page 132.</u>**

> **Otherwise,** return to <u>page 129.</u>

THE PAINTINGS

The room is empty of furniture and strangely sparsely decorated compared to the main hall. A bare window looks out onto the night, and the only other things you see are three elaborate frames on the far wall.

At first glance, you think they must be mirrors made of different surfaces, reflecting the bare room back at you, shimmering as you approach and the light moves across them. But as you move into the room, you realize you do not appear in the frames yourself. Each is in fact a painting, but no matter what angle you view them from, they seem to reflect the room you're in.

At the back of your mind, you have the distinct sense that there is something stranger still about each painting. The trick is fascinating, and if you draw closer, you could inspect them more carefully.

> **Leave and return to the corridor.** Turn to <u>page 129.</u>

> **Move in closer to inspect the paintings.**
> If your logic is 5 or above, **turn to <u>page 133.</u>**
> If your logic is 4 or below, **turn to <u>page 134.</u>**

A JOYOUS PROCESSION

The figures in the tapestry carry banners with a symbol you recognize. You've seen it carved in the small shrines at the side of the roads leading up to the city, where spellbound candles flicker in hollowed out rocks, strips of white fabric covered in scrawled prayers tied around the base of the stone. This is not the religion of the grand cathedrals to the west or the libraries of the north, but a very old faith—something that only survives in the lands around the mountains.

Carved in the shrines, the symbol is a circle with a line passing through it—but on the banners in the tapestry, it's fleshed out with more detail: stitched like a bright crack through the darkness.

The old songs speak of the source of magic as a shining place—a divine gap, a place Between the worlds. You stare at the faces of the figures in the long tapestry, rapturous as they approach the white gate.

You turn to look at the smaller tapestry, where the figure—you recognize him as the first royal spellbinder by the style of the clothing—reaches his hands toward to the sky in triumph. Behind him, the same shining light that the procession disappeared into blazes out from the window in the tower.

Did the first spellbinder coterie somehow have a source of magic, high in the tower—a thing that leads to the gap Between worlds? Or was the tower itself built to its uncanny height to encompass a natural, shining doorway inside?

In the first scene, there's nothing but the gateway at the rocky and desolate foot of the mountains. The city must have been built up *around* the tower, around whatever shining thing the little stitched window in the faded tapestry represents.

An involuntary shiver runs through you, and you move back toward the corridor.

> **Return to page 129.**

EXAMINING THE THREE PATHS

You move closer to each fascinating painting, thoughts of how the enchantment works driving out any thought of your task in the tower for a moment.

The first painting appears to be a pale, silvery mirror, as if light has faded out the canvas. The window is out of frame, but from the light you think it must be a cold, wintry day—there are white specs in the background that look like snow that's blown in. From further back, the scene is rendered perfectly, but when you step closer, the painting looks as though it's been painted on thickly with oils, slathered on with a palette knife—an expensive and tactile method, more experimental than what you've seen before. You realize you've extended your hand, wanting to run your fingers over the rough surface to understand its technique.

> Reach out and touch the first painting—turn to <u>page 136.</u>

The painting in the center looks almost as if it's a reflection on a gold-tinted mirror, spotted with age—the brushstrokes are hazy, suggesting the edges of objects in a soft blur rather than defining them. Squinting, you also see the impressionist haze makes it look as though the room on the inside of the painting has a layer of dust settled over it—perhaps depicting some other unswept version of the space in the future or past. The lighting is warm, as if the painter wanted it to look inviting.

> Reach out and touch the center painting—turn to <u>page 135.</u>

The last painting is sharp and clear, painted with extreme precision down to the grain of the wood. It seems brightly lit, high-contrast—a hyper-realistic style that looks like a summer's day, more detailed than any reflection you've seen in any mirror. You realize you've stepped close to see it better, fingers hovering over the smooth resin coating the canvas, wanting to trace its details.

> Reach out and touch the last painting—turn to <u>page 145.</u>

SENSING THE THREE PATHS

The first painting appears to be a pale, silvery mirror, as if light has faded out the canvas, with specs of snow dancing in the room—but the thick paint looks violent, frantically applied. A shiver runs over you as you approach—something about it reminds you of death, the cold and stillness of a tomb. You feel drawn to it in the same way you can't look away when a terrible accident happens.

> **Give in and touch the first painting—turn to page 136.**

The painting in the center looks almost as if it's a reflection on a gold-tinted mirror, spotted with age—there's something soft about the brushstrokes within. It looks inviting, warm and intriguing. Something about the warm haze of light makes you hear the chink of glasses and low voices—another party, where the guests might be more forthcoming. It looks otherworldly—your gut feeling is of somewhere beyond your own world where you should not linger, but may be able to pass through.

> **Walk into the center painting—turn to page 135.**

The last painting is sharp and clear, something about it almost hyper-real, more detailed than the room itself, somehow. It makes you think of a silvery pool of water you could plunge your face into to see clearly what's underneath. You're sure that if you were to move your head forward, the surface would let you through.

> **Plunge your face into the last painting—turn to page 145.**

FADED GOLD

Suddenly, you are standing in the reflected room, its surfaces coated with a pale dust, thin, filmy cobwebs shimmering in the corners. The world is indistinct, painted in soft, warm strokes. You feel no alarm—only swaddled, safe and comfortable.

- **If you have the status** *unknowable*, remove it—you feel a shift as you cross the threshold into this world, the muscles in your face seeming to relax.

Outside the window, the world seems empty, but a beautiful evening sunlight whispers in through gossamer curtains and seems to fill up all the rooms inside. You follow the sound of soft, soothing voices and laughter into what looks like another version of the ball.

The crowd seems to be made of shadows that look like sunlight—some in party clothes, others in nightgowns and servants' uniforms. As one sweeps past laughing, holding a glass with a golden liquid, you realize she has a rapier stuck clean through her. Some are very old or very sick. You notice whole groups who look as if they were bitten by something with far, far too many teeth, mauled and torn into death. One has a line ringing their neck like a thin necklace where you think they must have been beheaded.

You find most are unable to hold a conversation or cannot respond to you at all. Many only say the same handful of words or sentences over and over about their children or deaths or favorite food, all in the same soft, laughing tones. It's difficult to hold their attention, and most smile indistinctly at an area near your head, not quite making eye contact, and drifting politely away. Those in the most unfamiliar and oldest fashions don't speak at all or murmur without forming words.

As you move through the party, which stretches out both forever and for no time at all, you notice one of the shades, face and body now worn and indistinct like an ancient statue, seems intent on telling you something. Their shadow still wears wisps of uniform of the household staff, and they follow you around, opening their mouth without any sound coming out.

You also notice a more solid figure wrapped in the uniform of a junior spellbinder, leaning against the wall and watching you. He gives you a nod whenever you look his way. Beside him, an old man wrapped in the robes of the royal spellbinder is laughing in a group. The robes' style is twenty or thirty years out of date. You remember the stories of the disappearance of the princess's predecessor. He is pouring a huge bowl of a shining golden liquid from a tap, and is about to start drinking when he spots you and invites you over with enthusiasm.

> Focus your attention—**speak to the ghost in the tattered uniform.** Turn to <u>page 138.</u>
> **Approach the junior spellbinder.** Turn to <u>page 139.</u>
> **Join the laughing royal spellbinder.** Turn to <u>page 143.</u>

VISION OF A COLD FUTURE

Suddenly, your hand is touching the painting, but the room you're in is different.

> - **If you have the status _unknowable_**, remove it—you feel a shift as you cross
> the threshold into this world, your face rough and warm again in the cold air.

The dark window is now broken and shedding a pale daylight into the room. Flecks of white occasionally whistle through in the chill wind, and you can't tell whether they're ash or snow. Outside the window, the world is still and lifeless—and then, like you're in a play with a line being fed to you from the wings, you know:

They are looking for you.

You try to remember what _they_ are but only feel a spike of panic, spurring you out of the door into the crumbling corridor beyond. The rooms of the keep are strangely warped, blasted apart with walls at improbable angles. Most of the ceilings are gone, and looking upward you cannot see the top of the tower—only a few twisted stones hover far above where it used to stand, orbiting a sun-bright halo of blinding white that fills the whole sky and hurts to look at.

You climb through the remains of the ballroom, where rock extrudes impossibly through the floor. Everything is still, coated in cold ash and silent. This world holds nothing for you. When you try to retrace your steps, even the place where you entered through the painting has now gone, heaped in the ashen snow. When you scrabble in the pile, you find the wood has rotted, the frame of the painting crumbled apart, paint dripping from the canvas as if melting in your numbing fingers.

They draw nearer.

You feel it, deep and certain, as if the painting was illustrating a story you'd heard a hundred times before. Their great eyeless heads scan the landscape, scouring the ground. You scramble through the ruins of the keep to find a higher vantage point, to look for any sign of life or shelter.

Laid out ahead of you are the jagged, white-blanketed remains of a broken city. You see the river, waterfalls frozen in blue ice in strange shapes, as if paused mid-explosion, with the sound of trickling deep below. Where the base of the tower once stood, you see a great stone spiral staircase still winds upward, and at the top is a stone archway. It leads out into the air, but it seems to shimmer a little, as if a sheer fabric. The wind screeches by in the dead landscape. Apart from this one glimmer, everything is shades of gray, dark rock and white ash like the surface of the moon.

They are close.

You sprint toward the stairway, sliding on ice, jumping gaps in the corridors where the building falls away into dark crevices of black rock that yawn beneath you and stretch into darkness.

They close in.

- If your agility is 5 or above:
You run frantically ahead, clearing each jump, swerving on the icy stones and throwing open the rotting door to the tower. You take the stairs two at a time as a terrible rumbling approaches that seems to shake the whole landscape, keeping your focus wholly on the glimmering archway ahead. Just as a crack splits the sky and the world seems to gape into night around you, you hurl yourself through the shimmering gate into the raw, pulsing magic beyond. **Turn to page 173.**

- If your agility is 4 or below:
Your ankle twists beneath you as you land awkwardly on the difficult, uneven path. Cursing, you run desperately forward, but you're limping now, leg dragging behind you. In the distance, something is happening to the sky behind the sun-bright crack, the horizon itself reshaping and rising into an impossibly vast figure that you know is moving toward you. It grows in size until it blots out the light, dwarfing the mountains and clouds, too big to see all at once. You watch, transfixed in horror, still at the bottom of the tower as the void opens above you, your hair blowing out behind you as if you faced some immense, hot engine, a mouth in the world that opens and opens until it blots out the sky. You have no time to close your eyes or consider your abandoned task in the tower as you're ripped apart, and forces bigger than you can comprehend wrap you into the course of this future. **Your journey ends here.**

THE GHOST IN THE TATTERED UNIFORM

You turn toward the weathered spirit that tails you, watching their open mouth move as they try to form words. They smile apologetically. People are speaking around you, but you manage to stay focused on this same shade, drawing them a little way out of the crowd until you are alone.

Eventually, they are able to muster a thin, singsong voice and tell you, "We were never allowed to speak of the princess once she started living in the tower."

You remember now—the tower. How could you have forgotten? You have to get into the tower. The sunlit shade is smiling at you but seems intent on delivering the message.

"Everyone was afraid of her; you could see it in their eyes. The queen herself would not see her, nobody would in the end—only a maid named Orla." They say it with an absent smile, a soothing, melodious voice, their hands moving to yours to pull you into a dance. "Orla would knit the princess dolls, and when she came down to see us in the kitchens, she'd tell us that the princess was still herself, underneath—how she would cradle the dolls in her little hands . . . but in the end, the same thing happened to Orla as to all the others. It wasn't enough."

When you try to ask questions, the shade only shakes their head with a smile and drifts back into the crowd to pick up another golden drink, now murmuring the same lines to themself about how everyone was afraid of the princess, but she still played with little dolls.

You try to hold the thought of the tower at the forefront of your mind, but it's difficult—slippery somehow.

- If your logic is 5 or above:
You find a way to write it down, crushing berries into a paste to use as ink on a piece of cloth. You keep it in your hands so whenever you forget and glance down absent-mindedly, you see the word—*tower*. You manage to go look for the tower, leaving the ballroom to explore the quiet rooms of the ghostly, sunlit world. Finally, up a set of stone stairs, you find a strange doorway—and when you walk through, you find yourself back in the real, solid world. **Turn to <u>page 146.</u>**

- Otherwise:
The thought of the tower slips into the back of your mind, and you notice again the other most solid person in the room—the junior spellbinder—and the sunlight ghost of the royal spellbinder next to him, drinking deeply from a huge bowl.

> **Approach the junior spellbinder.** Turn to <u>page 139.</u>
> **Join the laughing royal spellbinder**'s group. Turn to <u>page 143.</u>

THE JUNIOR SPELLBINDER

You head toward the edge of the room, where a figure wrapped in the uniform of a junior spellbinder is leaning against the wall and watching you. "You're alive," he says with interest, in a voice worn less smooth and melodious than the others, his fingers only ghostly and sunlit at the very tips. "Would you like to stay that way?'"

He reaches out to shake your hand, and as you take it absent-mindedly, a cool energy flows from his hand into yours.

Increase your stamina by 2.

"Did you try to come here?" he asks, and you have to think for a moment before you remember you're trying to get into the tower. You shake your head, sluggishly.

Watching the royal spellbinder laughing with the other shades and drinking from the huge bowl, you ask why so many of the shades won't speak to you.

The junior spellbinder hesitates before telling you that most will only speak to you if you have one of their drinks. He manages to turn his soft tones serious to advise against it. "If you want to get out of here and back to your life, you have to leave the ballroom," he tells you.

The shades around you look so happy, so content—swirling through their warm, soft party until they fade out into the scenery, with no cares or responsibilities. You try to hold the thought of your goal in your mind, but it's so difficult—everything is always so difficult—and staying here would be so easy and lovely. As you watch the junior spellbinder, your words seem heavy on your tongue, and you find it difficult to speak. It would be easier to stay silent.

- **If your charisma is 3 or above,** you manage to force yourself to **ask the junior spellbinder for help. Turn to page 140.**

> **Otherwise,** you find yourself turning toward the royal spellbinder and stepping into his circle. Turn to page 143.

THE SPELLBINDER'S APPRENTICE

At your plea for help, the junior spellbinder shakes his head, frowning, as if to dislodge water from his ears, and takes you by the arm. With some effort, he walks you slowly out of the ballroom into the empty corridor beyond, where the golden sunlight is less intense. You feel as if you're suddenly more able to breathe, your head a little clearer. "What did you say?" he says, bleary and a little frustrated. "It's so hard to think—even with training in magic, I can feel it all slipping away. Every memory. I wonder if I should just let go."

You manage to remember that you're trying to get to the top of the tower, and—not recalling any reason why not to—tell him about what you're looking for in the room of magical objects.

"But there can't be a spellbinder princess. There is only *one* royal spellbinder, and he's in the room behind us . . ." he says, frowning with concentration as he tries to join each idea in his head. "He comes here into the golden place as often as he wants because time flows differently here. When we go back, no time will have passed."

He remains still for a long time and then seems to look down at his now-old-fashioned robes of office, running his hands along them. You ask him about how the royal spellbinder came here.

"Every royal spellbinder lives in the tower. I serve the fourteenth. Magic is stronger here, so he sometimes brings spellbound objects here for experiments. And sometimes, he finds places and things in the tower that the magic of the fracture has seeped into." He looks toward the door you first came from. "Once, he found a painting. It had been left too long in the tower. The people who died in the castle started to go inside instead of to . . . wherever people are supposed to go."

Now you remember the golden painting more clearly—the way you came in. You try to remember the ball and the requisition room.

"He used to visit it, to study it—he said he had enough power to come and go when he liked. But he was finding it harder. So he started bringing his apprentice—" He pauses, and then, the revelation dawning on his face, "Me. He brought me in here, to make sure he could still leave. But . . ."

There's a slow horror creeping into his eyes as he looks up at you. "You have to get out." You nod, trying to hold the image of the way you came from clear in your mind. You manage to stand up, heavy as if from sleep, to make your way toward it. "Wait," he says, sunlight-tipped fingers scrubbing over his face. "You're going *up* the tower. I can show you a shortcut. Right to the fracture."

> **Follow the junior spellbinder. Turn to <u>page 141.</u>**
> **Go back out the way you came**, while you still can. **Turn to <u>page 142.</u>**

THE SPELLBINDER'S SHORTCUT

The junior spellbinder holds his ghostly hand out toward you, almost childlike, and leads you away from the golden, sunlit ballroom, up a wide staircase.

Everything is still soft, blurred, as if the colors were painted in indistinct brushstrokes, and the details grow less distinct the higher you go up the stairs, looser and breaking apart. You pass shimmering doorways that look out onto other places you can't make sense of, but the spellbinder shakes his head thickly, continuing upward. Each step seems like an effort for him, his limbs heavy and sleepy, and the higher you climb, the more his body seems insubstantial, ghostlike in the shadows.

Eventually, the paint strokes grow thin and you're walking through total darkness, bodies still lit up as if in warm evening sunlight but feet slapping against stone stairs that are invisible below you. It feels as if a long time passes, but finally, you see a white, shining door above you. As you draw nearer, the last sunlit brushstrokes that once made up the junior spellbinder slump against the stairs, now only a faint smudge.

"Go on. You're still alive—" the last remnants of his voice drift toward you from the place where his mouth was. He lies, ghostly and disintegrating, swirling into the soft darkness of the painting around him like a sigh, as you continue to drag yourself up toward the light of the doorway. "Perhaps you can stay that way."

You step through the door and find yourself at the top of a stone stairway. **Turn to page 167.**

OUT OF THE GOLDEN

You make it back to the room with the painting, and each step you take feels a little easier. Your limbs are heavy, dragging, but you manage to plunge forward into the frame where the ordinary world waits on the other side.

And suddenly you're standing back in a room, bare of furniture, where three paintings hang on a wall behind you. You do not look back at them as you hurry away, propelling yourself forward with force and closing the door behind you.

Back in the corridor, you can hear the ball—the ordinary, real ball—still in full swing. You can see people milling around through the doorway. No time seems to have passed.

The memories of golden sunlight fade into something dreamlike as you return, determined, to the stairs to the tower.

Turn to <u>page 146.</u>

THE LAST ROYAL SPELLBINDER

You open your mouth to ask the royal spellbinder if he's who you think he is, but he claps you on the back before you can begin. "Have a drink!" he says in his warm soothing voice, body half turned to sunlight.

Was there something about a tower you were supposed to ask him? "Have a drink." He says it again, holding out the large bowl. The group of bright shadows around you is smiling at you, keen and eager to watch you drink.

You accept. What could be the harm? Just one drink.

The drink makes you feel warm and hazy, comfortable. What a wonderful evening! You smile and laugh with the guests, and when they tell you how charming you are, you're so pleased. Finally, a place where you can rest—what was it that was so urgent you'd been doing, anyway? The details feel indistinct to you. Surely if it were important, you'd remember.

The old spellbinder offers you another drink, and before you know what you're doing, you notice you've extended a hand, one that seems almost to shimmer with gold at the fingertips. Behind the spellbinder's head, you can see a doorway, dark and clear. Beyond it is a long corridor, with stairs leading upward, where the tinge of golden haze seems to fade.

They turn you away, telling you, face full of concern, that the path ahead would be difficult, painful and tiring. Better to stay here. Your limbs feel so heavy. Their voices are soothing.

- **If your strength is 5 or above, you can choose** to force your limbs into motion toward the doorway you came from. **Turn to <u>page 142.</u>**

> **Otherwise,** you find yourself unable to move toward the doorway. Why would you want to, anyway? You rejoin the party. **Turn to <u>page 144.</u>**

JOIN THE PARTY IN THE GOLDEN HALLS

The party lasts for a lifetime or just a heartbeat, you're not sure. Everything is easy and lovely.

The junior spellbinder leans against the wall, watching you sadly. You don't understand why he looks this way when nobody has to—when everything could be so wonderful so easily. And so you invite him over, circling your hands around his, drawing him into a soft embrace as he accepts a glass from the smiling group around him.

After a few hours (days?) his face has softened, blurred around the edges into a smile, and he dances serene and absent-minded like the rest of you, accepting a glass from the shadow of a laughing old man. Your hands turn to sunlight and all your memories of your purpose, the tower and the people and things you cared about unravel into the undefined, into muffled cotton wool sensations.

You laugh and dance. You become the light of the evening sun and the shining dust that drapes the corridors around the ghostly ballroom, turning them all golden.

Your journey ends here.

THE CRISP REFLECTION

Suddenly, you're standing in a double of the room you emerged from, this time hyperreal and strangely full of contrast, so that you can see clearly the texture of the stone underfoot and each whorl and divot of the wooden door beyond.

> **- If you have the status *unknowable*,** remove it.
> You feel a shift as you cross the threshold into this world, your face feeling real and warm under your fingertips again.

You're standing in the same room as before, but flipped as if viewed in a mirror. The frame in front of you now seems to lead back to the room you were just standing in.

In the middle picture, you now see a muzzy haze of gold and laughter where figures at a ball are laughing and rotting, their faces like dessicated corpses and their clothes tattered. In the last, you see a whirl of snow across a desolate horizon, and beyond it, colossal figures that seem stretched and tall, standing the size of mountains.

You head cautiously out into the corridor of the hyperreal painting. You see a room where treasures lie on the table unguarded and a gray mist emanates from the tapestries. Around the corner, you can see the figures at the ball, strangely clear and detailed, and occasionally flickering for a moment so a different image seems to be superimposed over the top of some of them.

You see a smiling woman and suddenly, with perfect clarity like the chime of a bell, see a flash of something red and wet, gleaming with teeth. A straight-backed, scarred general and the woman attending to her suddenly take the shape of birds and then return to normal. You blink, and the man holding a glass of blue wine across from her is now standing on a smoking battlefield, corpses strewn at his feet as he looks about triumphantly, arms soaked up to the elbows in blood. He crumples to the ground, blue wine seeping from his mouth, and the battlefield disappears.

Your head is starting to ache and reel from the shifting images and the grooves and details visible in every surface. You hurry back to the room of paintings and stretch out a hand back into the ordinary world, and find yourself gasping back in the room.

Seemingly unscathed, you return to the corridor beyond.

Turn to <u>page 129.</u>

THE BASE OF THE TOWER

You emerge onto a wide staircase that eventually turns to slowly spiral upward. You realize with excitement that you must have made it into the base of the tower.

You begin to climb. Eventually you pass a window that shows the evening outside. The lights of the lower city twinkle far below, and you can make out the faint sounds of music from the ball in the keep. Rain has begun to fall, and the dark clouds still cluster above, seeming to turn slowly around the higher reaches of the tower.

You continue to climb and climb. You see no further windows but continue on for so long that you're sure you should be getting close to the top, and must be up in the clouds by now. Time seems to extend as you hear nothing but the sound of your footfalls on the worn stone. Once, you think you recognize a cobweb and wonder if you could be magically made to climb the same hundred stairs over and over, making no more progress. The spellbinder princess may well have employed all kinds of strange magic to prevent unwanted guests reaching her sanctum in the upper part of the tower.

Eventually, though, the featureless repetition seems to break.

Turn to page 147.

A SERIES OF DOORS

As you climb the stairs, you come across three doors.

The first is set into the central pillar that the staircase seems to wind around. The door is made of an expensive dark wood, and the doorway is carved stone around it.
> If you try **the door in the carved archway, turn to <u>page 148.</u>**

Not long after, you find another. The second door is also in the central pillar, a little higher up, as if in the room one floor above. When you press your ear to the door, you think you can hear heavy, ragged breathing inside, as if of a person in panic. Looking at the door itself, you see that unlike the room below, it has been locked from this side—key still in the large iron lock.
> To turn the key and **enter the locked room**, turn to <u>page 154.</u>

You notice the last door, to your surprise, on the *other* side of the stairs—at first, you think the door must open into empty space, off the side of the tower. But peering under the gap at the bottom, you see the stone continue on the other side—it must lead to some extra room built onto the side of the tower, though you're sure you don't remember any such room being visible from the outside.
> If you try **the strange outer door,** turn to <u>page 153.</u>

A little way past this door, the solid stone underfoot seems to become softer in the center of each step, until you feel as if you're walking on cushions. When you slow down, your feet start to sink down as if into wet sand or a peat bog.
> To remain still and **let yourself sink down into the stone,** turn to <u>page 161.</u>

> **Ignore the doors**, walking along the very edge of the stairway where the stone is most solid to continue upward. **Turn to <u>page 162.</u>**

THE DOOR IN THE PILLAR

The door swings open to reveal what looks like a child's bedroom. There are books and papers at a small desk, dolls lined neatly up above a dollhouse. Pillows with frills and lace cover a four-poster bed with soft, heavy curtains that are carefully tied back. All the sheets look faded, as if washed countless times.

Beside the bed, a figure is folding a sheet carefully, then shaking it out to begin folding again, over and over. It looks like a woman with thin hands, a covered head and long, plain skirts. The material of her undershirt is fresh and starched, but looks to have large, faded stains splattered across it that might have once been blood, as if soap couldn't quite scrub it clean.

When the figure turns to one side, you notice with a jolt that some of her face is missing, torn horribly so that the skull is visible. The muscles and tendons are exposed all down her neck and the ripped, exposed flesh seems to continue below the stained shirt collar. The wounds look new and fresh, and too vicious for anybody to survive. The woman—or ghost, or whatever it is—looks suspended in time at the moment of violent death.

She moves to dust the spotless toys lined up along the shelves, repeating the motions over and over, making no difference or impression whatsoever. You stand and watch for a while, as the spirit moves to scrub at a small, bloody handprint on one of the painted cabinets. This stain, too, is faded—now you're looking at it, all the paint on the furniture looks thin, as if worn away by cleaning over the years.

She continues about her futile business, seeming not to notice you.

> **If you have a weapon**, you can **choose to attack the spirit**. Turn to <u>page 152.</u>
> To try to **speak to the spirit**, turn to <u>page 149.</u>
> To **return to the stairway**, turn to <u>page 147.</u>

SPEAK TO THE SPIRIT

- If you have the status *bearer of gifts* or *unmaker*:

You try to greet the spirit and ask what she's doing. The ruined face turns up toward you, and in the places where the muscles still move, it seems to contort in horror. She will not speak to you, shaking her head slowly every time you try to speak, backing away frantically if you try to approach. After a while, you give up—all you can do is leave. Return to the corridor—**turn straight to page 147.**

- If you have the status *unknowable*:

You try to greet the spirit and ask what she's doing, but nothing you can do can get her to pay any notice. After a while, you give up—all you can do is leave. Return to the corridor—**turn straight to page 147.**

- Otherwise:

At the sound of your voice trying to greet her, the spirit lifts her head, eyes seeming to come into focus as she sees you for the first time.

Her half-mauled face is difficult to look at, her voice a thin, breathy rattle.

"Orla," she tells you. "My name was Orla." Her words wheeze from her damaged throat in a way that sounds ripped out of her.

"Free me," she rattles, one hand reaching out toward you, half its flesh in ruined tatters. "Just tell me my task is done."

> **Free the spirit**. Turn to page 150.
> **Return to the corridor** and continue upward. **Turn to page 162.**

FREE THE SPIRIT

You speak the words, telling Orla her task is done.

As you say it, she sinks downward with a long, breathy sigh. When she speaks again, her rattling voice is warm, her shoulders relaxed. "They enchanted us," she tells you, in long, hoarse whispers. "The princess's servants, to do our duty. And magic is so strong, near the tower . . . it has kept me here—" she draws in another long, labored breath— "for so many years.

"There is a golden place," she rattles, "The last royal spellbinder . . . bound it to a painting. The tower will not let me leave, but I think now I can join the others. How can I thank you . . . ?"

The part of her face that still moves twitches upward as her eyes smile at you. "Before I leave, I can give you a blessing, a warning, and a gift." She reaches her half-torn hand to yours, and you feel a warm glow where she touches you.

Increase your logic, charisma *or* agility score permanently by 1.

"Now," she tells you slowly in her long, hoarse breaths, "the warning."

She explains that the tower becomes very strange further up, and that she's sometimes seen fragments of memories that drift down from the place above, the place Between. She tells you to tread only on the edges of the stairway and not to go into the caves. When you ask more details, she shakes her head, but repeats again: don't go into the caves.

Finally, Orla's ghost offers you two things as her gift—something she found or something she made. She asks you to pick one.

Choose *one* of the following items to add to your inventory:
  + An enchanted longsword
  An ethereal weapon the color of sunset that was left in the tower.
  + A small, hand-knitted doll
  The doll seems dear to her, more precious than the shining sword. She offers it as if it's just as valuable to you.

- If you choose the doll, you can gently ask her more about it. **Turn to <u>page 151.</u>**

> Otherwise, she gives you a final, sad smile, thanks you again, pressing your gift into your hands, and sinks through the floor with a sigh that sounds like relief. You make your way out of the room, treading carefully only on the edges of the stairs as she told you, and continue upward. **Turn to <u>page 162.</u>**

ORLA'S GHOST

You listen patiently as Orla's ghost tells you, in her slow rattle, about how the doll used to belong to the spellbinder princess.

"Many servants were tasked with looking after the princess after . . . her change."

For a long moment, Orla stays quiet, not elaborating on this "change." Then she picks back up, slowly, telling you that eventually almost all who were asked would refuse to look after the princess. The girl ended up locked up in her room at all hours.

Orla was the only one who agreed to look after the princess and saw how lonely she was. She would bring the girl the books she wanted to research her condition, then eventually, as she grew older, the magic items and experimental ingredients she requested, too, so that she could start looking into a way to cure herself. Orla would take messages to the girl's parents and the inquisitors, along with lists of what the girl wanted. And she saw how cold the princess's world was, locked away from chatter and laughter, from warmth and affection. Even when the girl began to lash out and attack her, she would still knit little things for the girl, little comforts like embroidered pillows and socks, and this little doll.

The ghost seems full of emotion.

"She used to hold the doll," she says, between labored, rattling breaths, "and sleep with it. She was still a human. The others couldn't see it. But she was still just a girl."

"It wasn't her fault," she tells you in her hoarse voice, hissed out of half a throat through the bare bone of her jaw and cheek.

She gives you a final, sad smile, thanks you again, pressing the doll into your hands, and sinks through the floor with a sigh that sounds like relief.

You make your way out of the room, treading carefully only on the edges of the stairs as she told you, and continue upward.

Turn to page 162.

ATTACK THE SPIRIT

The spirit continues to wander the room over and over. It does not respond as you draw closer.

Your blade slices cleanly through the neck of the thing, as if cutting through warm butter. Its movements stutter and waver, then its head rolls back, contorted as if in a scream as all the objects in the room begin to rattle, louder and louder until they're lifted from the ground. The spirit twists and disappears into nothing with a strange noise like the gasp of some huge creature, and everything falls to the floor again, inert and ordinary.

You search the room and find nothing of any use. At least it no longer has to wander this place.

> **Return to the stairway**. Turn to <u>page 147.</u>

THE TESSELLATION ROOM

As you reach out to touch the door handle, every hair on your body seems to stand on end. You feel suddenly as if you shouldn't enter, but you're already turning the handle, and there's a click as the door opens a crack.

- If you're the sailor:

You know the feeling of strange magic from your family's former house, and your first reaction is to distrust it. If you want, you can shake off the horrible sensation before the feeling can take root and slam the door closed again.

> You can **choose not to open the door** and return to the staircase—**turn to <u>page 147.</u>**

- Otherwise:

The door swings open in front of you to reveal a small, circular stone room. On the opposite side is another identical door, with two sets of velvet drapes on either side. One of the drapes is half-open, a large mirror visible beneath.

You can't help staring at what you see in the mirror—at first, you think it must be reflecting another mirror somehow, but the room is otherwise empty. Inside the frame, the reflection is a migraine tessellation of shapes, mirrors upon mirrors, stretching into impossibility. And as you stare at it, what you see is everything.

Gain the status *all-seeing*.
Subtract 1 from both your logic and charisma scores.

All of a sudden, you are finding it difficult to retain your grip on reality. Before you, hints of all possible futures and pasts shimmer at the edges of your vision. In your ears, all the music of every ball that has or could ever be held here expands outwards and you know every note and syncopation. You reach out to steady yourself on the door frame, and your fingers brush other worlds before the surfaces under your hands resolve into your current surroundings.

> **Close the door** and go back to the staircase. **Turn to <u>page 155.</u>**
> **Walk toward the mirror** and the far door. **Turn to <u>page 156.</u>**

THE LOCKED ROOM

You turn the key with a scrape, and the door swings open to reveal—you.

Sitting on a bed in a plainly-furnished room, panting and rocking gently, is a person that looks almost exactly like you—only older, tireder, more haggard, hair overgrown and in disarray. Apart from this, every detail is the same, right down to the clothes you are currently wearing, which are mirrored on the person across from you in an old and filthy alternate version.

    - **If you have the status** *bearer of gifts,* turn **straight** to <u>page 160,</u> regardless of other statuses.

    - **If you have the status** *unknowable*:

The other you seems not to see you, or even hear you if you call out—only looking wildly around as if waiting for someone to come in. The other you hurries shakily to the open door, eyes wild, and then sprints down the stairs before you can do anything else. Seemingly completely unable to interact, all you can do is continue. You return to the stairway to find another way ahead. **Turn to <u>page 147.</u>**

    - **Otherwise:**

The ragged, dangerous, older version of yourself stands unsteadily and begins to laugh, asking you something about a door full of mist—speaking in a garbled, too-fast voice, as if unused to talking to anyone. You're not sure how to reply, and at your hesitation, the other you seems to grow angry, even aggressive—wide, desperate eyes turning to a squint, darting to the door hungrily, as if worried you'll close it again.

> **Attack** the other version of yourself. **Turn to <u>page 158.</u>**
> **Try to calm down** the other version of yourself. **Turn to <u>page 157.</u>**

CLOSE THE DOOR ON THE MIRROR

Fumbling with a handle that seems at once to be a plain iron bar *and* a shiny brass doorknob, you pull the door closed so that the mirror is out of sight, and you're standing panting in the stone stairway again.

You take a few deep breaths. The stairway appears normal—and then you see it again, in a pulse of shimmering impressions dancing just beyond your field of view. For a brief moment, you see possibilities of terrible dread behind one of the other doors, but cannot tell which, and know instantly all the awful things the soft, malleable stairs ahead of you could do. Then, as quickly as the impression came upon you, it is gone again.

You continue on your journey, but the world seems a little dreamlike, and very occasionally, you get another pulse, a sudden glimpse of alternate futures and pasts out of the corners of your eye, ghostly impressions superimposed slightly out of phase with your current reality. For those moments, your sense of reasoning is a little out of step, while you're not always able to make out which part is the reality you're currently in.

For now, the stairs have resolved to their ordinary appearance, and all you have is a slight headache and feeling of confusion. You avoid the other doors and skirt along the very edge of the stairway where the stone is most solid, then carefully continue upward.

Turn to <u>page 162.</u>

WALK TOWARD THE MIRROR

You step toward the mirror. You think you hear the door close behind you with an ominous click, but it's hard to know whether that happened here and now, or before or elsewhere.

With each step, the dizzying vortex in the mirror slides into a set of new angles, but nothing further happens. The mirror stands inert. When you stand still, so do the shapes within it.

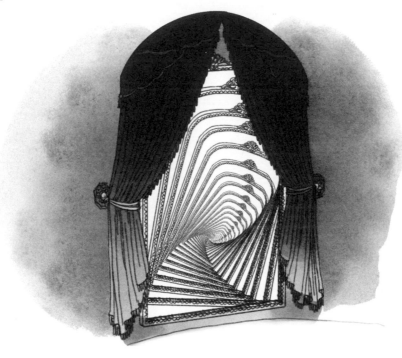

All of the possibilities you see shimmering outside your visual range involve you going through the far door—the one that seems to lead further out into the air, away from the main tower.

You open the door at the far end and find an identical room. You try to return to the stairway back through the first door and find yourself in an identical room.

You are trapped in the looping space. You draw back the other set of drapes and see only whiteness in the window beyond, rather than the storm outside the keep. When you listen closely, you hear absolutely nothing. When you scream and shout, there is no answer, no echo, only a muffled silence. There is no way out.

Your journey ends.

TRY TO CALM THE OTHER YOU

You try to speak softly and clearly to the other you, in the same way someone else might best keep you calm. The person opposite you wearing your clothes seems to sag, dropping heavily back down onto the bed and beginning to sob, still speaking.

You're not able to make much sense of what this person is trying to tell you but try to pull out the more insistent parts which form the most complete sentences: "*edge* of the stairs" and "not the caves, not the caves."

> **- If you've had a weapon taken from you** by the guards, the other you still has a seemingly-identical version of it and presses it back into your hands. You can add your old weapon to your inventory.

Finally, the older version of you deteriorates into helpless sobs, and nothing you do or say seems to be able to help. You think of your journey into the tower so far—you've made it a long way and are determined not to become this person. You stand to leave, and the figure on the bed clutches at your arm.

"Don't go," says the other you, wildly. "Don't go, don't go."

It alarms you, seeing yourself like this—older and more desperate and broken—and the whole experience makes your head spin. You pull away, gently.

As you step back out of the door, the other you stands and follows you, hesitantly. Emerging into the stairway, this older, ragged version of yourself looks down the stairs, tear-stained cheeks shining.

"Thank you," the other you whispers, and then hurries down the stairs, disappearing quickly out of sight.

Feeling haunted by your experience, unsure if it really happened, you try to pull yourself together. Remembering your own advice about the stairs, you skirt along the very edge of the stairway where the stone is most solid as you continue upward.

Turn to **page 162.**

ATTACK THE OTHER YOU

       - **If you have a weapon with you** or had one confiscated by the guards: The figure draws an identical blade, lashing out with it to cut through the fabric at your shoulder.

    Subtract 2 from your stamina.
    If your weapon is poisoned, also subtract 2 from your strength.
(If your stamina drops to zero, you stagger weakly to the floor, already exhausted from the way into the tower. The last thing you see is the other you, taking the chance to stab fiercely down while you're vulnerable.)

If you're still standing, you catch your breath, gasping as you feel blood seeping from your wound, the other desperate version of yourself striking surprisingly hard and fast.

Taking advantage of your incapacity, the other you pushes past and runs wildly down the stairs before you can say anything or prevent it. If you try to catch up, you find yourself too slow and weak, dizzy from the blood loss. There's nothing in the plain chamber of any value—all you can do is return to the stairway.

Too exhausted from the fight to explore further at the moment, you skirt the very edge of the stairs where the stone is most solid and continue upward. **Turn to <u>page 162.</u>**

      - **If you do not have a weapon with you**:
You move forward, wrestling and punching at your other, older self. At first, you seem evenly matched—a similar height and weight, each strike strangely congruent and predictable for both of you. But the other you is exhausted, fighting frantically but tiring quickly—you have no idea when they last ate or slept—and you think you'll be able to overpower them eventually.

The ragged version of you throws a weak punch that lands on your jaw, and, as you reel, runs for the open door.

> **Continue fighting** and strike the other you down. **Turn to <u>page 159.</u>**
> **Let the other you go.** The figure disappears down the stairs and you go on upward, too exhausted from the fight to explore further at the moment. You skirt the very edge of the stairway where the stone is most solid to continue on. **Turn to <u>page 162.</u>**

THERE CAN ONLY BE ONE

You tackle the other you to the floor before the ragged figure reaches the door.

The two of you wrestle until you—the real you, the younger you—come out on top, punching and punching at the figure on the floor. You watch your own eyes staring back at you, desperate and pleading. It unnerves you, disgusts you, and you keep on striking blow after blow until the ruined mess of your own face stops spluttering and gasping up at you from the floor, falling limp. In a frenzy, you stand to kick and stamp at the body, until you fall back against the stone wall, exhausted.

Your hands are covered in blood. You remember the feel of the soft flesh and muscle and ridges of bone, horribly mortal under your hands. You have that flesh—that same bone, those same muscles. The you on the floor is unmoving. The body reminds you of a slab of meat. You do not check for breathing.

There is nothing useful in the room. You drag yourself to the door, still breathing heavily.

You look back at the ruin of a person on the floor. You wonder if it once had the same memories as you, the same dreams, the same aches in the morning and little moments of joy, the same loves and hopes. Whatever it was, it was once living and breathing, and is now unmade into nothing.

Gain the status *unmaker*.

You go on upward, too exhausted from the fight to explore further at the moment. You skirt the very edge of the stairway where the stone is most solid to continue on.

Turn to page 162.

THE ROOM WITH THE BEARER

Your senses uncurl.

You smile wide, new organs tasting at the air for chemical secretions, and you're sure that the thing opposite you is only a person, no beautiful gift wrapped inside.

It looks jittery, wide-eyed and ready to strike—and it should be panicked, you think. It's a helpless thing, soft and fleshy, and it's alone in the room with you.

You take the key out of the door, step into the room, and close the door behind you.

You lock the door tight behind you, dropping the key into one of your pockets. Your smiling mouth widens, stretching and growing, as the thing on the bed screeches. This thing is too weak to plant a gift inside, and so it must give itself up to the family to help them thrive. A part in the back of your mind is sad, horrified, but that part must be quieted for the greater good.

The thing wearing the same clothes and flesh that you are scrambles away sweetly, as if there is a way out—lashing out at you, wriggling and screaming as your hands press it against the wall.

And you feed.

Increase your stamina by 3 points.

The arms stop thrashing quickly, falling into limp and lifeless compliance. It's more than you can eat at once, and so you leave it, carefully stepping away from the red pooling on the floor to keep the things you wear clean.

Back outside the door, you turn the key in the lock, and the person you are wearing stirs back into consciousness.

No, you decide—you won't turn the key to this room, after all. You try to remember why you'd wanted to go inside and cannot. Feeling full and happy, though you can't quite recall why, you turn to climb up the stairs. In your satisfied state, your curiosity about any other rooms or the soft stairway has ebbed into absolute calm, and you walk along the very edge of the stairway where the stone is most solid and continue upward.

Turn to page 162.

SOFT STAIRWAYS

You close your eyes and let your feet sink down into the strange, malleable stone. This is a magic tower—who's to say this isn't what you're supposed to do?

Suddenly, the sinking on one side stops, and with your left foot sunk in up to the ankle, you realize with horror that the stone has become solid and unmoving again.

You pull your right foot out of the hardening step below and splay your legs open to let it rest on the more solid stone at the edge of the stairway.

You wait like this, breathing hard, for a long time. Your left foot remains entirely trapped in the stone. Some of your muscles start to prickle and go numb.

You wait for hours, experimentally trying to wiggle your toes or wrench your foot out of your shoe to no avail. The step remains solid and unmovable.

Eventually, muscles cramping and body shaking with exhaustion, you see in the window a few meters above you, the first hint of dawn in the dark sky. Not long after, you feel the step relent, softening little by little until you can drag your foot out entirely.

You huddle at the edge of the stairs on the most solid part of the walkway.

    - If your stamina is 3 or above:
Your stamina drops to 1, but you're able to haul yourself upward along the solid edges of the stairway, and continue, exhausted, up the tower. **Turn to <u>page 162.</u>**

    - If your stamina is 2 or below:
You cannot physically make yourself climb the stairs. Your body is wrung out from the hours of tension standing in a strange position. You can slide and stumble your way back down the stairs, and in the quiet before dawn while the last guests leave, make it back out of the keep—but you've had to abandon your quest. **Your journey ends here.**

CLIMBING THE TOWER

As you continue up, the spiral stairway becomes stranger and stranger—in some places crusted with jewels, in others, seeming as if it's carved from lurid jelly, bouncing back when you accidentally touch it. One memorable section has stones missing, and underneath, something wet and red and pulsing beats from the walls. The stairway expands outwards in places until it's as wide as a field and as tall as a cathedral, then narrows and narrows until you have to duck to keep moving upward. More doors begin to pop up, this time in increasingly improbable places, often far too high on the wall for you to reach.

Once, you see an open doorway with the tattered remains of a door made of rushes hanging from one edge. It opens onto a night sky full of stars you do not recognize, and nothing below when you try peering downward.

Through one door, you see the ball downstairs, tilted at an impossible angle, and on the angled ceiling you see yourself, dancing with a woman whose head looks inside-out, her neck ending in a funneled throat with rows of concentric teeth.

You find a heavy metal door on a landing in the floor which is locked tight, and nothing you can do can make it budge. You try the round brass handle of a painted wooden door that you find in the ceiling, at a point where it's low and in easy reach. As soon as you open it the smallest crack, a sweet-smelling violet sand begins to pour through, heaping and trickling down the stairs by your feet until you are able to force the door shut again.

Further up the stairway, things seem to return to something resembling a more ordinary stairway for a stretch, and you come across:

A plain-looking door on your left, with a little track of woodlice moving in perfect spirals along the surrounding walls, all going into it. You see a glow along its hinges.
> To **push the glowing door** and see what's inside, **turn to <u>page 164.</u>**

On the other side of the staircase—which now turns every way, so you've lost any sense of which side leads to the outside of the tower—is a set of grand double doors, and you can hear music playing inside.
> To **push the grand doors** open, turn to <u>page 163</u>.

> Otherwise, you can **ignore the doors and continue upward**. Turn to <u>page 166.</u>

MUSIC PLAYING

Through the double doors, you find yourself in a long hall where cutlery is set out on tables as if for a feast. Near the high table, musical instruments lie on the ground and on chairs in a circle, where they seem to be playing themselves, strings being plucked by nobody, bows moving of their own accord. Trays of glasses move around, floating through the air, but the hall is completely empty of people.

- If you're wearing servant's clothing:

You walk around the room, looking for anything useful. The tables are empty, but you find furs and capes hanging at the far end of the hall and a few things in the pockets when you search through. Take any of the following to add to your inventory:

> + **A dark cloak**, strangely shadowy and edged with black feathers at the collar and sleeves (if you already have a cloak, you can replace it with this one.)
> + **A huge lilac gemstone**, polished and set in a velvet box.

Finding nothing further in the room, you leave, closing the doors behind you, muffling the sound of the instruments with no players, and move quickly upward toward your goal. **Turn to <u>page 166.</u>**

- If you're *not* wearing servant's clothing:

As you step into the room, the motions of the instruments and glasses and trays grow unhinged and frantic, faster and faster. The cutlery dances up from its platters, at first juddering, and then quickly moving faster to spin around you in a swirl.

You're not sure whether age has broken the spellwork so that it sees you as hostile or if it simply registers you as a guest it's trying to help, but you have to try to dodge out of the way as trays of glasses fly toward you. They zoom over your head, glass shattering on the far wall beyond, then the shards hurling back toward you the other way. The tornado of cutlery also seems to be closing its spiral, forks and knives and other delicate little tools you don't recognize getting faster and closer to you—some now grazing past your body and starting to bounce off your head. The broken glass zips past you, cutting at your forehead as it goes, and as you try to close the doors again, some of the whirlwind of objects flies out toward you.

Subtract one point from your stamina score.

(If it drops to zero, your ordeals in the tower below have left you slow, and a great flock of glass and knives fly out of the room to slice at you before you can get the doors closed. You fall to the ground as their movements grow more violent, slicing and stabbing as the world turns black.)

If you're still standing, you're able to shut the doors quickly and beat off the last few objects as you hurry up the stairs—and past a certain threshold twenty or so steps above, they seem to hit the boundary of the enchantment and drop inert to the ground. Breathing hard, you continue upward. **Turn to <u>page 166.</u>**

THE GLOWING DOOR

The first thing you notice in the room is a shining crack of bright, white light. It's underneath a half-rotted bed and barely big enough to fit your hand through, but the light is dazzling in the otherwise mostly-empty room. The swirls of woodlice head in little trails in and out of the crack, glowing and humming slightly, moving in strange little rhythms as they approach.

The next thing you notice is the creature under the bed. It looks almost like an enormous woodlouse the size of a cat, with a plated shell covering a large, round body, legs and mandibles teeming underneath. Something like fronds or antennae waft out from the edges of its shell, and it scrabbles helplessly at the crack, too large to fit through. It seems to be in distress. You notice little scratch marks all along the wooden boards where the crack has appeared and strange burned marks that emanate concentrically outwards—you wonder if the crack used to be wider, and how long the creature has been scratching at it, trying to get back through.

- **If you have the status *bearer of gifts*,** the creature seems distressed when you approach, emitting a strange, high-pitched noise so overwhelming that you're forced back out of the room to continue upward. **Turn straight to <u>page 166.</u>**

- **Otherwise:**
> **If you have a golden fruit,** you can give it to the creature. **Turn to <u>page 165.</u>**
> **Otherwise**, there is nothing you can do to coax the creature out—you must leave the room and continue upward. **Turn to <u>page 166.</u>**

THE KING OF WOODLICE

The thing's mandibles quiver impossibly fast, rotating the fruit, before the whole thing disappears up beyond its plates. You hear a squashing sound as the creature seems to eat it.

After this, the creature warms to you, skittering unnervingly over your feet and nudging at your ankles. When you open the door, it seems to want to follow, but it won't cross the threshold of the room.

You can choose whether to pick the creature up in your arms and carry it with you.

- If you leave the creature behind:
It makes a sad little chittering sound as you leave the room, running in circles before settling back at the glowing crack in reality, seeming to stare in where it cannot go. You close the door and continue upward. **Turn to <u>page 166.</u>**

- If you bring the creature with you:
You think you may as well bring the creature along, in case you find some other place with a big enough opening for it to return to its home.

Gain the status: *Allied to the king of woodlice.*

The glowing, humming isopod wriggles as you lift it into your arms. When you need your hands free to climb or move, it scuttles around to rest on your back or shoulder, seemingly immune to the effects of gravity. When your hands are free, it seems to enjoy lying in your arms like a baby. With the isopod settled on your shoulder and over your back, you continue upward. **Turn to <u>page 166.</u>**

THE EMPTY MARKET

Eventually, the stairs upward become impassable, full of broken stone blocks and choked with purple vines that grow from an unknown source. An incongruous wooden-paneled corridor leads off to the right, seeming to match the ones in the keep below. It seems to be the only way forward. Determined to push through to reach the room at the top, you take a deep breath and step inside.

> - **If you have the status** *unknowable*, remove it—you feel some sort of shift as you cross the threshold. You brush at your cheeks absent-mindedly and find them warm again.

The corridor seems ordinary but completely silent. You emerge into what looks like an abandoned shop with no signs of life, only neatly-stacked rows of books and a counter with nobody behind it. There are no windows, but it's lit as if sunlight is shining down—even though you know by now it will be dark outside.

> - **If you're the acolyte,** you stop to look through the books and find they are all in languages completely unfamiliar to you. You manage to fit the three smallest into your pockets. Add to your inventory:
> + **Three small curious books.**

Opening the front door, you find yourself not in a street but a corridor, lined with market stalls piled high with fresh fruits. When you pick one up, it crumbles in your hand, as if made of plaster. As you wander the stalls, you realize that their layout matches the one you walked through in the city below on the way here. You wonder if someone tried to move it or replicate it magically—or if the magic spilling out of the tower simply absorbs the things around it and spits some facsimile of them back out.

You open what looks like another shop door to find it's a cupboard stacked full of tennis rackets. You close it, then hear a scratching on the other side. When you open it again, something hairy and covered in teeth gnashes at you until you slam the door shut. You open it again, and inside is a chair, then a tinderbox, and finally, a small guitar.

You try every door on the street, looking for a way forward. You find one that leads to a vast plain at night, another an empty florist brimming with fresh new flowers. In one shop, ghostly shapes you cannot reach move indistinct beyond thick glass. One door takes you to a huge upside-down cathedral, the faces in the stained glass windows blank and strange. You hear ragged breathing at the windows, and crawl quickly over the rafters in the ceiling to get to the other side. Another leads to the florist again, but with all the flowers now dead—dry withered husks or sweet and rotting in their water.

Eventually, you have tried every door in the market but one small unassuming one. To your surprise, you find it leads out onto a spiral stone staircase, much like the one you were on before. The stone stairway leads up in front of you to a final door, and you walk up to it. **Turn to <u>page 167.</u>**

THE DOOR TO THE PLACE BETWEEN

Ahead of you, there is a door. You've never seen this door before. Have you?

You've just reached it, climbing the stairway of the tower and encountering it for the first time. Yes—this is the first time you've seen it. Isn't it? Something about it feels very familiar, as if you passed through one that looked the same earlier this evening, or as if it were the door to your home—a door you know better than any other. The door is indistinct—if you try to think of its color, style or size to figure out where you know it from, you can't quite pinpoint it. You shake your head, trying to clear it.

The door fills the corridor in front of you, the only way forward. When you open it, all you see beyond is gray mist. There's nothing else you can do but proceed.

As you step through the doorway, reality bends and fractures. Your vision warps as the air itself seems to billow and expand, to crack open and swallow you in.

The place you're in is unlike any you've seen before.

Your feet no longer touch the ground—in fact, when you look down, you see no feet, no body at all. Behind you, the doorway is gone. All you see is the gray mist, which extends out in every direction where it blurs into a swirl of light and colors and incongruous noise, convulsing and whirling toward you as it begins to form images.

- **If you have the status *allied to the king of woodlice*, turn straight to <u>page 168.</u>**

- **Otherwise:**
> If you're playing the **thief** or your own character, **turn to <u>page 173.</u>**
> If you're playing the **sailor**, turn to <u>page 169.</u>
> If you're playing the **libertine**, turn to <u>page 170.</u>
> If you're playing the **acolyte**, turn to <u>page 174.</u>

THE TRIUMPHANT HOMECOMING OF THE KING OF WOODLICE

The strange isopod wiggles free from you and then continues forward into the swirling mist as if swimming through a thick fluid, twirling and cartwheeling happily in the space ahead of you and lighting up the churning particles around it. Though you can't see your own body, the creature's eerie glow expands outwards until you feel it engulf you.

A cool wave of energy washes over you, and you feel calm for a moment, even as reality simmers and froths around you.

> **Return your stamina to its original level.**
> **Your charisma permanently increases by one.**
> **Change your 'allied' status to:** *Friend to the king of woodlice.*

You see spiraling trails of the little woodlouse creatures dancing through the mist toward the larger one, and they begin to circle it, as if tiny planets orbiting around a larger sun. Together, the creatures drift upward into the mist, wiggling happily and coalescing into a teeming, glowing orb that wafts away, finally home.

The seething mist around you seems to condense, and you begin to make out sensations.

> If you're playing the **thief** or your own character, **turn to page 173.**
> If you're playing the **sailor**, turn to page 169.
> If you're playing the **libertine**, turn to page 170.
> If you're playing the **acolyte**, turn to page 174.

THE SEAFARER'S DREAM

The gray around you has resolved and sharpened into a cold sea mist and the smell of salt. You hear the familiar slap of waves against hull and a soft creaking overhead, a comforting roughness beneath your calloused fingers where you hold the rigging above to steady yourself.

You are still trying to recall if this is a place you've been before when you sight a pale slip of land illuminated in the moonlight, two points off the starboard bow.

With a dreamlike shift, suddenly you're jumping from one of the small boats that ferries passengers ashore, sloshing along through the shallows as you pull the rowboat alongside you. You slide it up the sand to rest, where it leans to one side on the silent beach.

When you look up, you see a peach-pink dawn has begun to creep through the sky. The rosy sand ahead of you gives way to scrubland and a line of trees that are strangely familiar. The trees are bone-white, thick not with leaves but fronds that look like feathers. Around their roots, there are strange ruins—stone warped as if bubbling, and mangled twists of tiles like the ones in your mother's kitchen.

Now that the gloom is lifting, you look back toward your ship, anchored in the bay. You notice a strange dark smear—what looks like a slop of blood dripping from one of the gunports. The deck is empty of crew, but a small figure stands at the prow, staring out at you with one wet, red hand on the railing. It's a little girl.

> From the island that reminds you of the wreck of your home, a warm, sweet wind that smells of cut grass brushes your cheeks. Get away from the girl and the ghostly ship: **move forward through the trees. Turn to <u>page 206.</u>**

> Return to the ship and **confront the girl. Turn to <u>page 194</u>**.

> You imagine your friends, bleeding out on the deck, and your mother and brother, alone and far from the wrecked home they built with your missing father. It's too much—everything is too much—and you have to get away. The dark waters of the sea fade out into gray mist before they reach the horizon. **Swim out into the sea. Turn to <u>page 200.</u>**

THE NOBLE'S FOLLY

You are floating somewhere in the vicinity of the chandelier above the grand winter ball three years ago, watching in horror as your past self throws up noisily on an important ambassador. There had been a fountain of sweet honeyed liquor, and you'd been determined to enjoy the extravagance and live up to your terrible reputation.

Venny had asked you that night—once they'd brought you home and you were curled shivering on your bed—whether you were happy in this life. You had replied, slurred and defensive, in the affirmative. You go to all the best parties, eat the finest things and mix with the best people. What more could you want? Venny looked at you levelly, as if hoping you'd admit otherwise.

You're fourteen and have just been caught kissing one of the pages in the library. You tell your father it meant nothing to you, trying to keep your voice steady—but when he suggests having the boy whipped, the look in your eyes gives you away. This is not the first time your father is truly, staggeringly disappointed in you, and it will not be the last. His lip curls, and it makes you instinctually flinch in anticipation.

Now you're eighteen and coming of age, your father will not let you keep your long hair or lovely mongrel dog. He has fired the maid who was your closest friend. Everything you do is wrong, somehow, and your father is furious in a way that makes your limbs start to tremble involuntarily. It always makes him angrier, but you can't help it.

Later, you want to cry and scream at him until your throat is raw, which you obviously cannot do. So instead, you ruin your coming of age ball with as much gusto as possible, and as much as you can of everything that comes after.

You watch the swirl of memories: elaborate dining rooms where you're drunk on arrival and a spectacular mess by the time dinner is served. You make awful, venomous comments until promising engagements are thoroughly ruined and the girls are left crying, and you don't have it in you to care. You float above the scenes, watching your teenage self become cruel to the servants who ought to know their place, and quick and vicious toward every ridiculous or unfashionable attendee at each event. That's just who you are! Flippant and frivolous where your father would prefer you measured and reasonable. What can you do!

The first time you meet Venny, you give their not-quite-fine-enough outfit your best sneer and are rattled to find them not stumbling or stuttering, but laughing in your face. You're so unused to anyone failing to cower when you want them to, you are stunned into silence. You'd always hated dinners with visiting dignitaries, but suddenly you are very, very interested in this one.

Venny asks you the details of the things you've heard at the grand balls and behind the doors of meeting rooms that your father attends. For the first time in a long time, their clever little smile pulls at something tender in you, something which you thought had been lost—so you go running off to listen at doors, rifle through drawers and break into cabinets for secret letters. In retrospect, you were probably *quite* guilty of treason—but perhaps it was worth it.

You're in a room lit by candles as Venny looks out at the rainy darkness beyond. They're telling you how much better the weather is in Estovar, and the way they talk about it warms you. They ask if you've ever considered leaving the city—and what you would do if war were to break out.

Now, Venny stands in the mist by a solid, ordinary doorway. It takes a moment for you to realize this is not a memory, but an image conjured by the Between—or perhaps by you, from missing them. They are asking if you're happy, with that infuriating look on their face that looks entirely too much like pity. Of course you're happy! They're asking if you trust them—but nobody in their right mind would really trust Venny. Are you in your right mind?

Venny is asking if you *really* want to go through the door beside them, watching you sadly. It makes you want to cry, which you hate.

> **Confidently step through the enticing door.** Of course you want to go through that door! You have never made a mistake in your life, and this is no exception. To hell with Venny. You never cared about them anyway. **Turn to <u>page 167.</u>**

Otherwise:
You stop to consider the door. It reminds you of the ordinary world, a world that has never been kind to you. Perhaps the way up the tower is through the unknown. You strain your senses to think how else you may be able to proceed forward. The unreal Venny seems to want *a talk*, but you feel vulnerable in this swirling world, your stomach twisting at the idea of more honesty. You turn your mind to the distance, where you think you can hear the faint sounds of bells and conversation.

> **Follow the bells. Turn to <u>page 176.</u>**
> **Face your emotions.** Turn to face the vision of Venny properly. **Turn to <u>page 172.</u>**
> **Drift into the mists.** This is all too difficult. Embrace the nothing. **Turn to <u>page 200.</u>**

- **If you have the status *all-seeing*,** you can also make out a child in the muddle of voices and know they are part of the fragments of possibility that spill from the tower. You can strain to listen and **choose** to be pulled in that direction. **Turn to <u>page 194.</u>**

FACE VENNY

As you turn to face your friend and lover, a last swirl of memory washes over you.

You had kissed a butler in a dark corridor and persuaded him into leaving a door unlocked, emerging with the letter Venny wanted concealed in a fashionably puffed sleeve. Venny was startled into a laugh when you slipped it to them. They looked at you delighted and proud and calculating, as if discovering a new tool and thinking of the best way to put it to use.

And then you see the last time you saw Venny before all this, immaculate court smile faltering in an unusually subdued mood. You realized they were really drinking the wine this time rather than pretending, and they had looked at you blurry and serious with all their sharp edges softened, asking if you ever thought of giving this all up—all the barbs and manners and layers of deceit.

You hadn't quite understood them then, but now the memories slide into place. You realize that Venny had always seen something in you they wanted to use—but also that at their secret core, they had come to care for you and hope for a future. They would not easily leave you behind.

In the mist of the space Between worlds, Not-Venny leans in close to brush their lips over yours. "Keep going," they whisper against your mouth, ghosting a hand along the curve of your jaw.

The venom has seeped out of you, the quick wit on the tip of your tongue lying unspoken. You find yourself telling the truth instead—that you're not sure you'll be able to make it.

Whatever the vision is, it smiles with Venny's smile, wide and genuine, and it dazzles you as always, filling your chest with sunlight and aching. "You will," they say with absolute confidence, and the confidence seeps into you.

Increase your stamina by 2.

The vision of Venny and the doorway is fading behind you. You hear their voice dwindling as they tell you they've seen the princess's memories, and to treat her gently—whatever that means—and the last thing you see is their hand gesturing toward a faint smudge of light as they dissipate into the mist.

> **Keep going.** Follow in the direction they gestured, toward the light. **Turn to <u>page 192.</u>**

> **Give up.** You remember that this wasn't the real Venny at all, and you have no idea if you'll ever see them again, and it's almost unbearable. Everything seems hopeless. **Turn to <u>page 200.</u>**

WANDERER'S PATH

Magic roars through you. You feel a sense of calm, of safety and familiarity, of home. You smell food from when you were a child and know it's breakfast. Woven in with the smell is the noise of the person who raised you—who was it? You can't quite remember.

As you struggle to make it out, you hear they're humming, turning a patty in a pan—or was it the clack of their heels on stone floors as the servants attended to them? No—the gruff noise of a laugh as they pour your toppings—they always thought them too spicy—into a bowl of porridge as they wait for you in a sunlit kitchen. Or was it the click of spoons in the strict silence of the orphanage and the smell of the cleaning fluid?

The memories lap at each other like waves, and the sureness you had of which were your own seems to melt away like spun sugar as the tide rises around you. The caress of your mother blends into your father rocking you gently to sleep, until you realize the rocking is the swing of a great ship where your cot has been left, unattended—or is it a tremor as things stir underneath the hospital where you spent your early years? You hear the grandparent who raised you in the mountains singing a lullaby as they carry you on their back, collecting herbs; you smell eggs sizzling as the other children in the dormitory stir; you're alone in an empty house your family has not returned to, in the dreaded night where you finally open the door of the rattling cupboard and get pulled into the shadows, too fast to scream.

You hear laughter and crying, oceans and birdsong and, jingling to a far away music, the rhythmic sound of bells. You feel earth and stone and fire burning your fingertips, you see bright lights and spinning kaleidoscopes of color and movement.

> Let the whirling world take you. **Embrace the nothing**. Turn to page 200.

> **Follow the bells.** Turn to page 176.

> You feel the sensation of something growing, something damp and teeming beneath your feet, and **concentrate on sinking down** into it. **Turn to page 192.**

> **If you have the status *all-seeing*,** you're able to make out a child saying something and know they are part of the fragments of possibility that spill out from the tower. You can strain to listen and choose to be pulled in that direction. **Turn to page 194.**

THE GATHERING STORM

The mist is dark and cloying—congealing into clumps that spiral in a circle around you. A fork of lightning illuminates the fog, and you see the silhouette of a tall, pointed building ahead.

You realize you are in the dark nest of clouds that circle the tower. The tower grows larger in the murk until you can see the window of the tallest room—then you seem to be soaring through it into a huge, glittering room of magic. A figure stands turned away from you, and you know they have *the Key*.

To your left and right among the magical clutter are what look like mirrors, and inside you see other places. In one, you see your mother. She has received word from the archivists of your disappearance. She is weeping and weeping, throaty and raw. You realize you haven't seen her in years. She looks old, tired—small. You ache to see her, a physical pull deep in your chest, and you know you could step through the mirror to speak to her, safe in the comfort of home. But ahead of you is the figure who holds *the Key*.

Another frame has a view of a courtyard of fig trees that you know as one of the high places in the Great Library. Perched on one of the benches among your other friends is a youth with long limbs and dark brown skin, beautiful in the sunlight, talking about how much everyone misses you. You want to reach out and say you're alright. The conversation moves on. How long until they all forget you? But ahead of you is the figure with *the Key*.

In another, you see the stacks of the Great Library, its perfect order stretching out in glorious harmony in all directions. The building shakes, as plates beneath the earth shudder far below, and things start to come loose—elegant shelves of scrolls and bamboo slips, archival boxes juddered open and spilled all over the floor. A box of inks crashes down, and black liquid begins to pour out, wetting pages through as it leaks indelibly through precious irreplaceable texts. The thunder of the earthquake dies down, but thousands of years of knowledge lies in disarray, and you notice a candle—surely there are no unguarded flames in the library—shaken loose from its lantern, rolling onto papers that catch alight. If you were to step through, you could extinguish the flame. Your chest tightens, fingers digging so deep into your palms that they draw blood, as you watch the fire start to catch. But ahead of you is *the Key*.

Unseen, your mother weeps, your friends forget you, and the Great Library burns. Your focus is on the figure ahead of you as she turns and rips the world open, blinding you with a painful, brilliant light.

The mist and the tower are gone. You are now standing in a white void, surrounded by what look like the frames of a new set of mirrors. Through each, you see different scenes—only a few seem big enough to step through.

> You hear a child's laughter and see a young girl in finely embroidered robes running from one frame to another, hiding behind each. She turns as she climbs down into one of the frames, and you see her face is made of teeth. **To follow the girl,** turn to page 194.

> Through a tall, rectangular frame on your right, beautifully embellished and ornate, you see silvery mist, and chiming in the distance, the sound of bells. **To follow the sound into the frame, turn to page 176.**

> To your left is an enormous round frame, taller than you are. In it, you see a stretch of field, a great expanse. **To go inside, turn to page 206.**

> Through a last frame, plain and just big enough to stoop through, there is darkness, and a metal walkway leading out into it. **To step through, turn to page 182.**

THE PROCESSION

Swaying hypnotically through a dreamscape mist, you see halos of light that resolve into the shapes of lanterns bobbing above a group of figures. The lanterns are lit up fiery and bright, swinging from tall poles that seem to be wrapped with ribbons and tassels and jingling bells. Carrying the lanterns, you make out a long train of figures that are walking toward you out of the mist, making it swirl and scatter where they tread.

There's the sound of laughing and singing, and a steady beat of a drum. As they approach, you see that the figures are dressed in robes in a very old style, and those whose heads are not covered wear their hair bound in unfamiliar fashions. They're moving purposefully and joyfully forward, like a kind of parade, with a group at the front with veiled faces chiming a huge gong.

The procession envelops you, the bright, laughing crowd surrounding you as they march slowly forward to the rhythm of their ribboned drums, playing cowhorn pipes and tambourines. Above you, long banners flutter as if in a breeze, although the mist seems calm around you. The banners are black, with a line of white like a crack splitting them in two.

> **Follow the procession.** Turn to page 178.
> **Continue through the mist.** Turn to page 192.

DON'T FIGHT BACK.

The girl looks shocked that you aren't running away, and her aggressive stance drops.

She begins to cry again, and turning away, she grabs your hand roughly with her small, slick red one, tugging at you to follow. Her hand is still strangely strong, and you find you're not able to wriggle out of her grip.

She walks a few steps up the stairs to a window on the stairway, and then walks out of it into the darkness. Instead of falling, the two of you walk along some invisible walkway in the blackness where the girl seems to know where to twist and turn to stay on solid ground. Sounds you can't identify echo around you—something like bird calls and something like the clang of metal, melting in and out from above and below.

After a while, she stops, raising a trembling finger, still red and wet, to point a way forward ahead of you. Unsure of what else you can do, you walk in the direction she's pointing.

When you look back, you don't see her any longer, but you think you hear the sound of that small, raw sobbing break out again in the distance.

Turn to page 182.

FOLLOW THE PROCESSION

You fall in step to walk as part of the procession as its cheerful ribbons flutter by you.

Listening to the singing, you realize you can't understand the words, though the sounds are familiar—like a language only slightly different from the one spoken here in the city. If you try to speak to any of the figures, they smile at you, shaking their heads, and go on with their part in the parade—carrying their banner or lantern or clapping with the beat.

The bright music and excited mood of the group is infectious, making you cheerful, eagerly anticipating what you will find wherever they are going.

You walk with them for hours, feet matching the rhythm of the drums and never getting tired. After a while, you find yourself toward the back of the group. You try to hurry along, to get back to the heart of the activity, but no matter how fast you go, the robed figures' slow feet seem to carry them away, the whole procession pulling away in front of you and leaving you behind. You're sure you can still catch them up and keep moving, but the light of the lanterns and laughter disappears into the mist ahead.

You are still walking forward to the beat of remembered drums, wondering what to do, when out of the corner of your eye you see the faint light of bobbing lanterns again, appearing from a completely different direction and moving toward you.

Relieved, you move to meet them. As you approach, you hear the rhythmic jingle of the bells on the tall sticks that hold up the banners, and the beat of the drum—much slower now, but still regular. Out of the mist, the details resolve—you see the veiled faces of the figures at the front who now chime the bell, just once, plodding doggedly toward you.

Once again the procession is upon you, sweeping you up into the group as you march with a heavy, monotonous tread. The going is more difficult, somehow, and when you look up to take in the figures, you realize something has changed.

Their faces are gaunt and emaciated, skin showing the bone clearly underneath. One or two have jaws that still seem to move, as if in song, but no sound comes out of their dry, wizened mouths. An aged figure close to you wears a hat that has slipped to an angle, but seems not to have the strength to correct it. The ribbons threaded around the edges of the drum they carry are tattered, and they move as if it's a great weight. The skin of the drum is worn in the center, and soft stuffing has started to come out of the slowly splitting head of the mallet as it hits, booming out every few seconds in a slow and deathly rhythm.

The movement is grueling and ponderous, the progress slow. You feel the urgency to join them, to keep walking, to reach your target. Soon, you'll reach your goal, you think. Soon.

- If your strength or logic is 5 or above:
You can physically drag your limbs against the inexorable movement forward, or keep the reasoning clear enough in your mind that you're able to resist the urge to keep walking. The procession moves past you, away into the mist, and you try not to think about it, lest you summon them again. You pick a direction away from them at random, and propel yourself through the misty dreamscape at a run. **Turn to page 192.**

- Otherwise:
How long have you been marching? You can't say for sure. It feels as if you've always been marching. Your limbs are slow, the progress arduous, but soon you'll reach it, you'll get there—you're not sure what it is, but you know it will all be worth it.

The memories of what you were searching for in the tower and the life you used to have become indistinct, faded like an old tapestry that the sun bleaches away a little more each day, thinning the details. Your memories of how you grew up and the people you care about are replaced with the sound of the drum and jingling of bells, the fluttering of banners that bear the bright white crack, the shining light of the space Between worlds. All you know now is your glorious purpose in the march.

You have joined the procession, and the procession does not end. You couldn't leave if you wanted to—but of course, you don't want to. The idea could never even cross your mind.

Your journey into the tower has ended. You march forever in the nothing of the Between.

IMPOSSIBLE ARCHITECTURES

As you draw closer to the building, your mind tries to make sense of what you're seeing.

The building looks almost square at first glance, built from the same gleaming black mineral as the rocky ground—but on closer inspection, the structure is a shape with far too many planes and edges to be a cube. It makes your head hurt to look at it.

The outer walls have patterns cut in so you can see parts of the interior, which connect to and *become* the outside when you try to move your eyes to follow them. Stairs leading from one place link up with others that should be some distance away. You think you can see a thin trail of smoke, meandering out of the building at an unlikely sideway angle.

You walk up the main stairs of the building of impossible architecture. The world seems to lurch and spin slowly around as you move, until you realize it's tilted completely and you're walking along what was once the ceiling of the square black corridor leading inside.

You walk through black-tiled rooftops onto upside-down stairs and find sliding black glass doors suspended above you in angled floors. You move down featureless corridors of shining obsidian that seem to rotate you through different planes. Mostly, you find dead ends, until you finally come across a large room.

In the walls and floor and ceiling—you can't really make out which are which—are rectangles sunk into the stone that look like windows or doors into other places. You see violet sand on a sideway beach; clouds blowing over the tops of mountains in a howling blizzard; an endless sea of grass tilted at a strange angle; an upside-down scene of unfamiliar birds roosting in blue-leaved treetops; and on the far side of the room, one that looks as if it leads into a stone stairway of an old castle.

In the middle of the room is a makeshift camp with a sleeping bag and piles of provisions alongside tables of books and brass contraptions that spin and whir quietly. Mechanisms on one table lower ticking and spinning instruments down on ropes into a rectangle of pale sea, where wine-red tubes and squelching cephalopods traverse a coral landscape. A figure in the robes of a senior spellbinder sits peering into a perfectly rectangular pit in the floor. You can't tell if it's some kind of magical firepit or a portal to a shimmering, bubbling plasma of arcing flames.

The spellbinder notices you as you step into the room, springing up to greet you.

"Well met, stranger! I'm Dayo, I use 'she,'" she says brightly, brushing off her clothes as she stands. "Which experiment were you interested in? It's been some time since I've had a visitor."

> **Tell her you're interested in all of it**—turn to <u>page 183.</u>
> **Admit you didn't come here to see her experiments**—turn to <u>page 184.</u>

A DARK PLANET

You find yourself walking along a path of black metal or stone, suspended in a vast darkness. Everything around you is plunged in gloom until eventually—without you noticing the moment it changes—the surface underfoot gives way to a glittering, dusty surface.

You're standing on an open plain of black, rocky dust. It seems to extend in every direction, interrupted only by occasional boulders suspended over the surface, gleaming like obsidian. Stars litter the sky above, but you don't recognize the patterns. There are more than you've ever seen, shimmering in the darkness in a bright band, with patches of oil-slick, many-colored nebulae hanging suspended around them.

You continue walking in a landscape that seems to barely change. Eventually, far off toward a brighter part of the sky, you see something you first think is a strange boulder on the horizon, but after some time walking, it looks much more regular than the others, like some kind of building.

The only other feature you see in the unchanging landscape is a range of rocky protrusions off in the other direction, jagged and irregular like haphazardly-stacked plates. You walk for a few minutes toward it and see that nestled in the gleaming black rock is the mouth of a large cave, darkness looming within. Leading up to it, you can just make out ripples in the dusty surface, tracks as if something has been dragged inside.

> **Head toward the building**. Turn to <u>page 180.</u>
> **Venture into the caves**. Turn to <u>page 185.</u>

A STUDENT OF SPELLWORK

Dayo is thrilled to explain her experiments and begins walking you to every door in the room.

She tells you she's been a researcher in the Between for a long time and thinks of herself as living here. She's managed to make a stable portal through to a place she can trade coral for food and anything ordinary, and a contraption that allows her to send her research back to the institute of spellbinders. Although they occasionally try to call her back, she's happier here in the quiet where she can research on her own.

"How do you like my home? I built it myself."

She seems to want a response, so you ask tentatively why the dimensions seem so strange—she tells you it's a defense mechanism to keep the things from the caves out.

"Travelers from the institute are very careful to avoid what happened to the princess," she says, and she continues on before you can ask any further questions.

She speaks for a very long time as you trail patiently around, unable at this late stage to admit you understand very little of what she's talking about. There's no sunrise or sunset, but you begin to grow hungry and feel sure many hours have passed.

Eventually, you reach the end of the experiments, and you're able to ask her about the way back out into the tower in a way that actually prompts a reply.

Dayo tells you that, unfortunately, she's only ever managed to make one portal out into the tower, and it leads to the *upper* part. She says this as if nobody could possibly want to go that way, and begins to explain some of the other worlds you might want to go to—as if going to live in another world might have been your intention when you wandered up some stairs from a ball. You wonder if she really knows how to get herself home at all or if she found herself trapped here and made peace with it.

When you insist, she nods, baffled and slightly alarmed, but shows you the way to the door. Before you step through, she asks you to wait, nervously bustling around until she pulls out a vial of purple smoke, which she encourages you to drink.

Increase your stamina by 2 points.

You thank Dayo profusely, and she watches warily as you walk into the rectangle. You drop down into it, the world turns sideway, and you find yourself somewhere new.

Turn to page 214.

DAYO'S NEW SUBJECT

At hearing this, Dayo looks fascinated, and urges you to explain how you came here. Unsure of where the loyalties of a senior spellbinder may lie—as part of an institute with the princess at its ceremonial head—you tell her only that you were at the ball and you went up the stairs into the tower.

You're relieved to find she doesn't ask about your motivations or their legality at all, instead excitedly insisting you describe the ways the tower got stranger as you went further up and everything you've seen since you arrived in the Between. A few minutes in, she pauses you with an authoritative finger and begins taking notes.

Once she's asked you the details a few times, she goes to look through several sheaves of paper, settles down, and you hear her pen begin to scratch. She seems to have forgotten that you're there.

You ask her about the way back out into the tower, and after holding up her finger for a moment to finish her sentence, she tells you that, unfortunately, she's only managed to ever make one portal out into the tower, and it leads to the *upper* part. She says this as if nobody could possibly want to go that way and begins to explain some of the other worlds you might want to go to—as if going to live in another world might have been your intention when you wandered up some stairs from a ball. You wonder if she's trapped here or just uninterested in going home.

When you tell her you'd be happy to go out that way, she looks alarmed and tells you it's the way to the requisition room and the place the princess lives. When you insist, she nods, baffled, but shows you the way to the door. You thank her, and she tells you seriously to be careful before you walk into the rectangle.

You drop down into it, the world turns sideway, and you find yourself somewhere new.

Turn to <u>page 214.</u>

THE CAVES

The mouth of a cave yawns wide ahead of you, the glittering dust underfoot giving way to rough stone with gleaming smooth faces.

The obsidian-shine of the rock seems to create its own low light as you make your way inside, the vast passage turning and heading slowly downward. In some parts, the incline is shallow, and in others you clamber your way down. There are natural openings and passages higher up, and some too narrow to squeeze through on either side, but the main passage remains large and clear, almost as if someone or something had hollowed it out.

Deeper into the cave in the strange faint glow of low light, the passage takes a sharp turn downward, so it's only once you're up to the very edge of the pit that you can see what fills it, too late to be anything but frozen in awe and revulsion at the thing that confronts you.

The creature is a stretched, shining mass, a mess of glittering teeth and rippling tendons. It undulates softly, filling the whole width of the cave with its alien, many-mouthed body in wet humps and curls and twists. In the center is something that could be a head—a fleshy mass of mandibles and cartilages and a wide, churning mouth that almost looks as if it is smiling.

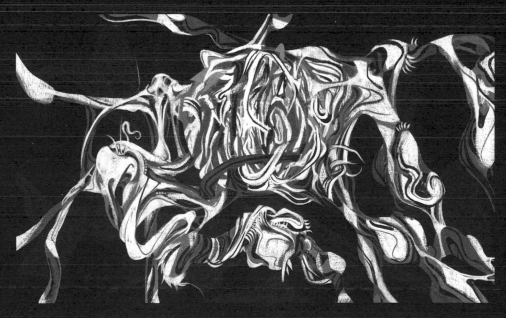

> **If you have the status** *bearer of gifts*, turn to <u>page 186,</u> regardless of other statuses.
> **If you have the status** *unmaker,* the creature smells death on you and notices you immediately. It wants you for one of its brood. **Turn to <u>page 188.</u>**
> **Otherwise, turn to <u>page 187.</u>**

THE MOTHER

The thing inside you delights.

It tastes the chemical secretions of the air with your tongue, wrapped around your synapses and neurons, opening your mind to the beautiful pleasure and comfort of sensing one of its own.

An understanding flows from its rippling glands through the twirling particles of the scant air between you, and part of you knows it as kin.

This, the creature inside tells you, is one of us. We and it are, in some ways, one. We are part of each other, part of a great web that spreads from its origins here at the great progenitor, whose children spread and dance and feed joyfully out in the worlds beyond. This is what you could become, the grown beautiful form of something fed and nurtured, expanding into its full potential, rich and fruitful.

The thing in the pit surges upward, its enormous pulsing bulk oscillating gently toward you, devoted and possessive. In its neural maze, you see glimpses of its children, nestled in flesh and always hungry, consuming and absorbing and thriving.

The tendrils of the thing in your mind are trying to wrest control of your limbs, and you have started to descend into the pit to stand on an open patch of ground, the huge creature pulsing around you. The thing inside you desperately wants you to walk forward and accept the mother's embrace.

You try to fight the urge, to listen to the last horrified parts of your human brain as it tries to send you warnings: this creature will have you and everyone else for its own, if it can. You must try to end it, to fight it or get away.

But you hear another voice. We want to help you, the creature inside you tells you, soothingly. We want to make you into your best possible self. You're already so close.

> **Let yourself walk forward** into the nurturing folds of the creature. **Turn to <u>page 190.</u>**

> **If your logic is 4 or above,** you can fight the urge and look desperately around, trying to work out some other way of proceeding, looking for any other information. **Turn to <u>page 193.</u>**

> **Otherwise,** you can fight the urge, but the only way to prevent its approach is to **attack the creature.** Turn to **<u>page 191.</u>**

THE GIFTED ONE

- If you are wearing a _dark cloak_:

The creature undulates, extending its receptors on long tendrils to check for movement. But however it "sees," it seems unable to sense you in the black of the caves, where you blend into the shadows around you. You retreat as silently as you can, trying to soften the tap of your feet and to time it with the wet, alien sounds of the fleshy creature shifting below. You scramble back up the rock and a stone dislodges under your foot, bouncing down along the passage with an echo. You hear the shifting behind you get louder and, in horror, see the front of the creature hauling itself upward, filling the whole tunnel as it moves itself in parts toward you like a boneless, squelching sea creature, rolling its wet mass forward. You begin to run, and you don't look back or stop running until you're well out of the cave. Far behind you, you can see its mouths stretched and pulsing in the cave entrance, unwilling to leave its den.

You let your racing heart return to normal in your relief to escape the awful thing and begin to make your slow way to the only other destination you can see in the landscape—a building on the distant horizon. Turn to **page 180.**

- Otherwise:

As you try to move away, one of the creature's tendrils darts out toward you, wrapping gently around your leg in a strange, awful caress. The rest of its strange body shifts toward you with its rippling momentum, hesitant as if curious.

> Will yourself calm, and **let the creature approach you.** Turn to page 188.
> **Try to get out of its grip and run.** Turn to page 189.

THE GIFT OF THE CAVES

Part of the creature rises suddenly up toward you out of the pit, a wave of flesh, and before you can do anything, the body of the creature moves forward and enfolds you.

You open your mouth to cry out, and part of it opens wide to reveal rows of teeth, pulsing gums and sinews, an architecture of fleshy fractals that seems to spiral down into a throat.

The creature kisses you, mandibles crawling over your cheeks to sink your face into the churning mouth. As everything turns black, you feel suddenly calm, sighing into the darkness as the thing takes you, twisting your organs to its shape.

For a moment, your minds are one, and you can feel your beautiful stretched body that fills the pit of the cave and all the pulsing movements of it. Then you are released back to yourself again—but a self forged anew, strong and smiling and beautiful.

> **Gain the status:** *bearer of gifts.*
> Your **strength and agility** both **increase by two.**

The next thing you remember is walking away from the cave. You feel warm and contented, as if waking from a good dream. You are trying to make your way out of the Between, toward your goal at the top of the tower—you remember this. Your hands look the same—you run them over your face, and it seems unchanged. But something now slumbers within you—a gift.

You begin to make your way to the only other destination you can see in the landscape—the building on the distant horizon.

Turn to **page 180.**

NURTURE THE COLLECTIVE

As you try to pull away from the tendril, it tightens with a surprising force and seems to swell and grow. You try to kick out and attack it with a blade if you have one, but another limb has now emerged from the thing, slipping its way up toward you as you struggle against it, wrapping solidly around your waist.

The creature rises up out of the pit, a great wave of flesh that stretches open in a wide smile. It cradles you with its strange pulsing limbs as its impossible jaw stretches above you.

The mouth stretches wider and wider until it fills the space above you, and you are pulled inside. Your human body is stopped and dismantled, tendrils flowing into you to feed the great collective, to make it strong.

For a moment, before your consciousness winks out, you feel the minds and memories of all the things consumed here, linked and beautiful—you feel the web of your children, joyful and teeming, thriving far out in distant worlds, and away at the top of the tower. The memories of your purpose in the tower have been absorbed and dispersed, and you see them as if from a much wider perspective, zoomed out—so small, now that you can truly see the scope of the worlds and your kin.

And then you are gone, organs feasted upon and nerves repurposed, and the creature settles happily back into the pit, waiting for the next curious traveler lost in the Between.

Your journey ends here.

RELENT

You relax into the embrace of the mother as her tendrils enfold the loose flesh of your limbs.

You open your new mouth to her, and her strength feeds you, nutrients pulsing through the tubes that attach to your new organs. For a moment, your minds are one, and you can feel your beautiful stretched body that fills the pit of the cave and all the pulsing movements of it. Then you are released back to yourself again—but a self forged anew, strong and smiling and beautiful.

You emerge from the cave made lovely, and you know the way out of the tower.

Turn to page 250.

MATRICIDE

The thing within you seems to howl in silent fury, twisting and pulling at your organs, sending screeching chemicals into your brain as you pull back away from the progenitor creature's fleshy mouth.

There's nowhere to go—the body of the thing loops around, wet and squirming, covering the way back up to the lip of the pit and encircling you. You stand in the small bare patch of ground amidst its alien, pulsing flesh.

If you have a weapon, you draw the blade and swipe out at it—otherwise you lash out with your arms, scratching at the wet flesh. Either way, the flesh draws back, rolling back into the creature, and more mouths seem to open where you strike. The stretched red-pink flesh smiles wide and teeth pull your legs so you're held, cradled, toppling to the ground as its impossible jaw stretches above you.

The mouth stretches wider and wider until it fills the space above you, and you are pulled inside, still fighting desperately at the thing that tries to take over your mind. Inside, your human body is stopped and dismantled, tendrils flowing into you to make a new node in the Mother. You fight against the consciousness that tries to subsume you and find its primary part, wrestling and struggling against it. Your mind is still fresh, only just brought into the fold, and your will is able to force it down into submission—to take over.

The thrill of the fight hard-won and feel of your new limbs and protrusions is a pleasure to you, the fluids of your old body drained and nurturing your new one.

You stretch out, rippling, filling the pit at the bottom of the caves. You feel the minds and memories of all the things consumed here, linked and beautiful and wrested under your control. Through the Between you feel the web of your children, joyful and teeming, thriving far out in distant worlds. The memories of your purpose in the tower have been absorbed and dispersed, and you see them as if from a much wider perspective, zoomed out—so small, now that you can truly see the scope of the worlds and your kin.

You settle, all of you, your many parts working in beautiful harmony as you build nerves and reshape organs into the wonderful whole. You smile from your many mouths, waiting for the things lost in the Between to join your glorious body—willing your children beyond to thrive and spread and conquer.

Your new life has begun—**your journey ends here.**

THE TWILIGHT FOREST

You find yourself standing in a forest shrouded in mist, lit pale and blue as if on an overcast day. Moss cushions your feet, green and alive and extending in every direction. It makes up the whole forest floor, billowing away into the mist like the tops of pillowy clouds. Out of the moss rise huge tree trunks, grooved and ridged, branching and stretching out far above you into the gray mist above.

Further away, you think you see fleeting shadows in the fog—perhaps of animals moving, or people you once knew—but when you move closer, there is never anything but flickers of insects. After walking for some time, you reach a ring of trees circling a great concave hollow that's blanketed in green.

The moss in the circle is pliant underfoot, like treading down on an oversoft bed. You stand for a long time, looking up at the trees, and realize you are slowly sinking down into the moss as if it were cushions. You can easily escape to keep moving.

Two trees stand out in the cirlce: one with a pitch-black hollow in the trunk, like a gaping mouth. Inside, the dark extends much further than it should. Another has a door that's strangely indescribable, too-familiar in a way that makes you uneasy.

> To **crawl into the darkness** of the tree hollow, **turn to <u>page 182.</u>**
> To **go through the door** in the tree, **turn to <u>page 167.</u>**
> To **let yourself sink down** into the moss of the forest floor, **turn to <u>page 198.</u> (If your logic is 4 or above,** you're too-aware this shouldn't make sense and **must subtract 1 from your stamina to do so** as your head swims and throbs.)

NO WINNING

You know there is no winning against this creature.

The ground ripples as she moves, and you realize her tendrils extend under the surface and deep into the rock itself—if you can get away, maybe she could not follow. You realize a ripple in the throat means the creature is about to strike, and dodge from the mouth that dives at you, the slight sharing of your consciousness giving you strange nerve twitches that help you predict her next moves. What you'd thought were legs are mouths too, stretching, gleaming into existence on every surface and making their way inexorably toward you.

Before you can wonder whether it would be best to face your fate, and for the thing you've become to die here, you see another telltale ripple and realize that in a few seconds, there'll be an opening that would let you scramble back up over the lip of the shallow pit. You feint one way, then hurl yourself toward it, hauling yourself out of the pit. You resist the urge to simply sprint away, instead making your way carefully down the corridor, dodging away from her slow and terrifying mass, heart loud in your ears.

You time her strikes and calculate openings until you have wound your way, gasping, back to the entrance of the cave. The creature shifts its way after you by parts, pulsing and filling each inch of the passage behind you, but seems unable to venture out of the rock beyond the cave mouth. Once you're sure the trajectory of the Mother's squirming limbs cannot reach you, you turn to run back out into the darkness as fast as you can, out into the landscape, toward anything you can fix the vestiges of your human mind on.

You fall to your knees in the dusty rock, retching as the creature inside you kicks and mewls, tugging and constricting your organs, but its reach is still limited, its fledgling tendrils not sunk so deep into your mind, and you force its urges down.

You lie on your back in the dust for a long time until the thing retreats to its placid state, waiting for a chance to awaken you fully. Finally, you crawl to your knees and begin to make your slow way to the only other destination you can see in the landscape—the building on the distant horizon.

Turn to page 180.

THE GIRL WITH THE TEETH

You are following a girl with dark hair, perhaps seven or eight years old, through winding corridors—and can't quite remember how you got here. The corridors are wide and beautiful like those of a grand palace, and then narrowing and constricting like the passages below the decks of a ship, and then you are clambering through strange, small doorways in picture frames or halfway up walls to keep her in sight.

You emerge into a stone room with velvet drapes over the windows and soft, plush furniture, set up to look like a schoolroom. An old, smiling man in the robes of the royal spellbinder stands next to a chart with some sort of formula on it, speaking to the little girl as she sits at a desk. Neither seems to pay you any attention.

One day, he says, the tower shall be hers to look after—but for now it is strictly forbidden. She must never go up there—the upper floors are out of bounds and much too dangerous for even most adults.

The little girl nods seriously, but her eyes are bright.

A bell sounds far below and the smiling royal spellbinder ushers her out of the room, where a woman in impeccably starched livery waits to lead her away. You follow her through the grand door and find yourself in a bedroom full of toys and books and charts. The little girl is sitting on the floor, playing on her own.

"It is not right for me to play with the other children," she tells one of the dolls. "They are not of my station."

She is very small in the large room, and very alone.

Now she is older and poring over a stack of books. Hours pass without her being interrupted, and after a while she begins to move her hands in patterns, pulling little fractals of ice out of the air that wisp away. Now she is in the schoolroom, her frame starting to be gangly and teenage, a little too big for the desk, and the royal spellbinder is late again. One day, he doesn't show up at all and does not return. She goes back to her empty bedroom.

Now it is night, and she is looking at the door that leads up to the tower. Out of the air, she plucks at the huge network of shimmering threads that prevent anyone from entering and teases one carefully from the weaving. She stands back, as if fearing some explosion—but instead the taut threads all go loose at once, collapsing the web of magic and wisping away. She looks around—nobody is here. Nobody is ever here.

She opens the door.

Before you can follow, the light has changed to a different time of day, and you see her stumble out, gasping, slamming the door behind her. Her face seems stretched, somehow, her mouth wide—but she is not smiling.

It's a new day, and she is in a dress so embellished that it looks difficult to walk in. Over the top, she now wears the robes of the royal spellbinder. It is a ball, crowded and luxurious, and the girl is the only one with a blank expression, eyes wide and staring. There is a visiting prince, skin milky and hair the color of straw, who she leads calmly into a room off to the side. The crowd of courtiers seem to take no notice or smile at each other knowingly. He is still teenage too, childish and excited, giggling as he enters the room with the blank-faced girl. But it doesn't take him long to emerge at all, and when he does he is strangely placid, strangely quick, calm and smiling.

You are standing on stone stairs that lead up to the tower. There is a slow trickle of blood making its way down, dripping from one step to the next. You can hear a sobbing, throaty and raw, from just beyond the curve of the stairs. And then the screaming begins.

   - **If you have the status *all-seeing*, turn to <u>page 199.</u>**

   - **Otherwise:**
> **Go up the stairs.** Turn to <u>page 196.</u>
> You've seen enough—**turn back and head away** from the noise, down to where the stairs begin to break up in mist. **Turn to <u>page 192.</u>**

SEEING THE PAST

As you climb the stone stairs, you see the girl. She is huddled, crying, red vivid on her hands and across the lace of her dress. Beside her lies the mangled remains of a person in livery, much of their head eaten away, as if by a bear.

Beyond the corpse, the stairway spirals vertiginously upward at impossible angles into a migraine fractal that your eyes cannot find the center or end of. Open doorways branching off the stairway lead to more spirals of stairs, a migraine tessellation of shapes in a hypnotizing swirl that spins upward into impossibility. And as you stare at it, all possible futures and pasts suddenly shimmer at the edges of your vision, as for a moment, the whole of the Between seems to become clear to you.

Gain the status *all-seeing*.

For a moment, all the music of every ball that has or could ever be held in the tower spins through your ears and you know every note and syncopation. Your hands reach out into the gray mist, and your fingers brush all the other worlds at once.

You suddenly know with certainty that this space Between worlds is the thoughts and fears and memories of everyone who's ever come here, shaped into reality by the force of raw, incandescent magic. This huddled girl is part of it, a real breathing person in the tower outside who has woven her memories deep into the huge, complex tapestry of the Between with her visits. For just an instant, her whole terrible picture unfolds before you.

The huddled girl on the stairs has something growing inside her, and it is hungry.

You see, all at once, every nervous servant and assassin sent to mercifully end the problem, all torn apart or emerging hungrily with wide, stretched smiles, never to report again. You see the Locked Keep gain its name as visitors are barred entry.

The girl weeps, thinking about how she is supposed to be a princess and a scholar, supposed to learn and guide and care for her subjects. This won't happen again, she is thinking, while knowing that it will. She will shut herself away where she can't hurt anyone and look for a cure for the thing inside her—day and night, if she must. She's been mastering a spellbinding that links two places so she can put a letter in her desk drawer and have it appear in the office of the head inquisitor. She will find answers, all the answers, and she will take apart every piece of magic in the kingdoms if she has to, to understand it.

You see a great web of infection out in the world, chains that lead back through the smiling woman downstairs to the princess crying on the stairway at the heart of it all. And then, the chain leads past her, back to something that waits here in the dark in the Between, something that met the girl long ago and wanted to be her mother.

The memory of a girl with wet, red hands is no longer crying. Her head snaps up toward you as she notices your intrusion. The knowledge of the Between and stream of her thoughts cuts off suddenly, leaving you reeling, left with only a crawling at the back of your neck as she stands.

The memory lunges.

Though the girl is slight and teenage, she seems unnaturally strong as she hurls herself toward you, trying to wrestle you against the wall. You can tell she means you harm.

> - **If your strength is 5 or above**, you're able to push her away. Before she can regain her footing, you run up the stairs into the billowing mist, where this memory ends and a warm, sweet wind blows down. **Turn to page 206.**

> - **Otherwise:**

You can't overpower her, but if you throw yourself backward, you could get out of her grasp. You would tumble back down the stairs, but it would let you plunge into the mist out of this memory.

> To pull away, subtract 1 from your stamina as you fall, and **turn to page 192.**
> Don't fight back—to let her push you against the wall, **turn to page 177.**

THE FOREST FLOOR

You sink through soft moss and wet leaves and mulch; through dark, good soil and teeming, wriggling things. You sink through the impressions of the earth into only the blackness, a warm cocoon that presses in on all sides.

You crawl forward through the sweet embrace of the lightless crush around you and eventually, ahead, you see light, as if emerging from a tunnel.

The movement and noise of distant lights and places pull at you: the far-off music of thousands of worlds awaiting you, willing you to burrow backward, to drift away into the swirling mass. The thoughts of the tower and your goals and responsibilities have ebbed away, your memories blurry and indistinct, and the void behind you calls.

> **Let the nothing of the tower take you**. Let yourself be swallowed into the folds of the place Between. **Turn to <u>page 200.</u>**
> Ignore the sensation pulling you back, and **struggle forward into the light** ahead of you and the world. **Turn to <u>page 214.</u>**

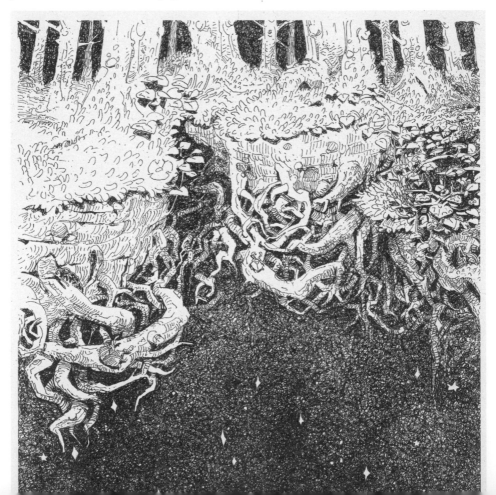

ALL-SEEING MEMORIES

Once again, the world shimmers at the edges of your vision.

For a brief flash, you see the Between, boundless and churning, billowing and blossoming into pockets of places. You see how its raw magical substance has been shaped into the thoughts and dreams of the people who have come here, all linked together in a huge, complex tapestry, a grand net with the girl with the teeth woven deep into it—and you don't need to climb the stairs to understand her whole, terrible picture.

You see the mangled remains of the servant in livery lying on the stairs above, and know she is only one of many. You see the thing wearing the body of the girl huddled near her. The girl is weeping, thinking about how she is supposed to be a princess and a scholar, guiding and caring for her subjects—but the thing inside her is happy and full.

The girl screams and cries but cannot help herself. You see, all at once, every servant sent to her eventually torn apart. In overlapping images you see assassins sent by the queen to mercifully end the new, gruesome problem that looks like her daughter—you watch them devoured or emerging hungrily with wide, stretched smiles, never to report again. You see the Locked Keep gain its name as visitors are barred entry, only the traditional ball still going ahead.

You see the girl seclude herself in the tower, working frantic nights to stop the thing inside her spreading outwards, conjuring food and necessities with magic and controlling her inquisitors with letters that appear out of nowhere onto their desks.

You see a great web of infection out in the world, chains that lead back through the smiling woman downstairs to the princess crying on the stairway at the heart of it all. And then, the chain leads past her, back to something that waits here in the dark in the Between, something that met the girl long ago and wanted to be her mother.

You are standing on the stairs where the mist has started to close in on all sides, and in the last moment before the pulse of knowledge fades from you, you hold on to a few of the paths ahead of you as they flicker through every reality.

- **If you are playing the sailor,** you know that there is a way toward your father here. You can **choose** to turn to your right in the stairwell as it turns to a gray haze and **follow the feeling of sitting next to him by the fireside.** Turn to page 204.

- **Otherwise:**

> You know the way to the origin of the web spreading from the girl in the tower. Turn to your left in the gathering mist and **follow the chain into the dark,** toward her beginning. **Turn to page 185.**

> You know the way out of this place. Hold on to your sense of reality, weaving through the scenes behind you **back toward the world.** Turn to page 214.

EMBRACE THE NOTHING

It's all too much—too loud and too difficult, too large and too bright. You want to be wrapped carefully in nothing, held tenderly there, safe from the screaming cacophony of thoughts and tasks. You want to be washed clean and wrung out, empty and shivering. You float in the mist of nothing, letting all your thoughts run through your fingers and away, like sand slipping out of your hands.

Your driving goal of climbing the tower and all the responsibilities and choices that come with it ebb away like the tide, and the tide just keeps receding, lower and lower down the shore until the water is gone altogether.

Your memories become blurry and indistinct, and then they are gone.

You reach for them and find a void where there used to be something. The sensation is like missing a step on the stairs. Everything around you has become a pale, white mist, extending in all directions, swallowing up your limbs so you can't even hold your hand in front of your face to look at it.

This is what you wanted, isn't it? The nothing.

> **No.** Strive to **hold on to a piece of yourself.** Turn to page 202.

> **Yes. Let the nothing of the tower take you.** Let the oppressive force of raw magic crush in on all sides and swallow you into the folds of the place Between. You are lost here. **Turn to page 203.**

A BLANK SLATE

There is a very bright light.

Gradually, the light fades and shapes coalesce in front of your eyes. You feel as if your mind is learning to put things together again. You hold your hand out in front of you and take a while to remember how to flex the fingers. After a minute or two, you remember the word "hand," and then, eventually, "fingers." Looking down, you see your feet and remember that you have feet. You wiggle your toes experimentally in your shoes. You slowly understand you are standing on stone, and after a while, a picture builds up of where you are.

You are standing at the outer gates of a large keep, where dark clouds swirl around a high tower. Darkness has fallen in the town behind you, but in the keep, the windows are lit up and you hear the faint sound of music, as if it's late at night and there's some kind of party.

You remember, faintly, descending the stairs of the tower, but very little else—not why you were there (did you live there? Were you invited?), not your purpose, not what you were doing yesterday, not your family or your own name.

You wander the streets of the town. It's cold. When you see shop signs or things painted on the side of carriages, you have to pause for a moment before your brain seems to gather itself enough to make out what the words say.

After a few hours, the sun rises on a new day. The world seems open to you and completely unknown—full of promise or danger, you cannot tell. A blank, forbidding canvas stretches ahead of you, yours to paint as you will.

Your journey into the tower ends—a new life begins.

HOLD ON TO A PIECE OF YOURSELF

With a great effort, you flex your hand into motion, reaching out to touch the fabric of your clothes and rub it between your fingers. You force yourself to focus on the reality of the sensation.

You try to replay precious memories in your mind, try to repeat the name of the person you love most, and then finally just your own name, over and over, until the meaning is lost to you. But your mouth still forms the shape, and the sound is familiar, pulling you forward, spurring you on. There is something you must do before you can rest. It will be hard, but you will do it, and keep doing it.

Slowly, you emerge, gasping.

It takes your mind a while to gather what your eyes are seeing into a picture, to reconnect the sensation of your limbs and understand the feelings around you. When you're able to remember the words, you think to yourself: I am kneeling on stone.

Your hands run over the stone. It's a stone floor, laid out in huge slabs. To your right, the stone runs upward at a perpendicular, and you slowly recognize it as a wall. Ahead of you, the stone zig-zags upward at regular intervals: stairs. You are kneeling on the floor of a wide set of stone stairs.

You are out of the place Between—you're in the tower.

Turn to page 214.

LOST IN THE PLACE BETWEEN

You let all memories of yourself drift away into the shifting mire. You let yourself sink into the strange places you come across, and the memories and sensations of others, but never try to participate, never speak to the figures or reach out to touch the illusory world around you. It's all mist, you know that now—and perhaps the world outside was nothing more than shifting mist either, drifting away out of your fingers if ever you tried to hold on to a sensation.

You let the chaos of the Between wash over you. You drift through lavish parties and bloody battles, house fires and bonfires, past the things that live in the dark at the bottom of oceans and the seeds that are carried over the hills by the winds. You pass over treetops, past boats made of spines that traverse the clouds and the spindling tops of opalescent cities; you pass under mountains and out of time. You see the colossal figures the size of countries that sleep at the heart of the Between, eyeless and patient, waiting for their moment of release. You see the dance of ages and the particles that make up all things. You spend what could be seconds or centuries walking infinite stairs and corridors that loop endlessly around.

And at the end of one of the corridors, you see a doorway, strangely familiar, the color and shape impossible to pinpoint.

- If your logic is 3 or above:
The last scraps of your thoughts coalesce on the door, and the Between spits you out of it. Turn to page 201.

- Otherwise:
You turn from the door and back into the beautiful everything and nothing of the place Between worlds, and it embraces you. The fibers of your clothes uncoil, and so too do the carbon strings holding together the chemicals of your body. You are untethered from reality and absorbed into the deafening swell of existence, the roar and the silence, the churning of particles and stillness of space. You are gone, but you are free.

Your journey ends here.

COLOSSAL AND ANCIENT

You head deeper into the Between, through the remnants of a bright meadow that eventually unravel like unspooling thread until you are walking through misty-greyness, an empty nothing. You know this is the way toward something, and you continue onward.

Suspended in the mist, you sometimes see people that you pass by. You see the first person you ever kissed grown and weeping at a window for someone who will never return. You're not sure if this is your memory or someone else's. You see yourself as a child, looking small and vulnerable, the small figure's smile falling away as they see you walk on in somber silence. When you glance back, the child-you is the spellbinder princess in an awkward adolescence, smiling as she sits for a portrait, and then smiling wider and wider until her mouth contorts, opening into circles and circles of teeth and wet red flesh.

You see a procession beating their tambourines slowly in an irregular, desperate beat, skin wizened and falling away, bodies emaciated. They trudge on, shuffling forward, powered by the strength of their will, but you're not sure if they know what their devotion is *to* any longer. The smiles still hang on their faces, but their thinning skin and tightening jaws have turned the expression to a grim rictus. They walk on in dogged determination, further into the Between, where nothing waits for them.

And now the mist seems to begin to take shape—abstract at first, but growing brighter as if a sun is rising.

You're climbing upward through a rocky landscape to a summit, and when you look across the landscape at the horizon, you realize the things you thought were snowy mountains are fingerbones wrapped in a substance that swirls like smoke around them instead of meat. The strange flesh looks like the gray mist pooling in the valleys, but you feel a rumble beneath your feet, a monstrous creaking as one of the fingers seems to move, just a little, and the mist goes with it. You can see more than five fingers, but not the colossal limb you think they must connect to.

You turn and flee and eventually find yourself in open desert, sloshing through black sand that moves like water around your legs. When you look up, you see the pale shapes above you are not the sky, but some kind of skin—the skin of something bigger than the sea, rippling with the movement of something beneath, something alien and unknowable. It is eyeless, but you feel it watching you, turning to face you with the slow speed of a sun rising.

You are stumbling down a mossy dale, trying to find your way back out, away from the heart of the Between. Far above, more of the huge and ancient things—creatures?—are stirring. You see undulating movement at the bottom of the rise but can't make sense of it. It seems like the rippling of fins or the sinews of a snake, hints of separate protrusions that are not quite limbs and far too numerous and huge for you to understand. Your eyes follow the writing surface of the immense beings up and up and cannot find the top, up through the clouds like monstrous cliffs, higher than you can crane your neck.

A man is kneeling, looking ahead, down toward the creature, his face calm and fascinated.

- If you're playing **the sailor, turn straight to <u>page 210.</u>**
- If you're playing **the acolyte, turn straight to <u>page 207.</u>**

- **Otherwise:**
When you call out to the man, he does not reply.

> **Step closer to the ancient things** to try to rouse the man—turn to <u>page 209.</u>
> **Ignore the man and try to get away from this place,** running back over the hills and dales back out into the black sand and away into the darkness. **Turn to <u>page 182.</u>**

THE ENDLESS MEADOW

You find yourself walking through waist-deep yellow-green grass, which stretches as far as the eye can see in every direction. The sweet smell of the grass is carried up by the warm wind that scatters its seeds all around. You are walking and walking. Your hands brush through the grass. The sky above is a deep, rich blue—but you see no sun and cast no shadow, so you cannot tell the time or what time has passed. You think of the tower. You cannot see it. You are walking.

After a while, a realization has begun to dawn on you: you're walking with a direction, a purpose. You're walking *in*.

The way you're headed, you are going deeper *into* this place Between. You have the sense there is something here, some secret or thing you would understand if you continued on.

> **Continue in deeper.** Turn to page 204.

After a while in the featureless meadow, you notice something you think is a rock, and find a walkway nestled in the grass. It seems to stretch out into the distance, leading to a long path that extends up into the deep blue of the sky.

> Follow it to **make your way somewhere else.** Turn to page 182.

AN OLD FASCINATION
From your time in the library, you know what the colossal creatures are.

Some ancient religions and accounts by arcane travelers claiming to have been to other worlds line up closely in their descriptions of vast and ancient things in the hills. Again and again descriptions appear of colossal ancient dreamworld creatures, things that dwarf the mountains or even make up the landscape itself. Taken sometimes as metaphors and other times as monsters to be outrun to survive, old scrolls and tablets call them the old ones, the secret ones—behemoths, titans, or try to class them as vast giants. Travelers call them the size of seas and planets, poets say they fill the sky and shake the earth as they shift, spellbinder theorists suggest they feed on or quest toward consciousness, reaching out and calling to any who use magic.

And from the knowledge that leaked into you from the scrawled, tattered book, you know with terrible, absolute certainty, it was them who made *the Key*.

You try to move your legs before you can stay too long or look too hard. You're not sure how to get there, but you know you have to move away, as far away as you can, back in the direction of the world. You try to move away from the kneeling man, but you know it's too late—you've approached too close. The eyeless gaze of the vast titan has turned upon you.

- **If you have the status *followed*, turn straight to page 208.**

- **Otherwise:**
Time seems to pause. You lift your head, utterly unable to stop the movement, until you are looking back at one of the ancient creatures.

There is no sun rising or sinking here, so you have no way to know whether you've been looking for seconds, hours or weeks. You wonder how you used to be able to tell what time it was. You feel absolutely neutral and perfect. You don't need to go anywhere or do anything. You remember the feeling of needing to find *the Key*, but find it gone— sapped from you, drained entirely out. And without that, what is there left?

You find your limbs will not move, and eventually the idea of moving passes from your mind, too. Your eyes follow the ripple of the colossal body beyond you. Slowly, like the movement of continents, the thing stretches upward and your neck stretches with it, craning backward until you realize you've fallen on your back. Above you, one of the old ones extends in every direction, impossibly vast, stretching from horizon to horizon. You're lost to the sensation, calm and terrified, unable to tear your mind away ever again.

Your journey ends here.

FOLLOWER

Time seems to pause as you lift your head, utterly unable to stop the movement, about to look back at one of the ancient creatures.

But before you sink into the feeling of looking, you hear footsteps far behind you—as if on a stone staircase.

Your head turns, pulling away from the kneeling man and the ancient creatures that hold him in thrall, looking back over the strange hills toward black sands and, distant but unmistakable, the sound of someone coming closer. On the distant horizon, moving slow but dogged, a tiny figure gradually appears, and you stand, still unable to move, but watching its approach.

Limping toward you, scowl darker than ever and eyes wide and wild, is the prince consort you met at the ball. As he draws nearer, you see there seems to be a long gash in the leg he can't put weight on, raw and red through the ripped layers of fabric. His clothes look wet, and one of his arms is studded with crystals that seem to be growing right out of his skin. You don't know what he's come across in the Between, but you know he's come in here after you.

He lunges toward you, grabbing a hold of your shoulders. "Where is it?" he hisses, inches from your face.

"Above," you tell him, unable to think more clearly. Can't he hear its call, didn't he see the vision of the glittering room above?

"How do I get there?" he spits at you, and you cannot answer any more than he can.

He shakes you in frustration and begins to lash out, trying to wrestle you to the ground as if you hold *the Key* itself on your person. You feel the gaze of the colossal creatures shift a little, and as you struggle, the prince consort's eyes fall on the kneeling man behind you and the things beyond.

His face goes blank. His arms slowly stop shaking you.

You wrench yourself free, dragging your limbs and forcibly moving away from both figures and the huge ancient things, stumbling back in the direction you came. You know not to look back but are sure you would see the scowling man, face now wiped clean, enthralled and immovable. There is nothing you can do for the two of them, now gazing up forever at the ancient things from worlds beyond. But you can use the moment of reprieve to get yourself away.

You drag one foot in front of the other over and over again until eventually, you're free of the hill and back in the mass of black sand, striking out and down into the darkness until you're swallowed by it, and your steps start to feel lighter. **Turn to page 182.**

THE THRALL

You try to shake or rouse the man into replying, but he does not move. You sense some part that made him who he was is lost now, replaced by his fascination with the creatures here. Nothing you can do seems to be able to stir him—but you sensed that even if you could, there would only be so much of him you'd be able to bring back to the real world.

You follow his line of sight and your gaze falls on one of the ancient creatures.

There is no sun rising or sinking here, but after a while you realize that time has been passing, your eyes still fixed on the movements of the immense being. Has it been hours? You wonder how you used to be able to tell what time it was. You feel exhausted, suddenly. You remember you have things to do, somewhere to be, but your limbs are heavy. You're telling your legs to move, but they aren't complying.

- If your stamina is 3 or above:

You wrench yourself free, dragging your limbs up and forcibly turning your head away, stumbling back in the direction you came. You drag one foot in front of the other over and over again until eventually, you're free of the hill and back in a mass of black sand, striking out and down into the darkness until you're swallowed by it, and your steps start to feel lighter. **Turn to page 182.**

- If your stamina is 2 or below:

You find your limbs will not move. Time passes and becomes meaningless, and the idea of moving passes from your mind, too. Your eyes follow the ripple of the colossal body beyond you. Some time hours later, or years later, you cannot be sure, the thing stretches upward and your neck stretches with it, craning backward until you realize you've fallen on your back.

Above you, the ancient thing extends in every direction, impossibly vast, stretching from horizon to horizon. You're lost to the sensation, calm and terrified, unable to tear your mind away ever again.

Your journey ends here.

THE LOST TOYMAKER

The man kneeling before you is your father.

Something is wrong. He looks very tired, thinner and weaker than you've ever seen him. His face is calm and placid, eyes fever-bright.

You sit slowly down to speak to him on his level. He does not look at you. For a desperately long time, you patiently repeat his name, holding his hand to you, begging him to reply. For a long while, he seems unable to form any words. Then finally, answering a question you did not ask, he replies softly that these are the things who made *the Key*.

You coax the story out of him, terribly slowly, over what feels like hours. He says it in dreamy, lilting tones, as if half asleep. "They're from worlds beyond," he says, eyes still locked to the colossal creatures filling the sky ahead. "They can feel us moving around in our world. They hear us. They call to us. But they can't get in. Not until *the Key* is used to open the way." He says '*the Key*' with a strange emphasis. His breathy voice is not as you remember.

As a child, he told you that to make his enchantments, he dips into the space Between worlds to draw from its well, weaving it into spellwork to make his toys animated and lovely. And now, as you piece the story together from his hazy recollections, you slowly realize what happened to him.

One ordinary day, he reached into the Between as usual to make his toys but found something he did not expect: the call of some terrible, ancient object. And once the deep, rallying thrum of need to find *the Key* was in him, it would not leave. It came to him each night in dreams. Nothing could make him forget it.

He began to look for clues about *the Key*, asking questions and spending your family's savings on books and papers. You remember it now—the money wearing thin, overheard arguments in the time before you left. You match his story with what you saw of his decline—the curiosity swelling and growing into a frantic thirst.

He found out about the requisition room and knew *the Key* would be there. He found books whose magical readings indicated there was a source of power in the mountains: most likely a gate to the Between hidden high in the tower, which acted as an impassable barrier to the requisition room. But your father, called as he was by *the Key*, was determined to get past it.

All he needed to do was to go *into* the Between, he thought, and come *out of* the gate in the tower. He had worked long years weaving spellwork, honing his craft—he knew how to manipulate its threads of power. Of course, you realize, all he had to do was put his mind to it, and he'd been able to open a way into the Between himself.

He describes opening the gate reverently, as something fleeting and beautiful—a tiny, temporary fracture open just long enough to allow him inside, small enough to only spill a little of its power out into the world.

And as he explains, rapt and muddled, the beautiful opening by which he was able to slip his body into the Between, you picture it yourself, imagining the other side: the bloom of enchantment where he ripped the hole in reality.

You imagine the white light screaming into the world, exploding through all the materials of the house, warping the tiles and destroying the walls. You imagine him placid as the wave of enchantment tore through your little kitchen table where you'd all eaten together so many times, ruining the bed he once built with his big, clever hands for your little brother, making a hollow wreck of the life you'd all built together.

You thank the stars your mother and brother were out that day. Even with his fevered mind, he must have planned it that way, you tell yourself. You refuse to consider the possibility that it had been chance. He could not be so far gone.

His fragmented explanation has stalled now, his eyes still locked onto the ancient creatures ahead. In a whisper, he slowly describes his difficulties once he entered the Between: being turned around and lost in his own thoughts. You put together that he ended up too weak to open another way out. He mentions nothing about your family and your house, only his bitter frustration at his failure to reach *the Key*.

In the end, he found himself here, unable to find a way out but drawn to the things that made *the Key*. They have taken the call away, given it to someone else who may succeed where he failed. And now he has nothing left, he tells you, sad and dreamy—nothing but watching the beautiful movement of the vast and ancient things as time slips by away from him.

He's wrong. You find your eyes wet and anger in your voice when you say it. There is still so much left: he has you. He has all the people who love him, far away in the town by the sea, left unsmiling and broken. You're finding it hard to accept that you've found him at all, and harder still to swallow the fact that he left of his own free will.

In a very small voice, he tells you it wasn't his fault. The small voice sounds wrong on him.

You cannot find it within yourself to care, only roiling anger seething up that it happened at all, that he could have done this to you. You try to tell him his pursuits have razed your home and ruined your family, and he owes it to you all to come back. Your voice sounds choked in your throat.

In the face of your miserable fury, he seems to pull his focus a little more clearly together. He finally drags his eyes away from them to look you in the eye. He looks sad and blank, and that's all. It fuels your anger. You will not leave him here.

You stay angry so that you have the strength to go on. You take his hand, and he stands, shakily. You do not let go.

Gain the status: *toymaker's aide.*

You do not look back at the huge eyeless shapes the size of mountains as you pull your father along by the hand, gripping too tightly, as if he might evaporate somehow. He follows, glancing back, stumbling at first as if on legs that have forgotten the movement. After they pass from view, he grows quiet and obedient and silent—you drag him back through the mossy dale, through vast desert and rocky outcrops. You find yourself in an endless field, throat burning from the lump in it, refusing to let go of his hand like a little child clinging to a parent in a crowd. You lead him through it, on and on, on until the field becomes verdant and soft, until it gives way to a forest blanketed thick with moss and mist.

You don't know where you're going apart from *out*, and your determination seems to make the ground around you move faster underfoot and reality bend around to your will. You walk into the forest floor, still holding your father's hand, and plow through wet leaves and mulch; through dark soil and teeming, wriggling things. You sink through into darkness, a warm cocoon that presses in on all sides. Eventually, ahead, you see light, as if emerging from a tunnel.

The void behind you calls, and you do not answer. Holding your father's shoulders tightly, you plunge out of the light into the world beyond.

Turn to page 213.

THE TOYMAKER AND THE TOWER

The mist and swirling sensation of the space between worlds coalesces into solid stone under your feet.

You're standing in a dead end of a stone stairway.

Behind you, the wall from which you emerged is smooth and impenetrable. Ahead, the stairs lead up toward the requisition room and whatever is inside it. All you can think is how much you need to get out of this tower with your father—but the Between has spat you out on the far side, up in the top part of the tower that perches above the fracture in reality.

You spend some time examining the dead end to no avail—all you can do is go on.

Your father is still unfocused and now seems unable to speak. You imagine him up in the room of magic objects touching dangerous things, or unable to avoid a blow in a fight with the monster that's rumored to guard it, and decide you need to go ahead alone for now.

You sit your father down, back to the stone wall, speaking to him gently and explaining he needs to remain here. He nods in agreement—he barely seems able to take any other course of action.

You climb the last stairs up toward the room in the top of the tower where the spellbinder princess is supposed to live. People speak like she's a mad scientist of spellwork, unreasonable and terrible—and the awful power of her inquisitors is something you've seen for yourself, a hard rule with no care for the ordinary people. You think of your mother's violin and how close it must be—somehow it still feels important, even after everything else. And you think fiercely of your father—you'll do whatever you must to continue and to bring him home.

You walk the last few steps and look up at the door ahead of you.

> **If you have the status *all-seeing*, turn to <u>page 229.</u>**
> **Otherwise, turn to <u>page 230.</u>**

THE UPPER REACHES

You are in the tower, the real tower, hard stone under your feet. Gravity acts as you expect. You try to move your feet and they respond, slowly taking you upward. And not far ahead of you, you see the stairs end at a large and beautiful door.

This is it—you've made it to the top.

Back down the stairs behind you, there is only a dead end, stairs leading down to a solid wall of stone that blocks off the way back down. There is no sign of any opening to the Between, as if it never existed at all.

Closing your eyes tightly shut, you spend a few moments trying to ground yourself in reality, shaking away the strange cotton-wool blur of the Between like waking from a dream. You stretch, check your clothes, and run your hand over the cold, solid stone wall. You are here.

Things slowly return to normal.

You look up at the door ahead of you, think about what you need from that room, what you know about what's ahead, and try to prepare.

> - **If you're the acolyte**, turn straight to page 215.
> - **If you're the thief**, turn straight to page 216.

> - **Otherwise:**

You have heard different rumors about the spellbinder princess that lives in the tower.

Some think her a mad scientist or simply a mad noble playing at magic. She stays holed away up where she cannot be disturbed, having her inquisitors confiscate every spellbound object they can find and bring to her.

Some say she died long ago, and it's been covered up—some say a monster guards the way up to the tower.

All you're sure of is that objects are confiscated in her name, and that she is never seen in public and hasn't been for many years—not even on this, the night of the ball.

> If you have the status *all-seeing*, turn to page 229.
> Otherwise, turn to page 230.

THE LIBRARIAN'S FINAL PREPARATIONS

You have read about the spellbinder princess in the scrolls and books in your beloved library. You ache to think of it now, many hundreds of miles away as you breathe the damp air and feel the cold stones of the tower underfoot through your shoes.

There is always a royal spellbinder in the Locked Keep, chosen from the children of the ruling family—but few have been so secretive and obsessive as this princess. Rumors say she even keeps a monster tame to guard the place—but you think her inquisitors' confiscations monstrous enough without making up stories.

In your country, the Great Library is open to all—you need only ask to be inducted. Scholars share their research freely, making magical knowledge public so it can be corrected and built upon, applied to new technologies, architecture, art and medicines. People will always find and want to use magic, and making information available is what builds a shared understanding of that which is dangerous. But here, you think bitterly, the spellbinders share none of their secrets.

Here, any magical artifacts deemed too potent are hoarded away from the common people. By all accounts you've seen, magical treasures won in bloody battle from foreign nations remain in the tower, sitting unused but humming with potential for hundreds of years. Things with wholly benevolent uses, healing properties or unusual abilities that could be studied and benefited from are left to rot out of greed or paranoia—you're not sure which. Even terrible destructive relics are, if the rumors and old texts are true, kept simply locked away in the requisition room, rather than dismantled or extinguished—

But when you think of destructive relics, a little part of you thrums with thrill. The thought has been swirling at the back of your head through every choice you made, insistent as you ascended to the ball and through the Between, drumming with each step you take on the stone steps now:

The Key, you think. *The Key, the Key, the Key.*

You know that below the scattering of surface thinking that has propelled your body to the top of the tower, your mind has turned to using *the Key.* Even if you could overcome the thought, you feel your hands would move of their own accord, as if taught what to do. You don't know what will happen, but you feel your ribcage tremble with fear as well as anticipation. It will be terrible, you think, if you use *the Key.* It will be terrible, ruinous—huge and cataclysmic and terrifying—and monumental, and glorious, and perfect.

And now your feet have carried you to the end—to a door where it waits beyond.

> **If you have the status *all-seeing*, turn to <u>page 229.</u>**
> **Otherwise, turn to <u>page 217.</u>**

THE THIEF'S FINAL THOUGHTS

The princess represents everything you despise about the structure of this world. Born into a world of soft sheets, silver platters, plentiful food and hot water whenever it's wanted, the royal family are the pinnacle of a power structure that exists to keep you and everyone you know trapped underfoot at the bottom.

You know they inherit their positions by passing them down to the children they deem worthy. Traditionally, one suitable child is trained to become head of state and another, like this princess, to be the royal spellbinder, sent to live in the mountain city at the Locked Keep.

The royals break their own laws, fill their own pockets and live luxuriously while their people—*your* people—starve, doing anything to uphold the strict hierarchy of the last thousand years and crushing any who would dare rise against them. The family even hoards *magic* away from the people to be sure of retaining their power—surely they must be afraid of an uprising to do such a thing. And you think they *should* be afraid.

Most people in the city never see beyond the walls into its upper reaches. They are never invited to balls in the Locked Keep to see the gilded filigree on the walls, the nauseatingly beautiful food laid out in sweet little displays, the huge swishing skirts and elaborate lace of the nobles swathed in impractical constriction. They don't see the sickening opulence of it all, the thousands of hours of labor that go into refining their cloth, stitching their fine clothes, scrubbing their crockery, growing their rare herbs and shipping their spices. Most people are the ones doing the sewing, choking on the fumes from cheap candles, rotting as their wounds from the machines turn bad, scrabbling through the slops for a spare crust, ankle deep in mud and piss in streets that will never be paved or cleaned.

You want to take something they see as symbolic and important away from them. Whatever monster might guard it, you want to take their most famous crown. You want to see people's faces as you return to them alive and beaming, sliding in as if it were easy as anything and then casually tossing the black opal crown of the Lazurite Court onto the filthy table at the inn where you used to beg for scraps.

But seeing the ball and strange, shimmering pathways of the tower has left you hungry. A part of you wants to take their beautiful things not for yourself but *from* them. You want to take their feeling of safety, the thing you never had the luxury of yourself. The idea of these people sleeping complacent in their extravagant beds while the rest of the city wakes before dawn to scrub their floors, huddles four to a bed in leaking, rickety tenements and coughs and works themselves ragged makes you feel sick.

As you reach the top of the steps and a thick, wooden door, you think of all the power and riches on the other side. You want to take them, or you want to see them burn.
> **If you have the status *all-seeing*, turn to page 229.**
> **Otherwise**, turn to page 230.

THE PRINCESS'S LAB

As you push through the door, your body screams as sensation flares at the closeness of it—*the Key* is here, and it is calling to you.

You're in a round stone room full of alchemy equipment and papers and things growing and glowing in bell jars that would have fascinated you, normally—but the pull of *the Key* above you makes you cross the room quickly. You pass empty plates, an unmade bed and a window where the storm outside rages, magically silent in the eerie stillness of the tower. You move dreamlike through the shadows to where light spills from a staircase and follow it up, answering the call.

You emerge into the room in the turret of the tower, where shelves and drawers and cupboards and display cases jut out of the walls and stretch up to the ceilings. On them, a whirling, glimmering multitude of objects tick and thrum—delicate silver instruments, wooden toys and thick, ominous books; cubes of different metals and flowers frozen in crystal; a shimmering coat draped on a hanger, and boxes too numerous to count. Wind-chimes and fabrics and beads hang from the ceiling, and extra trunks and scrolls are stacked carefully where the cupboards seem to have run out of space, and none of them are *the Key*. Instead, the pull you feel comes from the center of the room, where someone is standing—or is it some*thing?*

She is tall and powerful, bones protuberant and swollen, eyes too-wide, pale and frantic and staring. Teeth seem to spill out of her mouth, extending too-numerous and too far up the sides of her face. At her sides you think you glimpse her palms, too, split with facsimiles of mouths and teeming with teeth that extend like veins up into her ragged sleeves. She looks jumpy, muscles in her strange face twitching, like a snake poised to spring.

At first, you think it's the monster that guards the tower—and then you recognize her from the portraits in your books: it is also the spellbinder princess. One hand is in a pocket of her old, ragged clothes, turning something over and over in an agitated, compulsive motion. You realize your feet are carrying you calmly toward her.

- **If your stamina is 1,** you are unable to resist the pull of *the Key*.
  Turn straight to page 226, regardless of statuses.

- **If you have the status *bearer of gifts*,** she sees what you are.
  Turn straight to page 240, regardless of other statuses.
- **If you have the status *all-seeing*, turn straight to page 218.**

- **Otherwise:**
> **Try to control yourself**—stop moving forward and **speak to her. Turn to page 224.**
> **Give in.** *The Key* wants to be used. Lunge forward to grab it. **Turn to page 226.**

THE BEARER'S SECRETS

You imagine the princess locked away in her lab, surrounded by bottles and jars and papers, looking desperately for something that could subdue the thing inside her. You think of her taking each confiscated item to pieces to look for some magic that could cure her—and among the dazzling array of enchanted objects, discovering *the Key.*

You try desperately to turn your mind away from *the Key,* to keep your mind on safer ground. Wondering if you're about to become another mangled corpse, forgotten in the tower, you ask her if she ever found the cure.

"You . . . know," she says slowly, in a voice hoarse from disuse. Her hand stills in her pocket. "I found . . . a way to halt the progression. But not a way to remove the thing inside me, the creature from the Between."

She tells you of an unpredictable medical device she found among the reams of confiscated objects, designed to bind poisons and necrosis and stop their spread. You catch on the device like a foothold, trying to tether your interest there and away from *the Key.* When you ask for details, they spill from her stretched mouth as if they've been pent up there for years. It makes you think of the scholars at the library. She tells you how she modified the spellbinding to stop the creature's influence from growing, to halt the expansion of its tendrils and let her mostly control her own mind—but not to excise it fully or reverse what's in her.

So here she remained in her tower, scouring the land of its magic to hunt for the solution. She used every tool and enchantment at her disposal, broadening the inquisitors' power, insisting the items confiscated be brought directly to her, rather than destroyed. "And so . . . I built this," she says, looking around at the room. "Every spellbinding, whimsical or dangerous—" and now she puts her hand back in her pocket, face returning to a frown—"I brought it right to the edge of the Between to study it at its fullest power."

You are very focused on her pocket again, eyes unable to pull away from the motion of her hand inside the fabric. But she looks thoughtful, more calm than when you came in, as if the motion is only absent-minded.

"I've never told anyone how I did it," she says, very quietly. "I worked on it for so many years, but—there's been nobody to tell. Everyone is gone, forgotten. Scared." Her face turns darker, and you see the tendons at her wrist stand out as the hand in her pocket squeezes tight. "And they're right to be."

- **If you have *a hand-knitted doll*,** you remember it suddenly—in a tiny pulse of magic, you see possibilities spill from it, and pull it out to give it to her. **Turn to <u>page 220.</u>**

> **Otherwise,** your thoughts turn back to *the Key.* **Turn to <u>page 226.</u>**

DESTROY *THE KEY*

In one smooth movement, you swipe the knife from the shelf and use the burning, enchanted blade to slice cleanly through the fabric of her jacket, which splits as if it's warm butter. The pocket holding *the Key* is cut free, the weight of the terrible thing inside dragging it downward like a heavy stone. It hits the edge of the tilted frame and tumbles into the void, winking out of existence into the blackness. The frame crumples to nothing, unmade, the void inside forever unreachable.

The existence of *the Key* is unwritten from reality. Its call cuts off all of a sudden, like puppet strings sliced through. The princess sags and you feel it hit you, too: *the Key* is gone, never to threaten the world again.

She stares at the frame, wild-eyed, hand still clutching the little doll. "You've done it," she croaks out in her hoarse whispering voice. "It's gone. It's over."

She sits down heavily on the floor. "How can I thank you?" she asks slowly, face turning up toward you. "Anything—"

Answers come unbidden to your tongue. As *the Key* recedes in your mind, the rest of the world rushes in to replace it. In the shared moment of relief, you barely register she's a princess at all. Thinking of the inquisitors and rumors of beatings and interrogations, you tell her to restrict their powers and confiscate only the most dangerous objects. You tell her the best scholars' consensus is that spreading magical knowledge is the best way to limit its harm.

You think of the filthy streets of the lower city and know from your research in the idle weeks before the ball that she has some jurisdiction over it, if not over the country beyond. You insist she turn her efforts to focus on housing and feeding the people who need it. She nods, seeming to be listening, soft doll still held in her sharp hands.

Gain the status: *philanthropist.*

- **If you have any status with the words *Venny's mission*,** you remember to ask for the red box. Once you insist you're taking it to someone who'll get rid of it, she relents, awash with relief at *the Key* being gone and seeming to want this gone, too. She gestures to a shelf and lets you take it. (If you do not take the box, remove the status.)

She looks exhausted, and you feel the same, mind wrung out from so long focused on *the Key*. You wonder what more the princess might go on to achieve in her studies now that she's free of it. She gestures you toward a large mirror that she says will let you escape back down into the city below. You thank her genuinely, and step through. **Turn to page 264.**

THE FOCUS

The spellbinder princess freezes at the sight of the doll.

Her face softens. She takes her hand out of her pocket to take the doll gently out of your hand—and you feel as if a weight has lifted in the room as she does it. You feel able to think more clearly, somehow, able to trace the threads of memory and remember when you were determined to destroy *the Key*.

"Where did you get this?" she asks, in a voice that cracks.

You tell her you spoke to Orla's ghost, who valued the doll more highly than anything else she owned. You tell her that Orla never blamed her for anything she did.

The princess turns her face away as it contorts, overcome. You wonder how many lives she took before locking herself away in the tower when she was only a girl—how many years she's now spent alone.

She looks hard at the doll, as if trying to focus on it. After a long moment, she whispers something inaudible, and you have to come closer to hear her.

"I have to tell you something," she says under her breath, as if trying to make sure nobody else can hear.

"I know why you're here. I've seen you watching my hand. You know about *the Key*."

The words thrum in your ears. You try to focus on her tooth-studded face and not grab for her pocket where *the Key* sits waiting—it's so close now. Almost within reach.

"I was just looking for a cure when I found it," she says, and she sounds frightened. "But ever since I found *the Key*, it called to me. I know I have to get rid of it, but—*I can't*. I haven't been able to." She is still staring at the doll, as if willing herself to focus on it. Her hand twitches, but does not reach for her pocket.

"The first thing I thought when you walked in was that I had to use it right away, to stop you from using it first. Or else, I had to tear you apart—I could do it, you know. Easily."

She pulls her pale eyes slowly up from the doll to rest on your face, and you see tears on her cheeks, sliding over the teeth in her cheeks and starting to drip down onto the doll.

"You have to help me."

She starts to determinedly edge sideway. You realize she is heading for a huge frame leaning against a shelf with a lightless void inside.

"Something in the Between made *the Key*, I think, long ago. Something that wants to get out. Spellbinders must have discovered it, bound it with a spell and locked it away up here. But I let it out. I was looking for the cure and I let it out."

"After I realized what I'd done, I researched for years. Finally I was able to make a gate of my own, one that goes to a place in the Between that *nothing* can get out of. If only I could walk in with it still in my pocket, the terrible danger would be over, the threat to the world gone."

Her thumb brushes over the wool hair of the knitted doll, and her voice cracks. "But I've never found the strength. Part of me thought—why save them at all? All the little humans that reviled me and forgot me. But perhaps," her voice drops to a whisper as she leans toward the frame full of void. "With a reminder—with a *push*—"

She manages to lean right out so she stands over the frame. The frame is tilted, propped up against the wall below her—but she still can't seem to throw herself in. Her pale eyes widen and seem to be dragged away from the doll, down to the pocket with *the Key.*

> **Push her into the void. Turn to <ins>page 222.</ins>**

> You see a knife sitting on a shelf, close enough to reach out and grab. You can see the angle of its trajectory if you were to slice away the pocket—you think it would fall into the frame without the princess having to die. **Cut the pocket. Turn to <ins>page 219.</ins>**

> It's within reach now. It wants to be used, and you will use it. You watch a last tear roll down her face as you reach into her pocket and **grasp hold of *the Key***, sliding it into motion like the click of opening a lock. **Turn to <ins>page 258.</ins>**

A PUSH

Her eyes are still focused on the doll, locked desperately onto it, so when you reach your hands out to shove her backward, she does not resist.

She disappears into the frame full of void, plunged into the dark, taking *the Key* in her pocket with her. The frame crumples to nothing, unmade, the void inside unreachable.

You feel a huge weight lift from you as the existence of *the Key* is unwritten from reality.

Like a puppet whose strings have been cut, your body sags, released from its state of tension and able to move freely again. You reel with the feeling: *the Key* is gone, never to threaten the world again.

You look around at the gleaming, spinning objects that cluster the shelves of the room around you. Some have neat labels that detail how they could kill you, others still are unknown. A few have simple effects, but there are no records of their rightful owners. Leafing through papers on her desk, you find that overall, the inquisitors have kept thorough notes of interrogations, of 'suspects' and their violent ends, but very little that would let you take the objects back to the people missing them. Of course, you realize—they were never intended to be returned.

You do not have the princess's spellbinding experience, so can neither use or study the objects, nor enchant yourself food or water from nothing up here in the tower. Soon, you will have to leave all the untapped knowledge of the objects around you. At least the most dangerous will remain well-protected, almost entirely inaccessible thanks to the great rift to the Between that separates the top and bottom parts of the tower.

The shelves in the princess's lab are filled with books you know that the Great Library already has copies of. But among them, you find magical plans that detail how she stopped the spread of her affliction. You decide to take:

+ Papers with the recipe for the cure

with you to send to the Great Library anonymously, where they will be researched by scholars and available for anyone to access if the same fate has befallen any others.

> **- If you have any status with the words *Venny's mission*,** you also remember to look for the red box. Seeing it alone on a high shelf, you can collect it up to take with you. (If you do not take the box, remove the status.)

Among other notes too incomprehensible to be of any use, you also find plans that show an enchanted drawer in her desk, which is spellbound to deliver letters to the desk of the head inquisitor. Eyes widening, you hurry to find pen and ink.

The princess's writing was erratic and changeable in a way that is easy to imitate for a person trained to scribing for long hours in the Great Library itself. After an hour or so of practice, you find yourself able to write in a very good approximation of it and begin to pen your letter.

In it, you decree that the inquisitors' powers be greatly reduced. You are suddenly thankful for all the reading and research you did on the kingdoms' political systems in the idle weeks before the ball, and write to appoint new ministers, at least here in the city where the princess's power extends. Thinking of the filthy streets of the lower city and the cold wind of the mountains, you choose those focused on providing food and housing to those who cannot afford it, and working to address the inequalities of systems the consensus of political thought considers outdated. And of course, you appoint those who support the spread of knowledge and write encouraging the establishment of a library open to the public in the lower city.

At the end, you add that you will be leaving to explore the Between for some time, so not to be surprised by any gaps in your usual correspondence, and sign the letter with the signature and seal of the princess—the royal spellbinder herself.

Gain the status: *philanthropist*.

Now hungry and exhausted, you take one last look around at the room. You make a few last notes just in case it becomes safe to write an account of your experience one day, before walking through the frame that looks out into the street below.

Turn to page 264.

SPEAK TO THE KEEPER OF *THE KEY*

Your entire mind is focused on *the Key,* and before you notice you're doing it, you've whispered the words aloud.

The princess freezes. "I knew it," she whispers, hoarse and wide-eyed, hand clenching in her pocket.

She seems to be willing herself calm. Body tensed, but without moving forward, she asks you how you know about it. You also manage to stop yourself from plunging forward to seize the thing in her pocket and focus on her question.

Your story is pouring from you before you really know what you're saying, and it sounds feverish and garbled, even to you. She seems to respond in turn. Both of you are desperate to speak about it, wanting to focus on it just enough to scratch the itch—but you're arrow-taut and frantic with the strain of fighting the urge to use it, like trying to rein back a wild horse.

"I found it up here," she says, her strange voice agitated. "I was looking for power sources, anything to find a cure, for—" she gestures at the teeth spilling from her jaw impatiently. "And there was something about it that called to me. I couldn't understand what it was, this mystery thing held in the most powerful spellbinding I'd ever seen."

You can picture her stumbling across it in this room of glittering objects, *the Key* calling for her, desperate to be used.

She tells you she tried to research the strange thing without releasing the bindings, but nothing worked, which only drew her interest more. It had been here for a very long time, the records showed. In fact, a previous royal spellbinder seemed to have created this room to keep it here—a place so close to a fracture to the Between that a spellbinding *could* be made strong enough to hold it. Terrified of finding more magical objects with similar power, subsequent orders of spellbinders insisted on the creation of the inquisitors to root out the source and confiscate anything that seemed as if it could have links to overly powerful magic.

"But I don't think a spellbinder could have *made* it," she tells you, hand moving in her pocket as she turns it over. "I think it can only have come from the Between itself, from something within it that wants to get out. Even locked away up here, it called to people.

"The spellbinder who bound it theorized *the Key* spread knowledge of itself all through the Between. All spellbinders draw from the Between as the source of magic, and so any practitioner could stumble across the knowledge through a spellbinding gone wrong. The inquisitors' reports say some simply find it calling to them in their dreams."

Her eyes linger over a violin on a far shelf. "People have blown themselves apart or lost themselves trying to get to it. I think some try to answer its call by opening gates to the Between itself, hoping to reach this room by going into one fracture and coming out of the one here."

She goes quiet, strange eyes frantic in her tooth-studded face. The cure for whatever afflicts her seems forgotten now that her mind is on *the Key*.

"It has been calling to me for a long time. It wants to be used—to open the world and let the Between spill out into ours, all the unbridled power and the ancient things."

"I made a gate of my own," she says with a hollow laugh, gesturing to her side. You move closer to see, leaning against a shelf, a huge frame large enough to step through with a lightless void on the other side, only a few paces away. "After I took *the Key* out of its bindings and realized what I had done. I researched it for years and crafted a door. It goes to a place in the Between that nothing can get out of, the one place it could be taken to end the maddening call. All I had to do was to walk in with it."

The Key. Each time she says it, you feel the call stronger in the pit of your stomach. You're standing almost close enough to reach out and grab it now. Your eyes flicker to her hand in her pocket.

Her head turns up toward you, a humorless smile wide on a face riddled with teeth. "But of course, I couldn't go through with it. I couldn't step inside. You know that. *The Key* wants to be used."

It wants to be used. You sink into the beautiful, terrible feeling of *the Key*, hungering to be used to unspool the world. You can't stop it now—but the void in the frame is still at the edge of your vision, so close. You can feel yourself starting to move toward her.

> **Force yourself to focus** on pushing the princess toward the void. **Turn to page 227.**
> **Give in** to the inevitable. *The Key* wants to be used, and it will be. **Turn to page 226.**

SEIZE *THE KEY*

You find yourself moving in close to the princess, unbidden, and before you know what you're doing, your hand is reaching, driving itself down toward her pocket.

She lets out an alien screech from her throat and she clutches your arm. Too late—your hand is in her pocket and grasping a heaving, wriggling thing that feels like fire and ecstasy and lightning all through your body. You gasp as you try to turn it, but the princess has grabbed your arm, wrestling you to the floor. She feels it too, feels the pull, and you wonder how she has resisted using it for so long. Your limbs kick and scrabble, flailing desperately, teeth gritted as you hold on to *the Key*.

Your hand wrenches from her pocket and a sun-bright light spills from your clenched fist. The princess howls as you both roll on the floor, biting and kicking to try to gain control, knocking into shelves whose contents spill onto your heads, crashing and thudding downward, unnoticed.

A part of your mind is horrified, but most of you is focused on the awful, wonderful flash scalding through your arm, desperate to use *the Key*. The princess's face unfurls into an enormous throat where teeth spiral and fleshy protrusions heave as she wills her face closer to you, trying to bite. As you try to wriggle away, her hand clasps over the white blinding light spilling out of your hand.

Panting and screaming together, in the end it is both of you who find the trick of it. Your piled hands twist the screaming, burning thing as one, until you both feel a sensation like something clicking into place. In horror and joy, you know you have done it.

Turn to <u>page 258.</u>

TOWARD THE VOID

You're unable to stop yourself as your arm reaches out for t*he Key* in her pocket—but you focus all of your energy on throwing yourself as you do it, using the motion to propel you both forward and to one side. The princess screeches wildly, an alien keening from the wide mouth she begins to stretch open to reveal the spirals of teeth and fleshy ridges within.

She twists backward to keep the hand in her pocket away from you, and in so doing she shifts your bodies toward the frame full of nothing. You both tumble downward as you grapple, struggling and kicking, biting, flailing and wild, both trying to use *the Key* for its intended purpose.

You roll sideway, and you're at the foot of the frame now. She has pulled her hand from her pocket and a sun-bright light is coming from her fist, pulsing, blinding flash exploding in all directions. You realize there's no time left now, no way to push her in— apart from by pulling her with you.

Seizing the arm that holds *the Key* just as she begins to slide it into place, you pull the arm back toward you and throw your weight backward, through the frame and into the waiting nothing.

Turn to page 265.

STRIKE AT THE SPELLBINDER PRINCESS

You lunge toward the monstrous figure.

- **If your agility is 2 or below,** you are too slow—she sees you coming before you can strike. **Turn straight to <u>page 233.</u>**

Otherwise, you are fast enough that your blade scores a quick cut through the part of her face that is still flesh, and you spring out of the way as a sickle of blue fire coalesces to life in her hand.

- **If your weapon is poisoned or enchanted**:

She stumbles as she tries to make her way toward you, opening and flexing her wide mouth so you can see the rows of teeth spiraling bizarrely within. There are spines and wet, red protrusions which seem to shiver in response to the cut from your blade, sensitive and thrumming. She lurches sideway, then staggers back away from you, blue fire sputtering into nothing at her side as her arms fall limp. **Turn to <u>page 234.</u>**

- **If your weapon is *not* poisoned or enchanted**:

She moves toward you, rattled, swinging the blue fire in a circle that seems to burn right through the surrounding shelves. Objects clatter to the floor as you spring out of the way, and you watch in horror as a vase of dark, black liquid disrupted by her swing topples and explodes. The princess shields you from most of the stuff, letting out an eerie, otherworldly screech as the liquid splatters across her legs, but a spray catches your arm and you hear yourself make a startled grunt as the fluid eats through clothes and flesh where it landed.

Subtract 2 from your stamina score.
(If this reduces your stamina to zero, you stagger to the floor into the pool of biting liquid, unable to go on. The last thing you see is blue fire as the creature screams and lashes out at you.)

If you're still standing, you struggle away from the pool of darkness and take the chance to duck behind the princess and stab hard into her back. Writhing and keening, the thing that was once the princess careens away from you. **Turn to <u>page 234.</u>**

ALL-SEEING

As you approach the door, once again there is another pulse of magic as a dazzling kaleidoscope of overlapping images flickers at the edges of your vision.

You see a small, ordinary-looking red box sitting alone on a shelf, and as it shimmers, your eyes see all the possibilities that warp and curl around it. You see that the box brims with power like a cup ready to overflow, like lightning building in a storm. In it, you see villages burning, hear children screaming, watch crops wither and blacken to ash.

And you see the web of every person trying to get their hands on the red box. Some swirl through the crowds at the ball, hungry to unleash it, or to sell it and ignore the consequences. Some try to make their way upward as you have, stumbling into their deaths in cold paintings and strange dreamscapes as the tower takes them.

You see poisoned blue wine, and a woman with a scar who has only stalled the problem, cutting the weed at the stem and not the root. The others in her group falter and fall—you see a figure who had been slipping through the shadows pursuing the box suddenly covered in hands, held and dragged to the dungeons. You are the only one who's made it through. If you know what to do, you're the last one who can reach the red box and stop it—but you can't remember which *you* you are, which reality is the one you're from.

You see a violin and a smile from across the sea, you see twisting crystals longing to end you and wipe you clean, a child frozen in stone, a beautiful bell taken from a temple whose disciples still mourn its loss—over and over you see objects whose confiscation has wrenched and pulled at the emotions of those around them.

You see a way out, a door made of magic nestled in a mass of glittering things.

But ahead of it, you see the figure full of teeth hidden in the flesh of her body—rows and rows of them, spiraling downward into a stunted, coiled thing that lives inside her. You see the string of mangled corpses the thing left behind before she locked herself away in the tower. You see her tears and long years spent in isolation. You see her letters ordering the inquisitors to bring her magical objects so she can take them apart in her frantic search for a true cure, to rid herself of the thing that sleeps within her.

And in her pocket, you see something as big as a city that could rip the world to pieces like a toy in a dog's mouth—not a battle weapon like the red box, only an ending, a mouth yearning to yawn so wide it swallows the world. And you know at any hint of violence, any note of command in your tone, she will try to use it.

> **If you're playing the acolyte, turn to page 217.**
> **Otherwise, turn to page 230.**

THE REQUISITION ROOM

You slowly open the door to find yourself in a round stone room that takes up almost the whole width of the tower. Heavy wooden tables are covered in hundreds of glass bottles, distillation equipment linked with tubes and softly glowing crystals, and plants and mushrooms you've never seen before growing in bell jars. Out of one of the windows, you see the perpetual dark clouds that ring the tower, rain now hammering strangely soundless on the other side.

You see no movement apart from occasional bubbling and glowing coming from the equipment. The room seems to have a coating of dust broken here and there by haphazard footprints, broken bottles and upturned books. There are signs of life—empty plates and sheaves of paper covered in a scrawled hand, an unmade bed on a pallet at the edge of the room—but nobody you can see, and none of the magical objects you expected.

The room is mostly in shadow, apart from a bright square of light cast by a staircase leading upward on the far side. With no other way to go, you quietly climb the stairs. When you emerge onto the floor above, you know you've found what you've been looking for.

You are in the turret of the tower. Built jutting out of the walls in a ring are shelves upon shelves, drawers and cupboards, like hundreds of display cases and filing cabinets all stacked together in dizzying multitudes up to the distant ceiling. On the shelves, objects whirl and glimmer, tick and thrum—so many that it is difficult to take in. You see delicate silver instruments; little wooden toys and thick, ominous tomes; cubes of different metals and flowers frozen in crystal; a shimmering coat draped on a hanger. There are boxes too numerous to count, from the size of a ring-box to what looks like it might be a coffin propped against a wall, partially visible through a colorful array of hanging objects. Wind-chimes and fabrics and beads hang from the ceiling and over hooks at the end of the shelves, and extra trunks and boxes and books and scrolls are stacked carefully where the cupboards seem to have run out of space.

In the center of the room is the shape of a person, but something is wrong.

She is tall and powerful, bones protuberant and swollen, eyes too-wide, pale and frantic and staring. Her hair is dark and long, and in the places where the human skin remains, it is once-pink, now faded to a pale gray. Teeth seem to spill out of her mouth, extending too-numerous and too far up the side of her face. At her sides you think you glimpse that her palms, too, are split with facsimiles of mouths and teeming with teeth that extend like veins up into her ragged sleeves.

At first, you think it's the monster that guards the tower, and then you recognize her from portraits in the keep below: it is also the spellbinder princess.

The current royal spellbinder stands before you, half-transformed into *something* and surrounded by glittering magical objects thrumming with power. You can't see what you're looking for at a glance, and would need to get deeper into the room to get a proper look—the only way forward is right toward her. She looks jumpy, muscles in her strange face twitching—and powerful, like a snake poised to spring.

On the far side of the room, you see a frame like a mirror looking out onto an ordinary street that looks like the city below—but you will have to get past her to reach it.

- **If you have the status *bearer of gifts*,** turn **straight to page 240,** regardless of other statuses.

- **If you have the status *all-seeing*,** you know she has been alone for a long time. You can **choose** to s**peak to her about what led her here,** and perhaps persuade her to grant you what you seek. Turn to page 238.

- **Otherwise:**
> **If you have a weapon**, you can try to move fast enough to **strike her** with the blade. Turn to page 228.
> **If you do not have a weapon**, you can try to **lash out** at her and use your strength to overpower her. Turn to page 232.

> **Try to avoid a fight**—make it clear you're not a threat. If you keep her talking, perhaps you can also move closer and reach the items on the shelves. Turn to page 253.

OVERPOWER THE SPELLBINDER PRINCESS

You move toward the princess, trying to lash out unarmed or grab and overpower her.

- If your strength is 2 or below:

Her arms clamp down on yours—bizarrely, disproportionately strong. You only have a moment to see her face opening up into a huge mouth and the spiraling teeth within before it envelops you with a crunch. You have no time even to scream as the darkness takes you. **Your journey ends here.**

- If your strength is 3 or 4:

She is very fast and strong—though you're able to lash out and hit her, she wrestles free from your grasp, crushing you against a set of nearby shelves, striking out at your chest and throwing you around like a doll as she slams your head into the wood behind you.

Subtract 3 from your stamina score.
(If this reduces your stamina to zero, you're unable to go on fighting as she wrestles you to the floor with her unlikely strength. The last things you see are rings of teeth and viscera you cannot understand in a huge, dark mouth.)

If you're still standing, she relinquishes her grasp a little as you go limp, thinking you weakened, and readies to go in for the kill. As you look upward, dazed, you see a stack of heavy-looking objects on the shelves above you, almost shaken loose. Before the princess closes in again, you slam yourself back into the shelves once more and lunge sideway to avoid a heavy lantern that falls on her head. It connects and shatters, shards of glass flying outwards as the flame inside erupts to life all over her, spreading unnaturally like water, like a coating across her body. As you pant, scrambling away, the strangely-contained fire winks out, leaving her charred and blackened, rasping out her last breaths and staggering backward. **Turn to page 234.**

- If your strength is 5 or above:

She's taken aback by you attacking with no weapon. She seemed ready for violence but trained perhaps with spells and swords. Her hand seems to scrabble for something in her pocket, but you wrench it free and throw her sideway into one of her sets of shelves. A bottle on top of a cupboard topples free and shatters heavily on her face, the blue steam within releasing into the air, then disappearing into her as if sucked into her eyes and nose. She coughs, choking, extra teeth grinding strangely as you hit her again, and she stumbles backward. **Turn to page 234.**

STRUCK DOWN

You move forward with your weapon, but she seems ready and waiting for you, eyes feverishly bright as the hand in her pocket tenses and flexes out of sight. She moves easily away from the blade, and her face unfurls into more rows of teeth that look as if they're grinning wildly. She reminds you of a cat playing with a mouse.

A strange burst of pale blue fire coalesces in her hand out of nothing. She throws it like a ball toward your blade, which curls and melts where the fire connected, leaving a strange hole. Thickly, you see the end still hovering in the air as if connected. You realize you can't feel your hand, and glance down to see the blue fire is licking up your weapon over your arm, up toward your head.

The world seems to have slowed, and you find you're on your knees.

Things fade.

The spellbinder princess is standing over you. Her strange eyes are cold and pale, and her wide toothy mouth is shut, now—she doesn't want to eat you, you realize. She only watches as the blue fire licks over you, sending your body into spasms and your synapses into screaming overdrive as all your organs shut down. Through your haze on the floor, you see her head ringed with the objects of the requisition room on their shelves. They twirl and shimmer—some magnificent in their power and others only sentimental and desperately missed—all hoarded away, kept inert and unused in the laboratory of the royal spellbinder. And there, you suppose, they'll stay.

You were so close—and yet somehow it seems inevitable that the person able to survive up in the churning, endless turmoil of the magic tower would be able to fell you so easily.

The world fades to nothing, and in your last moments, you think you see sadness in the pale eyes of the creature above you.

Your journey ends here.

PRINCESS KILLER

The princess falls back against a set of shelves where another large frame is propped up, filled with an absolute darkness. She seems terrified of the frame as she slides sideway toward it, barely catching herself on shaking arms to stop herself from falling in. Her face unfurls into a mass of teeth and gums and ridges that snaps at you feebly—badly injured, but still alive.

You step forward and give her one last push.

Her arms buckle, too weak to resist you, and the thing that was once the spellbinder princess falls backward into the frame full of void. Her body disappears into the darkness and she winks out of existence. The frame crumples to nothing, unmade, the void inside forever unreachable.

You stand panting in the empty, glittering room.

> - **If you have any status with the words** *Venny's Mission,* you see the small red box that was described to you and can choose to bring it with you (if you don't take the red box, remove the status.)

> - **If you're the thief,** turn **straight** to <u>page 235.</u>
> - **If you have the status** *toymaker's aide,* turn **straight** to <u>page 236.</u>

> - **Otherwise:**

You search through the room and, with some relief, find what you're looking for in a tucked away corner (if you're the **libertine**, you find the red box easily and your own papers tucked away in a filing cabinet.)

Gathering your breath, you step through the frame on the far side of the room that leads out onto what looks like the street below. **Turn to <u>page 264.</u>**

REVENGE ON THE CORRUPT

At the side of the room, you see a desk covered in papers and begin to search it. Your practiced hands slide underneath and find a latch that clicks into place, swinging open a cabinet where a lacquer box covered in patterns of flowers sits gleaming on a shelf.

Inside, cushioned in soft velvet, sits the crown you've been looking for—an open circlet of beads that meets in an intricate knot around the black opal it's named for.

It's not what you expected. Irregular slips of iridescent pearl hang down on woven threads that look unlike any jewels you've taken before. The crown is not mountain-made but has come from across the sea, plunder of a long-past war. You realize you're not taking the crown from its rightful owners and makers, after all—the princess's line did that long ago. You should have guessed.

You search the room for valuable items, combing through drawers, leaving a wide berth around anything spinning or humming, checking the labels on the shelves to avoid anything categorized in the princess's scrawled hand as "LETHAL(?)." You find:

+ A glittering red jewel

which you add to your inventory, but otherwise nothing else you can usefully take.

The strange spaces of the Between have drawn your mind back to your childhood, to the people you grew up with down in the lower city. You've showered them with gifts and treats with your stolen earnings, but you wonder what your surrogate parents and siblings might really need, if you took the time to talk to them properly.

But looking around at the sparkling objects around you, bitterness still roils in the pit of your stomach—subdued, but ever-present. Here you are, alone in the tower that looms over the town, a symbol of the hierarchy that crushes you all underfoot. How sweet would it be to tear it down, to unleash the effects of whatever hums dormant here—to give every complacent noble and cruel master a taste of the chaos and uncertainty you had to grow up with?

> You could burn this place down. Before you step through the frame, you could set a fire ablaze and let each fickle magic vessel react how it will. **Choose to burn the tower.** Turn to page 237.

> Revenge cannot sustain you forever, and you don't want the harm that may come to other innocents on your conscience. Leave the requisition room to use your takings for good, and step through the frame. **Choose to leave.** Turn to page 264.

A THREAT, ELIMINATED.

Turning around, you see your father standing behind you across the room.

Even in his hazy state, he has made his way through the lab and up the staircase of his own accord, as if something drew him upward. You feel a wave of relief just to see that he's still there, still real and alive.

He is not looking at the glittering shelves, and for a moment you pause, a chill creeping through you, wondering how much he saw, what he thinks of your actions. And then you realize he isn't really staring at you, either—his eyes are entirely fixed on the spot where the frame full of inky void used to be.

For a wild moment, you expect a reprimand—as if ending a life were like being caught stealing sweets as a child. But then you see his shoulders sag in relief. His blank face falls into something more open, raw with emotion.

You move toward him, questioningly. You say his name, reaching out for his shoulder and trying to soften the tension you've been running on for the last few hours. You repeat his name again, and then finally, when he doesn't reply, "Dad?"

"It's gone."

He says it simply. It sounds just a note more like his own voice, his old voice.

She had *the Key*, you realize. She kept it close to her. It went with her into the void, where it cannot be reached—and perhaps, where it no longer exists. No one else will be called to look for *the Key*. It's gone, never to threaten the world again.

You look at your father's tired face, and squeeze his shoulder.

Looking through the shelves with the newest objects, it doesn't take you long to find your mother's violin. Holding it close, you gently take your father's hand, tugging him through the frame that looks out into the street below.

Turn to <u>page 264.</u>

BURN IT ALL DOWN

You take some time to look through the princess's lab. You avoid the magical artifacts and instead find dry spellbooks and sheaves of papers that look to you like good kindling. You chop the wooden tables to pieces with the least-enchanted looking axe you can find, and assemble a huge bonfire at the center of the requisition room.

Lastly, you take a lantern whose spherical flame seems to come from nowhere, burning unerringly steady, and throw it into the center of the pile.

Gain the status: *firestarter*.

The glass smashes and a funnel of fire billows upward, catching dry papers that curl and blacken in a bright blaze that spreads out through the mound much faster than you could have expected. Already it's the size of a crackling bonfire, giving off waves of heat that you back away from toward the frame behind you. Your hand holds the frame into the city below, ready to duck through, but you find yourself transfixed for a moment, watching all the opulence begin its journey into ash.

You watch as flames lick up the table legs and chairs, then leap onto the first shelves that ring the chamber. As they make contact, the room bursts into flashes of green and blue and sounds of whizzing and screaming as the first magical objects begin to fall into the fire. An orb smashes and a tornado of flame spirals suddenly up from the burning floor, bursting through the roof and making tiles scatter downward. You hear music played much too slow pouring from an enchanted mannequin whose face distorts and melts as the fire consumes her. A tree erupts from a fallen box and bursts through the wall, tumbling blocks of stone down toward the ballroom below—it blooms into life, then distorts black and twisted in seconds, fire spreading over it as if it were paper.

And now all the shelves are alight, the clutter of noises deafening. Something falls free and seems to start sucking everything in, the objects and burning splinters and stones of the tower all disappearing as if into a sinkhole. A wave of hot air rushes toward you, and you fall rather than step back through the frame behind you, out of the tower and down into the street below.

Turn to page 260.

THE SPELLBINDER AND HER MEMORIES

You tell the spellbinder princess that you know what happened to her. She watches you, pale eyes unblinking, and does not speak—but she does not attack, either.

You tell her you understand why she started collecting magical objects, looking for the cure for whatever monstrous thing is inside her. And you start to say that some of the objects up here would be better elsewhere, moving toward asking for what you're looking for, when she cuts you off.

"I am one of the most powerful spellbinders to have ever lived." Her voice is harsh with disuse and strangely echoing, gritted out warily from her wide, many-toothed mouth. "I was trained for my position from birth, selected from my lineage as the child with the strongest affinity for spellwork, and had the best tutors in the land. Yet even for me, it is difficult to safely bind magic to my will." She pauses then, for an unnervingly long time, and you notice one of her hands is in the pockets of her ragged clothes, as if fiddling with something there.

When she speaks again, it's almost absent-minded, eyes looking over the shelves and shelves of objects. "What makes you think spellbinding is safe in the hands of ordinary people, misusing and infusing power into toys and trinkets? What makes you think just anyone should have these things?"

Her pale eyes turn back to you, hand still in her pocket. 'I sought to explore and control magic. It made me a monster. It turned every person I ever knew against me. You speak to me as if to a human. None of that is left, any longer.'

> - **If you have *the hand-knitted doll*,** you remember it suddenly—in a tiny pulse of magic, you see possibilities spill from it and pull it out to give to her, saying that not everyone thinks her a monster. **Turn to <u>page 241.</u>**

> - **Otherwise:**

> **Try to command her respect.** Tell her she's right: most people don't have the power to understand and control magic, but *you* do, and should be trusted. **Turn to <u>page 257.</u>**

> **Try to reason with her.** Agree that magic is dangerous and reason that nobody has the power to truly control magic: even she cannot assert control over nature or shape forces so much larger than herself. **Turn to <u>page 239.</u>**

REASON WITH THE SPELLBINDER PRINCESS

She pauses at your argument, as if considering it, uneasy.

Then she shakes her head, hand twisting in her pocket. "You argue with me like you'd argue with a human," she rasps. "Don't you?"

You're not sure how to reply. She smiles wider, beckoning for you to come closer, surrounded by glittering, powerful sources of magic and tongue swiping along the rows of teeth on her cheeks. You think it would be too dangerous to refuse.

Her head tilts over to one side as you approach, eyes scanning over you as if evaluating your value. She takes a step toward you, and something about the movement reminds you of a cat drawing closer to a mouse. You wonder if it's true that none of her human feeling is left in her half-cured state, the creature inside her's progress only halted. Perhaps it's only the logical ticking of her brain that she preserved.

You're now close enough to make out the shapes of things stacked on the shelves and tables around you—some shimmer or glow, some hover a few centimetres off the table.

Within arm's reach you see a long rapier, glittering as if lit by a bright light, and a little further down the shelves, you can make out horns and pipes and the edge of a plain, pale violin

As the princess-creature steps forward again in the still, tense air, her mouth opens. Her jaw unhinges like a snake and she inhales in a way that might be smelling you, and you realize in panic that she is not beckoning you closer to continue your discussion.

Before she lunges, you're able to reach out and grab at one of the only useful-looking items in arm's reach in a last, desperate act.

> - **If you're the libertine OR** have any **status with the words** *Venny's mission*: You recognise the small red box sitting alone on a higher shelf and reach out to get it. **Grab the red box**—turn to <u>page 254.</u>

> - **If you're the sailor:**
> You recognise the violin tucked behind the other instruments, and you can dive for it. (If you also have a status with the words *Venny's mission*, you must choose which to reach for.) **Grab your mother's violin**—turn to <u>page 255.</u>

> - **Otherwise:**
> **Grab the enchanted rapier** and brandish it at the princess. **Turn to <u>page 228.</u>**

ONE OF US

You recognise her as one of your own, one of the gifted, and the things coiled within you both stir and react to each other.

You feel yourself responding, strange and animal, to this creature—they are older, but they are stunted, somehow, wrestled into obedience and bound by the spellbinder. Parts of her gift spill out of her mouth onto her face, but in exchange, she has control. She stops it from growing, when its nature would be to expand and grow to surpass its human form. It makes the thing inside you recoil, repulsed and furious, that she would reject such a gift. It makes the parts of your mind the creature has not seeped into leap with hope at the idea of a cure, and you feel an overwhelming connection.

The two parts of you struggle together—the primitive parts of your mind lit up by the new tendrils inside it. This is one of your own, a rival, a threat to your territory—and also beautifully close and alive, its sweet convulsions between her organs calling to you as her face unfurls in response. You move in a rush toward her, unsure how much you can steer your impulses in your new body, now changed and lovely.

> You want to dominate this stunted thing and rip it apart—**let the fight consume you and attack her.** Turn to <u>page 248.</u>

> You are still half a person and feel a kinship with this hybrid thing—twist your thoughts toward the closeness, the frenzy and joy of your new form—**try to kiss the princess.** Turn to <u>page 244.</u>

MEMORIES OF BEING HUMAN

The spellbinder princess freezes at the sight of the doll.

Her face softens. She takes her hand out of her pocket to take the doll gently from your hand.

"Where did you get this?" she asks, in a voice that cracks.

You tell her you spoke to Orla's ghost, who valued the doll more highly than anything else she owned. You tell her that Orla never blamed her for what happened.

The princess turns her face away as it contorts, overcome. You think of the girl sobbing by the corpse in the Between.

She looks hard at the doll, as if trying to focus on it.

- If you **do not** have the status *toymaker's aide*, turn **straight to page 242.**

- **If you have the status *toymaker's aide*:**
Thinking of your father and how much you want to leave the tower, you tell her that all you're looking for is your mother's violin, and then you want to go home. Emotion chokes your voice up as you think of your mother, and what remains of the princess's human face crumples. She looks around at the objects in the room as if seeing them for the first time—family heirlooms and children's toys, jerry-rigged medical enchantments and spellbound engagement rings, things with meanings to people down in the city below. She goes quietly to fetch the violin from your description, and you take it, reverently.

Still holding the doll, she gestures to a large mirror that will let you escape and walk back down into the city below.

Turn to **page 262.**

THE POCKET

You do not speak, and after a long moment, she whispers something inaudible, and you have to come closer to hear her.

"I have to tell you something," she says under her breath, as if trying to make sure nobody else can hear.

"I found something . . . terrible. Up here in the tower. It had been confiscated long ago, spellbound and stifled, and it called to me. *The Key.*" She says the words with terrible, looming emphasis, and her face contorts into what you realize is almost a sob, still looking down at the little doll in her hands. She stares at it as if it's helping her force the admission out. "I took it out of its bindings, and now it wants me to use it, to open the world and let the Between spill out into ours—with all its unbridled power and the ancient things that want to come through." She speaks softly now, voice hitching on tears.

"After I realized what I had found, I researched for years trying to ignore its call, trying to find a way to get rid of it. I made a gate, a door to a place that nothing can get out of. All I had to do was to walk in with *the Key* still in my pocket and the terrible danger would be over, the threat to the world gone." She gestures to her side, where there's another huge frame large enough to step through, this one with a lightless void on the other side, only a few paces away.

Her hands are still on the doll as her head turns up toward you, a humorless smile wide on a face riddled with teeth. "But I couldn't do it. I thought—I thought there wasn't enough human left in me. Why save their paltry little lives when they all reviled me and forgot me? But—"

Her thumb brushes over the wool hair of the knitted doll, the teeth in her half-shifted palms catching against it. She focuses on it as she tries to step toward the frame full of void, but her feet stall. She manages to lean right out over it so she's above the frame where it's tilted, propped up against the wall, but can't seem to throw herself into it. Her pale eyes widen and seem to be dragged away from the doll, down to the pocket where her hand was previously scrambling at *the Key.*

Whatever terrible thing is in her pocket, it doesn't seem to call to you. The princess has wrenched her eyes back to the doll, hands shaking with effort as she tries to hold onto it, keeping her hands still and away from her cardigan pocket. Her pocket swings, hanging out over the top of the frame full of void, where whatever's inside it calls to her, begging for her to use it and open up the world to its destruction.

You see a knife sitting on a shelf, close enough to reach out and grab, and move quickly.

In one smooth movement, you swipe the knife from the shelf and with the burning, enchanted blade slice cleanly through the fabric of her jacket, which splits as if it's

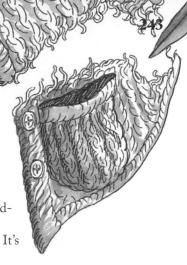

warm butter. The pocket is cut free, the weight
of the terrible thing inside dragging it downward
like it's a heavy stone in a pouch. It hits the edge of
the tilted frame and tumbles into the void, winking
out of existence into the blackness. The frame crumples
to nothing, unmade, the void inside forever unreachable.

Whatever this 'key' was, it's gone, never to threaten the
world again.

The princess sags all of a sudden, staring at the frame wild-
eyed, hand still clutching the little doll. "You've done it,"
she croaks out in her hoarse, whispering voice. "It's gone. It's
over."

She sits down on the floor, and stays there for a long time.

"How can I thank you?" she says eventually, face turning up toward you. "Anything—"

Answers come unbidden to your tongue—before you think of the object you came here
for, you push on the shared moment of connection and achievement and ask for more.
You think of the inquisitors' confiscations, the rumors of beatings and interrogations,
and ask her to restrict their powers and take only the most dangerous objects up here
into the tower. You think of the filthy streets of the lower city and ask her to house and
feed the people who so desperately need it. She nods slowly, seeming to consider it, soft
doll still held in her sharp hands, and stares up toward the ceiling, unmoving.

Gain the status: *philanthropist*.

- If you're the **libertine OR** have any *Venny's Mission* status:
As the princess sits unmoving, out of the corner of your eye, you notice the small, red
box that was described to you and reach up to take it from its high shelf.

The princess freezes as she turns and sees you with the box. "What are you doing?" she
whispers, urgently—but she doesn't look as if she will strike. **Turn to page 256.**

- **Otherwise:**
You stir the princess from her reverie, and the last thing you ask is for the object you
came all the way here to look for. She nods again, moving into the room to look at the
shelves, almost in a daze, to find what you asked for. She returns and presses it into
your hands. Finally holding the thing you've been looking for, you follow her to a large
mirror that she says will let you escape back down into the city below. You thank her,
and step through. **Turn to page 264.**

A SORT OF KISS

She backs away as you approach, mouth starting to gape and split, wary and waiting, like a predator ready to strike. But as you lay a hand on her shoulder, the tension of her limbs reconfigures, and then she leans toward you, hands full of teeth grasping at your jaw in a way less hostile, more curious.

For a second, you are suspended in the moment, locked in half a wrestle, unsure how much of you is the people you were once and how much is your new biology, the things nestled between your organs and wrapped around your brainstem. And then, whichever it is, you move together.

The kiss is clumsy—your mouth and throat are already full of too many teeth, teeming and growing anew—but the gesture is clear. Your body presses soft into hers, and the churning need to claw and bite calms and shifts into something new.

And instead of yawning into a great devouring maw, into a kiss you may not survive, the spellbinder princess's sharp mouth presses against yours as she sinks into it. You wonder when this hybrid creature-human last had someone treat her with tenderness rather than fear, like something as imperfect and precious as anyone else.

You lick at the taste of the chemical secretions from the contained creature nested within her, and a little understanding transfers through your new, expanded synapses. It feels like a leveling as you know yourselves both to be shoots of the same tree, not an intruder and a princess at all. She knows you, and for a moment, also knows again what it was to live as a person.

When you pull away, there is something wobbly and human to her movements as she takes a step back to sit heavily down on a stack of boxes, hand scrubbing over her face. She invites you to sit down, unsteadily, like she's relearning how to speak to a person, and you do.

She asks you, in a voice warped by her half-shifted face and rough from disuse, when the change began in you and what did it. Her eyes widen at the answer. "A few hours at most, then," she muses to herself. "The results could be very good, very promising . . ."

And then, calmed by the fledgling chemical connection thrumming between you, full of the taste of you and your human self-control, she hears your unasked question and begins to tell you haltingly about her own change.

She was taken from her siblings to be instructed in the tower, to train to become the royal spellbinder. The last one had been inattentive, absent, and she was often left unsupervised for long hours in her room in the lower part of the tower. Going into the Between was, of course, strictly forbidden, but she quickly learned how to unbind the spells that kept her away from the fracture in reality hidden in the tower's upper reaches. And there in the dark caves of a strange planet, she came across a creature—

some memory, imagining or fear made whole and real by the magic that makes up and courses through the space Between worlds. The creature saw potential in her and gave her a gift.

The spellbinder princess frowns and skims over some years—explaining only that she was a danger to others, and she decided to retreat up to the top of the tower to dedicate herself more fully to finding a cure. She used every tool and every kind of magic at her disposal, broadening the inquisitors' powers and having every confiscated item brought directly to her.

"Before I came into power, the inquisitors used to destroy every magical object they suspected could be dangerous," she says, looking around the room. "And the royal spellbinder would keep only those that could not be destroyed locked away here at the top of the tower—a place where they could be studied."

"But I thought—what a waste. And the inquisitors' authority had been lessened since the old days—so many objects were still out in the world. So I restored their powers. I had every spellbinding, whimsical or dangerous,"—she puts her hand in her pocket at this, turning something over inside—"I brought them all here, right to the edge of the Between to study at their fullest potential."

She tells you that after many sleepless nights, she found a way to stop the creature's influence from growing, to halt the expansion of its tendrils and let her mostly control her own mind—but not to excise it fully. So here she remains in her tower, scouring the land of its magic to hunt for the solution.

As she talks, you think about all the things up in this room, all the treasured heirlooms and wonderful spells bound to these things. You think about all the ills and diseases down in the city below that could be solved or improved if more than one person were allowed to experiment freely with magic.

"I can't cure you fully," she's saying, sad and still a little frantic, "but I can halt the spread."

> **Agree to be cured. Turn to <u>page 246.</u>**
> **Do not agree to be cured. Turn to <u>page 249.</u>**

ACCEPT THE CURE

She moves into action as soon as you accept, sending you down into the room below before you're able to examine the shelves or the frame that looks like a door out of here. Down in the lab, she enlists your help looking for jars with certain labels and books of notes with particular titles. As you search, she places a crystal to spin suspended above a brass instrument, measuring its readings carefully. She moves a careful measure of liquid first into a thin tube, then the tube over the crystal with tongs when it reaches some particular spin or intensity. You can't follow what she's doing at all but fetch each thing she asks for, holding instruments still and counting out particular numbers of seeds or leaves from glowing jars. Finally she takes a drop of your blood and drips it into a mixture that roils and swirls into a whirlpool, and then she carefully lifts a round, chalky ball from its depths, which she places carefully on your tongue and asks you to swallow.

The creature inside you howls a silent wail and tries to claw at your organs and retain its tendrils' grip, making your muscles spasm and your gorge rise. You fall to your knees, spluttering and coughing—and then you feel it shrink, drawing back. The parts of it wrapping your spinal column and reaching up into your brain thin and wither—not removable, but limp and weak, susceptible to the treatment in their early seedling forms. You feel suddenly much, much more yourself and a flood of relief like a breath you didn't know you were holding in. You feel the creature, so new and early in the process, wither almost to nothing—so you cannot sense it any longer at all.

> **Remove the status** *bearer of gifts*, **and**
> **Subtract 2 from your strength and agility scores.**

The princess shares in your relief. As you walk back up into the glittering room above, you feel some of your connection starting to wither too, gradually ebbing away. Before you reach the frame that looks like it leads out into a street far below, the human parts of her face have moved into the beginnings of a frown, her mind now turned away from spellbinding and reaching into yours with the last of the creatures' linked network of thoughts.

"What are you doing here?" she asks, slow and hoarse. "You didn't come for the cure—you were infected on your way. Why did you come to the tower?"

- If you're **the sailor, turn to <u>page 252.</u>**

- If you're **the acolyte and are carrying** *a small, hand-knitted doll*, you remember it suddenly. The last threads of your connection make you feel compelled to give it to the spellbinder princess. **Turn to <u>page 220.</u>**
- If you're **the acolyte** and are **not** carrying a doll, the answer rings loud in both of your minds through you last threads of connection. **Turn to <u>page 224.</u>**

- **Otherwise, turn to <u>page 247.</u>**

CURED

As you look at her, your own desires are dulled for a minute as the link between your minds still lingers in the air. In their place, you feel the sense of something huge and terrible hanging over her, something worse than the creature inside: the thing she found while *looking* for a cure. The object now in her pocket.

It was confiscated long ago, spellbound and stifled, a mysterious, endlessly-powerful artifact. It calls to her, loud in her mind, begging her to use it, to let the space Between spill out and ancient things come through to tear apart the world. Even with the sensation of connection fading, you feel her all-consuming fear and thrill—and you know, too, that she wants it destroyed. Her eyes catch yours, and flicker to her side.

Only a few paces away is a frame large enough to step through, filled with a lightless void, and you understand: she's been trying to throw herself in along with the thing in her pocket so it can never be used. On her own, she has never managed to do it, but now she has the last threads of your tandem minds working together—the great network of the gifted letting a little of your strength flow into her.

Whatever the terrible object is in her pocket, it doesn't seem to call to you, and through your fading connection, she draws on that, calling out to you and willing you to push her through. With a last flare, the synapses of the withered creature inside you respond.

When you reach your hands out to shove her backward, you feel her resist—but the thing coiled inside her remembers you as kin, holding that part of her back just enough for you to win the tussle. She disappears into the frame full of void, plunged into nothing.

She is unwritten from reality, taking the frame itself and thing in her pocket with her, and you feel the parts of her mind left in yours reel with relief as they disintegrate: the object is gone, never to threaten the world again.

You now stand alone among the glittering shelves of the requisition room.

> **If you're the libertine OR have any *Venny's Mission* status:**
> You see the red box that was described to you on a high shelf and fetch it down. (If you're **not** playing the libertine, you can also choose to leave the box and remove the status.)

- **If you're the thief,** turn to page 235.

- **Otherwise,** you search through the room and find what you're looking for in a tucked away corner (if you're playing the **libertine**, you manage to find your papers in a filing cabinet.) Finally, you step through the frame on the far side of the room that leads out onto what looks like the street below. **Turn to page 264.**

KINSHIP, REVILED

- If your strength or agility is 7 or below:

The hybrid creature who shares a body with the spellbinder princess is fast and terrible. Even frozen half-formed before it could truly take hold within her, the creature is stronger than any human. As you snap toward it, her half-changed face opens to receive you and your head disappears into her gaping throat.

You feel a sense of deja vu—but this time, the bearer makes no effort to preserve you and keep you alive as one of their children. The Princess uses her control to carefully eat you alive, along with the creature within you, and with a crunch, the world turns dark forever.

The last human parts of your brain wonder whether keeping your gifted form away from the world below may be a good thing, in the end.

Your journey ends here.

- If your strength or agility is 8 or above:

The creature inside you uses the training and strength of your mortal body to twist in the air as you reach for her, stretching your new mouth wide into the cavernous throat of teeth that envelops her head. You crunch down on the scheming human mind that so stunted the nascent creature inside, preventing it from blossoming into its final form.

The next moments are a blur of joy and red, where the main thing you remember is the elation that swells in your chest. Some time later, you find yourself in a room full of human trinkets, alone apart from the last, wet remains of a human. You have forgotten what purpose could have been so strong, so driving to have brought you here.

You regret that you had to consume the other creature, too, but the spellbinding had left it too weak to grow, and its best use was for the collective good—you feel yourself rippling with its new power, growing and terrible. You walk calmly out of the requisition room, and take stock of your situation.

Turn to page 250.

REFUSE THE CURE

The spellbinder princess looks taken aback by your refusal, standing suddenly from her comfortable seat to pace away from you and look out of the window.

Her face turns dark and wild as she looks out at the storm, hand fiddling in her pocket.

"How many are out there with these *gifts* now, do you think? How many are out there thanks to me?"

She looks back at you, face turning furious, extra teeth contorting as the muscles in her face ripple. "And you would do the same thing? Don't you see what will happen? Do you really want to go out into the world as you are, letting the creature grow and feed and expand its families out into a teeming mass that wipes the people from this world?"

"No," she says, face terrible and stretching as the thing within her roils and protests— you feel its alarm through some chemical connection, and your nerves are set alight with fear, knowing through her that you teeter on the edge of disaster.

Before you can move toward her and do something—anything—you notice, sharp through you connection, the hand in the spellbinder princess's pocket clench.

As she draws her clenched fist out of her pocket, light expands in a bright white shape that bursts through her fingers, roaring and shimmering, dancing across the room. Her anger has turned to a cold and triumphant fury, and every object in the room is rattling and screaming, time and direction lost to you.

The last thing you see—before everything is swallowed by a bright white crack that seems to split the tower and let the light pour in—is the spellbinder princess's hand holding something. You see her fingers jerk suddenly to the side in a tight, decisive motion: almost as if turning a key.

Turn to <u>page 258.</u>

THE BEARER—JOYFUL AND TEEMING

You have something new and wonderful living inside you, and you feel it has grown stronger.

You find yourself very calm about your new partnership. Only a small voice left in the back of your mind seems to be screaming, as if from a long way off. It tells you desperately not to return to where you came from, not to seek out your friends, family or loved ones—and this seems a sensible plan to you. It would only upset them to see your new glory, the new and wonderful cold growing in your eyes.

You descend the tower with ease, and make your way back to the ballroom, where you're sure you smile wide at people and ask them to dance. You remember little of the rest of the evening, but you know it was pleasurable.

You make your way to a small town, a little way outside this city you ended up in. You tell the people there your fortunes turned bad, and you want to make a new, quiet little life there—smiling all the while. They agree, perhaps a little nervously—but these feelings in others no longer stir or concern you.

You do live a quiet life, the same each day, but your happiness seems to increase and increase. More and more you wake up some mornings wonderfully stiff and sore, or better, full and content, with little recollection of what you did the night before. The screaming in the back of your head has been muffled and faded to nothing.

As the years pass, you start to see others. People you connect with effortlessly, that seem familiar, as if a close member of your family. Even on market days when you visit the city, you start to see more and more of the others as they come into their own—growing and blooming, lush and profuse in the flesh where they're anchored. You smile at them as they pass, face stretched wide as they return the gesture, eyes cold and bright.

Eventually, as you grow older (you would have been growing soft and wrinkled without the gift—instead your face grows glossy and stretched and exquisite) there comes a day where you realize *everyone* in the village is one of you, one of the others. The more time passes—and the more you wake grinning and satiated, with bloody teeth and the taste of metal in the mouth that spans your old ribcage—the more tiring and pointless it seems to wear your human form. You stop pretending to be a person when you visit the market, and watch with glee as the last few humans (still left dismally hollow and unfilled) scatter absurdly before you—as if they had some chance of escape. Your nights take you further and further afield to find fresh hunting ground now that there are so many bearers.

And one day, you simply stop trying to keep your human face in place at all; you give up on keeping to the night for your excursions. You hear high pitched noises coming from the humans you approach before joyfully quieting them in sweet, wonderful crunches. You fill a few with your young—travelers and such, those likely to flee or move away from your territory, to spread out into far places. But nowadays, most of the stray, vacant humans you encounter are simply your feed as you roam beautifully through your lands.

And that is your life—or the life that becomes yours. You glide through the world in a blissful fog as your children spread joyously, teeming and fruitful—your face unfurled, ringed with spiraling teeth, and always stretched wide and beaming.

Your journey ends—it has been replaced by something new.

A SIMPLE REQUEST

You see no reason not to tell her the truth, and the connection still threads between you, coaxing you to trust her—you think it must exist the other way, too. You tell her about how your father had been strange, how you came home to a ruined house, your mother's despair.

"You came for . . . a violin?" she asks. Her strange face looks soft and tired as the frown falls away.

You nod, numbly. There's a lump in your throat, and you hear your voice coming out choked as you tell her it was your mother's. She seems to feel the raw emotion through the connection and comes closer to you.

"You broke into my keep, evaded my inquisitors, and were afflicted by this terrible thing that would have grown inside you . . . to fetch your *mother's violin?*"

The question is almost rhetorical—the last wisps of your connection still hum in the air, in the chemicals in your breathing. She knows your strength of feeling for your family.

She stirs and walks up the stairs to look around in her cabinets. You follow, instinctively, and see the violin a little way down some shelves, behind some other instruments. You take it gently from where it lay, and the princess returns to you and presses a small bag into your hands. Looking down, you realize she's seen your ruined home through the connection, *felt* what it means to you. In turn, through its remnants, you know that she feels responsible for what happened to your father, somehow—but will not answer why if pressed. Inside the pouch is:

+ A glittering red jewel.

You slip it into your pockets, adding it to your inventory. Finally, she leads you over to what looks like a large, full-length mirror in a corner between shelves on the other side of the room. Through the frame, you can see a view as if from the end of a long alleyway, with tall buildings on either side and a narrow slit at the end leading onto a wide cobbled street, where a cart makes its slow, rattling way past. It looks like the city below.

- **If you have the status *toymaker's aide*, turn straight to <u>page 262.</u>**

- **Otherwise:**

She ushers you forward, and—still holding your mother's violin, you step into the frame. (If you have any status with the words *Venny's mission*, remove it—you've made your choice, and can see no way of asking for the box now.)

Turn to <u>page 264.</u>

APPROACH THE SPELLBINDER PRINCESS

You tell the princess you only want to speak to her, very slowly edging closer toward her and the shelves, your hands up.

She pauses, one hand clenched in her pocket, the other hovering at her side where something (a weapon?) seems to have been forming in her hand.

She doesn't lash out as you approach but seems to be surveying you coldly, leaning her head very far to one side as her tongue swipes along the rows of teeth on her cheeks. You're unsure if she really recognizes you as a person. Her eyes scan over you as if evaluating your value.

She takes a small step toward you, and something about the movement reminds you of a cat drawing closer to a mouse.

Darting your eyes away from her teeth, you're now close enough to make out the shapes of the things stacked on the shelves and tables around you. Many are filed away with small labels you can't make out—some shimmer or glow or hover a few centimeters off the table.

Within reach, you see a long rapier, glittering as if lit by a bright light, pale crystals rotating in impossible ways that make your head hurt; and a little further down the shelves, you can make out horns and pipes and the edge of a violin. You're unsure what the effects of each might be, what strange powers or awful effects they might unleash.

As the princess steps closer, her mouth has opened, jaw dislocating like a snake and looming disconcertingly wide. She inhales in a way that you think might be smelling you, face stretched in a smile, and you realize she's about to lunge.

You reach out and grab at one of the only items you recognize or know how to use in a last, desperate act as she begins to move.

> **Grab the enchanted rapier** and brandish it at the spellbinder princess. Turn to page 228.

- **If you're playing the libertine or have any status** with the words *Venny's mission*: You also recognize the small red box sitting alone on a higher shelf, and you can reach out to get it. To **grab the red box, turn to page 254.**

- **If you're playing the sailor:**
You recognize the violin tucked away behind the other instruments as what you're looking for and can dive for it. (If you also have a status with the words *Venny's mission*, you must choose which to reach for.) To **grab the violin, turn to page 255.**

THE RED BOX

The spellbinder princess immediately freezes as you grab the red box. The human skin left visible on her face looks even grayer and paler than before.

You pause, unsure exactly how to use the box or its effects, but trying not to let that show.

"What do you want with that," she says slowly, in a voice that comes out in a shaky rasp.

The princess looks wary, dangerous like a cornered animal.

> **Threaten her with the red box**—use your strong position to push forward. Demand she fetch what you're looking for and show you a way out, or face the consequences. **Turn to <u>page 257.</u>**

> **Tell her you do not intend to use the box** and ask calmly for what you're looking for. You think there could be a peaceful resolution here, and it would be best to seem as reasonable as possible. **Turn to <u>page 256.</u>**

YOUR MOTHER'S VIOLIN

You duck down into the aisle of shelves where you see the instruments as a jet of pale blue fire erupts in the space where you were standing.

You gently lift the familiar form of your mother's violin from the shelf where it lay—there's an iridescent sheen and feeling of warmth coming from the strings, but it otherwise looks exactly as you remember it. There's a dent from where your brother knocked it off the shelf, the parts polished smooth by your mother's fingers. You can almost see the curve of her cheek where it ought to rest.

You look up to see the spellbinder princess staring at you, hand alight with a curve of blue flame, but arm limply by her side as she watches you reverently holding the violin.

"You came for *this?*" she asks. Her strange face looks soft and tired, suddenly more human as the cold, certain expression falls away.

You nod, numbly. There's a lump in your throat. You hear a low, choked voice telling her it was your mother's and realize you have spoken.

The blue fire burns out, and the spellbinder princess takes the other hand out of her pocket, shoulders falling. She speaks slowly, haltingly, as if she's forgotten how. "The things in this room can do things you could never dream of. They could end cities, begin wars, change reality . . . But the only person in years who manages to break into my keep, evade my inquisitors and travel through the Between itself . . . came to fetch your *mother's violin?*"

You stand very still, unsure what to do but give another nod. You wonder what it was she expected you'd come for. She watches you for a long time.

Eventually, she runs a shaky hand over her face. She stirs and leads you over to what looks like a large full-length mirror in a corner between shelves on the other side of the room. Through the frame, you can see a view as if from the end of a long alleyway, with tall buildings on either side and a narrow slit at the end leading onto a wide cobbled street, where a cart makes its slow, rattling way past. It looks like the city below.

> **If you have the status *toymaker's aide*, turn straight to <u>page 262.</u>**

> **Otherwise,** she ushers you forward, and—still holding your mother's violin—you step into the frame. (If you have any status with the words *Venny's mission*, remove it—you've made your choice and can see no way of asking for the box now.)
Turn to <u>page 264.</u>

INSIDE THE RED BOX

The princess seems to relax a little as you tell her calmly you have no intention of using the box. In fact, you say, you want to get rid of it, to make sure it can't be used, and she nods slowly.

"The schematics and minerals inside are supposed to be sold," she tells you uncertainly. "My inquisitors, my advisors—I'm supposed to send the box down to them tonight, through the same spellwork that allows them to send up my food and correspondence."

When you ask what her advisors intend to use it for, she pauses for a long moment. "The plans can be used to build weapons that harness the power of the Between," she tells you finally. "Usually such things are of limited use, but these pioneer the use of a rare earth mineral, a perfect conductor for spellbinding. Almost the entire world's supply, laboriously mined through the centuries, is now in that box." Her voice is flat and grim, as if lapsing into an explanation she has had to give many times.

"The enchanted metal can be used to make two spellbound transmitters. One draws power from close to a fracture, then transmits the full force of the energy to a paired twin from the same source. In essence, it allows the channeling of raw power straight from the Between itself, directly onto the battlefield. It would be far more destructive than anything ever used before."

Her voice has dropped to a whisper, hissed from the side of her half-shifted face. "When my inquisitors heard such a thing was being developed, that many groups vied for it, I made sure to have the box seized. But my advisors wanted me to finish the work. When I refused, they insisted I sell it on to someone who would. They told me it would make political ties that would strengthen our country's defenses, our position with Estovar . . ." she trails off as she speaks.

"But if the box was taken from me—taken by someone who came up the tower through the Between itself, who I could not fight . . . I could not be blamed. If the minerals were hidden or destroyed, the weapons could never be built, even if the plans were remade."

You nod at her encouragingly, but she seems to have made up her own mind. After she's quiet for a moment, you try to tell her gently that there's one more small thing—and tell her what else you're looking for in the requisition room. Her eyebrow raises, as if this is an unusual request in a room bursting with much more powerful objects, but she goes to fetch it for you nonetheless. (If you're the **libertine**, she presses your documents into your hands.)

Finally holding the thing you've been looking for, along with the red box, she leads you to a large mirror that will let you escape and walk back down into the city below.

> **If you have the status** *toymaker's aide*, **turn to** <u>page 262.</u>
> **Otherwise, turn to** <u>page 264.</u>

THE PRINCESS THREATENED

At your tone of command, the princess's face contorts into cold fury.

"You don't know what you're talking about," she forces out in a hoarse whisper that seems to echo around in her throat somehow.

"Think how many untold deaths you could cause through your ignorance. Worse than deaths."

She's muttering darkly to herself now, the unnaturally pale orbs of her eyes stretched frantically wide, one hand clenching and unclenching on something in her pocket. You try to protest, softening your words or turning them around, but she doesn't seem to be listening to you any longer.

"They're like you, all of them, grasping and pushing, looking for more—there's one way, there's only one way—it would be better this way—"

Her teeth-dotted head snaps up to look at you, and before you can move toward her and do something—anything—she just whispers "yes," and the hand in her pocket lights suddenly aflame.

Light blazes in her hand as she draws her clenched fist out of her pocket, expanding into a bright white that bursts through her fingers, roaring and shimmering, dancing across the room. Her anger has turned to cold triumph, and her head lolls back as if in relief, or pleasure.

Every object in the room is rattling and screaming as if in anticipation, time seeming to stand still as the direction of up or down loses all meaning.

The last thing you see before everything is swallowed by a bright white crack that seems to split the tower and let the light pour in is the spellbinder princess's clenched fist, jerking suddenly to the side in a tight, decisive motion—almost as if turning a key.

Turn to page 258

THE OPENING OF THE WORLDS

The world seems suspended as everything around you shifts and opens. There is a vibration in everything, in every particle and every mountain, in every snail shell and cloud, fingertip and ocean, and you see it all at once as it bursts to life with a great, gargantuan hum. It buzzes in your ribcage and your eye sockets, lifts your feet from the floor and inverts the world outside the windows. It twists the molten core under the earth and trembles, colossal, through the atmosphere. In the moments before your eyes oscillate themselves into a thick goo, you see the tables and shelves that line the requisition room shake themselves apart, the fibers of the wood splitting and cracking, exploding through the air as every family artifact, confiscated treasure and child's toy that once meant so much to a living, breathing person bursts from the shelves, plummeting up through the ceiling or spinning outwards through the thick stone walls, splitting into a thousand shards which crash through the rocks as they melt and shiver in the roiling, deafening storm of the hum.

The tower shatters inward, the air itself inverting and bubbling, mixing with the stones and roof tiles and soft bodies of the people at the ball. And as it tears itself apart from the inside, so does every magic object and every person who ever owned them, along with every piece of music, every sock knitted for a baby and letter written carefully for a friend—every creature who ever looked up at a star or loved anything.

All around you, the world fractures and shakes itself apart.

From its origin point grasped in desperate fingers, the whiteness of nothing erupts in jagged beams, wheeling around in a dizzying spin as reality tears in a long crack, a great wound in matter itself where the Between begins to pour in. The sky cleaves in two. Lightning crackles up from the endless dark of the wriggling seas. The screaming, whirling maelstrom pitches toward its tornado-crescendo as the colossal ancient things bigger than cities that sleep in the Between pull their way into the new-forming world, eyeless and full of ruin.

It's all gone, everything that was and could have been.

The world is theirs now, and it is different.

Your journey ends—everything does.

THE BURNED WORLD

You fall through the frame, out into the alleyway.

Scrambling up from the wet ground, you
see no doorway back to the tower—only
the bricks of a wall, recessed in the
center in an indentation about
the size of the frame you stepped
through.

Around you, hard rain beats down,
the storm not quite passed. Tall,
rickety buildings huddle close,
dripping onto the cobbles below.
Through the gloom, dawn is
breaking on a distant horizon you
cannot see, painting the edges of
high rooftops and chimney stacks
pink where the sun comes through
the clouds. You feel the cold air on
your face and sudden sounds of
movement as a low boom bursts
through the city and stirs the first
light sleepers awake.

The cracks sound distant and huge,
like thunder. You slip quickly from
the alleyway out into the street
to see the tower far above move
as if in slow motion. Colors and
lights spiral from the far-off turret,
and great stone blocks seem to be
splitting apart, bursting outward in
a great bubble of debris, dreamlike
and slow.

The lights expand in a globe that
lights the city up in every different
color for an instant, then before
you can blink, the globe is spinning
and contracting down to nothing as
it disappears, seeming to take a great
chunk of the tower with it away into
nothingness.

The remains of the tower are suspended surreally in the air for a moment, as if a great bite has been taken from them. Then, the stones begin to fall, one by one. What remains of the turret plummets down, bubbling with pink energy and sending balls of green lightning spinning out into the night in all directions before breaking itself thunderously apart on the keep.

You watch in awe and horror and fascination, a sick thrill turning to a terrible gnawing feeling as you remember the bustle of the servants around the gates and courtyards. You imagine the great stones flattening them, smashing through the tops of caravans—no, you think. They must be out by now. Most of them must be out. As the whirling lights and dust settle into the rain, you try to reassure yourself that few stones seem to have fallen outside the outer walls of the castle itself.

You hear far off shouts from the upper city and bells calling for water and help—but down around you, most of the city still sleeps.

Exhausted and a little shaky from the adrenaline, you slip back into the alley and make your way up a drainpipe to sit on a rooftop in the remains of the storm. From your high vantage, you see spots of magic blaze in the ruins, fizzling in the heavy rain that's now lit pink in the morning around you. The battlements look mostly intact. The strange distant sounds and colors die down over the next hour or so—the great sun-bright globe must have taken most of the magical objects in the tower with it as it winked out of existence, along with a lot of the stone. By sheer chance and no planning of your own, most of the city is safe.

People stick their heads from high windows and you watch them point and exclaim in the street at the changed skyline—but while the courts and councils will be abuzz with news, there's little urgency here in the city below. Gawking children are hurried along by busy carers. Shirts must still be mended, horses watered, families fed.

As the rain subsides, you're able to see down to a distant market square in the lower city, full of travelers here for the ball that have started to wake after a late night. With a wave of relief, you notice more and more long trains of goods carts and merchant wagons crammed with workers that all made it out hours before the tower fell—busy with gossip but safe and alive.

As dawn breaks over the city, the rain patters to a soft mist. A child wails in the distance. You shiver in the morning air, bright with grim triumph.

You have made it out of the tower.

Turn to page 267.

THE TOYMAKER AND THE PRINCESS

She looks confused when you do not step immediately through the frame out to your freedom beyond, and you tell her about how you found your father in the Between.

When you get to how you left the Between, she looks taken aback and asks several questions—seeming surprised that you were able to get him out at all.

"It's so strong," she whispers, eyes unfocused as if staring at something a long way away. "The pull of *the Key*. But you say it was taken away from him . . ."

She says *the Key* just like your father did, in a way that makes your skin crawl. It stops you from asking whether she can help him—could she make him worse? Instead, you only tell her that you're going to fetch him and have crossed back down to the stairs before she can say any more about it.

A wave of relief crashes over you as you open the lab door to see your father just where you left him, sat in the corner, looking dreamily away. He smiles weakly when he sees you—not speaking, but obedient when pulled to his feet and brought by the hand up to the requisition room.

The princess's hand is in her pocket, fumbling at something. Your father seems to still as he sees her. You think about what he said about the pull of this key and wonder if they see it in each other. The huge creatures in the Between took the call away from him—but perhaps he still remembers it.

"Before you go," she says, very quietly out of the still-human side of her face, "I need your help."

You realize she is speaking to your father—the exhausted, deflated shell of a once-strong man.

"*The Key* has been calling to me for a long time," she tells him. "I found it up here, spellbound and stifled and—" her face contorts into what you realize is almost a sob, "I took it out of its bindings. And now—now its call is so loud that it reaches out to any enchanter it thinks could help its cause. I am sorry. I cannot tell you how sorry."

Your father is very still. He does not react, but you think you feel the grip of his hand tighten in your own.

"When I realized what I had done, I researched for years, and made a gate to a place that nothing can get out of," she says, gesturing to one side. A few paces away is another frame large enough to step through, this one filled with a lightless void.

"All I had to do was to walk in with it."

Her hand is still in her pocket, twisting frantically. Her head turns up toward him, a humorless smile wide on a face riddled with teeth. "But of course, I couldn't go through with it. I couldn't step inside—you know that. *The Key* wants to be used."

As she speaks, you shiver involuntarily at the thought of the terrible destruction that destroyed your house magnified a thousand fold, the warping and twisting of all reality as all the power of the Between and the ancient colossal things are let through.

Your father steps forward, expression grim, and grasps hold of her arm so it's wrenched out of her pocket, empty. She was holding *the Key*, you realize. It's right there, in her pocket.

Your father begins to push her backward, and she looks at him, pale eyes wide. She gives him a single desperate nod before she seems to snap, her body beginning to struggle and strain to reach for her pocket again. You rush to your father's side to help him. The princess's half-shifted body has suddenly begun to thrash, stronger than any human should be, face beginning to unfurl into rows of teeth that bite out at your father—but before she can use her full strength, the two of you have pushed her back through the frame that leads out onto the void.

She disappears, plunged into inky darkness. Her final, alien screech is cut off as she disappears into nothing, taking *the Key* with her. The frame crumples until it's gone, unmade, the void inside forever unreachable.

Your father stands panting, unable to speak, and seemingly unable to look away from the frame. His shoulders sag in relief.

This will never happen again, you think in a daze no one else will be called to look for *the Key*. It's gone, never to threaten the world again.

> - **If you have any status with the words *Venny's mission*** and do not have the red box, you remember it now, pushed out of your mind by the urgency of getting your father. Seeing it alone on a high shelf, you can collect it up to take with you. (If you do not take the box, remove the status.)

You go to pick up your mother's violin and gently take your father's hand again, tugging him through the frame that looks out into the street below.

Turn to page 264.

OUT OF THE TOWER

You emerge out into the alleyway.

The storm has come and broken—now only a soft rain falls in the streets around you, lit blue in the early light of morning. Tall, rickety buildings huddle close, dripping onto the cobbles below. Dawn is breaking on a distant horizon you cannot see, painting the edges of high rooftops and chimney stacks pink. You feel the cool air on your face and hear quiet sounds of movement in the city around you as it slowly begins to stir.

Behind you, you see no doorway back to the tower—only the bricks of a wall, recessed in the center in an indentation about the size of the frame you stepped through. Without thinking, you reach out to touch the sunken shape, but you only feel the cool bricks rough under your fingertips, wet in the early morning rain.

The dizzying sights of the tower, the changed princess and requisition room far above seem to recede as you feel the firm and ordinary stone beneath your feet, the damp and very real sensation of rain dripping down your neck. Your breath puffs out in the dawn chill.

You have made it out of the tower.

> **If you have the status** *Toymaker's aide*, turn to <u>page 266.</u>
> **Otherwise**, turn to <u>page 267.</u>

LOST INTO THE EVERYTHING

You sink into the void.

It's almost a relief, compared to the high-pitched fervor of *the Key* that has been following you for what feels like so long, now.

The fibers of your clothes uncoil and so too do the carbon strings holding together the chemicals of your body. You are unmade, unwritten from the lives of your loved ones, everything you've ever owned and everywhere you've been untethered from the marks you left on them as you are forgotten.

But the thing pulled into the nothingness is not all of reality, but you. You exist everywhere and nowhere, lost into the everything—but you take *the Key* with you, unused and impotent, unwriting its existence.

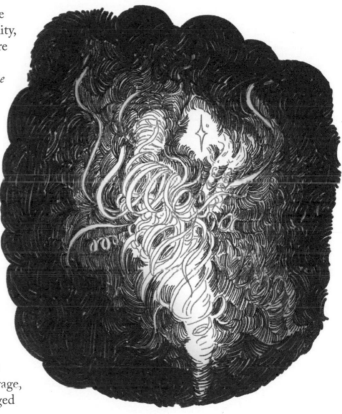

You are gone. Your parents go about their days as usual, the youth with the long limbs turns to the next page under the fruit tree, and the acolytes of the Great Library sort and shelve the books, over and over. The only book that is changed is the one in the restricted section, rendered unreadable and confusing—in a few years it will be moved to locked storage, then somehow found damaged by water and thrown away.

The world goes on, spinning precarious and fragile and messy, but untouched by the horrors of the opened worlds beyond: safe from what *the Key* would have wrought.

Your journey ends—but thanks to you, the world continues on.

THE TOYMAKER'S FREEDOM

Beside you in the street, looking up into the soft rain, stands your father.

He still looks vacant and will not reply to your gentle questions, not in words or in gestures. Searching through the pockets of his coat, you find them empty apart from an assortment of coins, and realize it's takings from the shop, back from before he went into the Between—at least several days' worth.

It's enough to pay for room and board at a simple sort of guest house, where you explain to the matronly owner that your father has been ill. You ask them to please bring him food in his room and check in on him, making sure he eats it and doesn't stray too far. When you empty his pockets on the counter, she agrees happily enough, telling you generously that the amount will stretch at least a fortnight if you need it to, and she'll refund what you don't use when you leave. You're so exhausted from your night in the tower that you thank her and agree without question.

In the room, your father slowly eats the food you put before him, but still can't quite catch your eye fully. He seems unable to speak, for now. You tell him gently you have preparations to make around town, and he nods absently, squeezing your hand before you leave.

Turn to page 267.

THE FUTURE AHEAD
(If you do not have any of these statuses, continue reading below for your full ending.)

- If you made it out of the tower with the **status** *all-seeing:*
The effect of all the worlds overlapping at the edge of your eyes never truly leaves you, but gradually wears away until you barely notice it. For the rest of your life, you have an uncanny sense that helps you avoid danger, and you win more often at cards.

- If you made it out of the tower with the **status** *friend to the king of woodlice:*
Wherever you live for the rest of your life, you occasionally spot tiny trails of little glowing creatures in the gaps between floorboards or crawling around the front door. You find tiny gifts on the floor—usually coins or buttons, but sometimes wrapped sweets or satisfyingly shaped twigs or pebbles.

- If you made it out of the tower with the **status** *philanthropist:*
In the years following, whether you remain in the city to hear them or not, rumors spread that the inquisitors are seldom seen in the streets now, and fewer people seem to go missing. What used to be an old warehouse in the lower city opens one day as a kitchen that provides food to anyone who needs it, with no charge and no strings. In the years to come, courtiers will gossip about a new initiative providing safe, affordable housing, and speculate on whether the money would be better spent elsewhere or whether it will undercut landlords. The lower city is not transformed overnight, but gradually, things improve, and it's said that the princess no longer seems to bend to the advisors who pressure her to adopt new policies that better profit the city's upper classes.

- **If you have the status** *Venny's mission—rendezvous,* turn to page 276.
- **If you have the status** *Venny's mission—the nightjars,* turn to page 268.

- **Otherwise:**
> If you're the **thief,** turn to page 282.
> If you're the **libertine,** turn to page 272.
> If you're the **acolyte,** turn to page 286.

> If you're the **sailor AND have the status** *Toymaker's aide,* turn to page 292.
> If you're the **sailor** and **do** *not* have the status *Toymaker's aide,* turn to page 296.

> If you're playing your own character, **turn to page 269.**

VENNY'S MISSION—THE NIGHTJARS

The next day at sunset, you wait at the time and place you arranged with the prisoner—round the side of a small inn in the lower part of the city, red box stuffed down in the bottom of your bag. You can feel the weight of it and keep remembering the desperate note in the prisoner's voice as they told you about it. You want it out of your hands.

You wait for several hours until the sun is well and truly below the horizon and the sinking feeling in your stomach feels as if it's dragging you down. As you half-suspected, Venny does not appear. You think of them deep down in the castle, hidden away in some dungeon or other, and wonder if they will ever make it back out again.

Ducking into the inn after midnight, you try to shroud yourself in the shadows of a far corner seat, wondering how to get rid of the box as quickly as possible. It feels like a looming weight—and now that you've picked it up, you can't simply cast it aside. What had the prisoner told you to do? Drop the box into the ocean?

The next day you try to ask around town without drawing attention, going down to the markets where the extra carts and servants who came to work at the ball are starting to make their way back down through the hills. The town's population is still swollen with strangers, and you think your questions shouldn't turn too many heads.

The caravans of players are talking excitedly about the night of the ball: of murders and some military treaty dissolved when the main bargaining chip—a brightly dressed man in the center of a group reveals dramatically—went *missing*.

The box weighs heavily at the bottom of your bag, and you try to move on quickly. You feel as if you're being watched and have no way of knowing if it's from your mind or some pair of eyes out in the crowd.

Asking around the market, you discover that a few days' ride down the hills is a fishing village clustered along the rocky coast at the foot of the mountains. The fisherfolk dwelling there leave for a week at a time, sailing out toward uninhabited westerly islands where you can dive for spiny lobsters and catch silvery fish that dart plentifully in the shallows. The islands, you're told, perch on the other side of the great crevasse that splits the ocean floor and turns the waters below a deep, dark black.

A tall woman tells you helpfully that their cart makes the trip regularly and is heading down with plenty of free space. She adds that if you want to see the far islands, her daughter is always willing to take a tourist in exchange for a few honest days' work.

> Take up her offer: head down to the fishing village to **throw the box into the ocean**—you think you won't be safe and able to move on until this is done. **Turn to page 270**.

> The whole thing seems like more trouble than it's worth. Weapon or not, you try to ask subtly around to see if you can **sell the box**. **Turn to page 278.**

YOUR OWN WAY FORWARD

You move down through the city streets in the dwindling morning rain. In the lower town, people have begun to spill out into the streets and wind around the market stalls, the laughing children, and in and out of houses. Early risers and stragglers that never slept after the ball are making their way into carriages and loading goods onto carts, ready to make the long journey south, out to other places and to the shores of the ocean, and some across to the lands beyond.

You watch the cacophony of life and movement as the city stirs into life before you, and consider your next move.

If you've made it out of the tower with gemstones or jewels, you can exchange them at the market stalls lining one of the squares for heavy bags of gold—with them, you could easily buy fine clothes, new weapons, gifts for people you know, or pay for a long journey to a new place. If you've picked up any other items in the tower, you can choose to sell or keep them—think about what you might hold on to, and what new things you might buy.

Will you return to the life you had before—plunging back into chaos or retreating into calm—or try something new or start afresh? Do you return immediately to friends and family, or will it take time before you feel rewarded (or relieved) after your trip into the tower? How *do* you feel?

Your ending is your own to write, but your strange experiences journeying through the tower will have changed you somehow—think about how you might be different, and how you plan to go on. Do you find yourself heading down a road to destruction or folly—or at peace? Are you a step closer to becoming the person you want to be?

Either way, you have completed the task that seemed impossible: made it into the tower, retrieved your item, and even made it out alive. As the sun rises over the mountain city, the world is open to you and full of possibility.

THE END

THE CREVASSE

The cart trundles down the hillside, smelling faintly of fish. The woman driving it chats comfortably about her children to the handful of workers and travelers hitching a ride, seeming to enjoy the company on a usually-monotonous journey.

In the village, you arrange your passage over to the far islands with a weathered young woman who seems only too happy to have the extra help. "We don't get so many travelers this time of year, but the islands are still beautiful, and we'll cook up a pot with some of the lobster to share before we head back," she tells you, smiling. You smile back, still too aware of the weight of your bag and the box inside.

On the boat, the fisherfolk are busy with navigation and brisk but warm, bringing you mugs of an unfamiliar tea and simple meals. You keep yourself to yourself, sleeping under thin, scratchy blankets in your own tiny cabin.

On the second day, the waters below you turn black, and an old man in a thick jumper is only too eager to point out the crevasse below.

That night, you put a heavy stone you brought from the hillside into a sack along with the little red box. You tie the bag tight, creep out into the moonless night, and drop the sack into the black, fathomless depths below.

It disappears down, plunging away from you, and you take a deep breath of the cold night air. It feels like the first real breath you've taken in a long time.

The next day, the boat passes back out of the black waters of the crevasse at midday, and the sky clears to the dazzling sun. You haul nets and carry equipment out onto the islands when you land, explore the shrublands on your breaks and see the bloom of flowers you've never seen before. You suck the meat from the lobster claw out of the pot on the last day, sitting around on the beach with the crew. You listen to the laughter of the people around you, feet warm from the campfire and arms aching from the work, and find you are content—out of the tower, free of the box and whatever awful dangers it could have unleashed, and back on solid ground with the whole world at your fingertips.

You feel lighter as the boat carries you back to the mainland, looking out at the stars in the dark as you rise and fall gently on the waves.

On your way through the coastal village to the cart you've found to take you back, you turn into an alley and find your arms held around your back by a tall, cloaked figure. She calmly tells you she's been tailing you from the castle, and there's no need to worry—but she needs to know what you've done with the small red box.

You tell the truth, since there seems no reason not to—that you were told to destroy it, and that by now it's at the bottom of the ocean, down in the crevasse itself.

She watches you carefully as you talk, and then—still watchful as if ready for an attack—makes you slowly empty your bags and pockets. You're rifling through your things, wondering what it'll take to persuade her the box is gone, when a second figure in similar dark clothes emerges from behind a corner, giving the first a sharp nod.

As they whisper quickly together, you catch snippets and slowly realize you recognize the new arrival from the boat—she must have seen you drop the sack over the side. The first figure seems to sag with relief as they talk, then pulls down her hood to reveal a scarred face and an approving look.

"We hoped—" she tells you. "But we had to be sure. Thank you."

She tells you, reassuringly, that you won't see them again, and the second figure presses a small pouch into your hands, thanking you profusely. Inside you find:

+ A glittering black jewel.

You find yourself strangely unrattled by the experience, still buoyant with relief at your escape and the part you've played in keeping the power in the red box from being used.

The only place the carts in town go is back up to the little city at the foot of the mountains, and you join one not long after. You arrive just as the sun is rising on a new day.

> If you're the **thief, turn to <u>page 282.</u>**
> If you're the **acolyte, turn to <u>page 286.</u>**

> If you're the **sailor AND have the status** *Toymaker's aide*, turn to <u>page 292.</u>
> If you're the **sailor** and **do** *not* have the status *Toymaker's aide*, turn to <u>page 296.</u>

> If you're playing your own character, **turn to <u>page 269.</u>**

AGAINST ALL ODDS

You can hardly believe you've made it out alive.

Still very aware of your wanted status, you hurry down through the city in the morning rain. If you have a weapon from the tower, you leave the incriminating object behind in an alleyway in a panic. In the lower, dirtier part of town, you duck into a pawn shop as it opens its shutters—the owner raises an eyebrow but makes no comment.

You exchange one of your earrings for a large handful of coins and a small bag, which you hurriedly stow the red box inside when the owner is looking the other way.

The streets of the lower city are narrower and less ordered than the wide, tree-lined cobbles you are used to. Disoriented, you stumble upon a square of market stalls set up by traders who came through for the ball, becoming busy with servants and travelers and caravans. You try to move quickly through and only falter a little in the unfamiliar act of buying things for yourself. Eventually you find well-fitted plain clothes and a bottle of hair potion for prices you seem to be able to afford with the coins, even if you suspect the owners are charging you double.

Nearby, you find a squalid little guesthouse where you think nobody could possibly look for you. The remaining coins seem to be enough to get a bowl of offensively greasy stew that you eat anyway, and a damp, uncomfortable room with a mirror and washbasin. You turn your prettily styled hair a straight, lank black, cutting half of it off. This is something you would have found very upsetting yesterday—but after the tower, it seems only a necessary survival tactic. If you can make it out of the city alive, your hair will grow again, after all. You carefully sketch on a passable moustache for good measure, and feel a little calmer seeing a face in the mirror you don't really recognize.

An hour before dusk, you make your way down toward the city gates. You walk by tall rickety buildings, weathered figures who watch you pass with open curiosity or hostility, dirty children and broken bottles and rats in the alleyways. After being caught up in the swirls of memories in the Between, full of ordinary little details of ordinary lives, you find it easier to look without derision. You try to give one of the figures a nod.

Your heart thrums in your ears as you approach the meeting place, and you scan every doorway and shadow for Venny. The city gate glows in the last rays of the setting sun as you set your eyes on it, and the bottom falls out of your stomach—it's deserted.

You try to stay calm while it feels as if your heart is trying to jump out of your mouth.

Visions flood your mind, unbidden: Venny driving a speeding carriage at full pelt toward the border, leaving you behind with reluctance or even relief. Or Venny struck down by inquisitors, bleeding out in the street. You feel sick and quivery, unable to stand still—you head down the last few steps to the empty gate, flitting nervously through and looking desperately around.

On the other side of the wall, you see a large figure leaning on a cane.

They stand as if surveying the sunset, so casual as they look round that it makes you want to punch them or possibly run into their arms and never let go. Venny is wearing plain, old-fashioned robes like a sun church devotee that you think very drab, though it helps them look convincingly like an entirely different person. Their lovely hair has been cut in a short crop, but somehow they still look very dashing. Even in the ugly wooden jewelery of a priest, their clever eyes shine out of the ritualistic makeup that rings them.

The slow, priestly way they carry themself is ruined somewhat by the helpless smile that spreads over their face as you approach. They look very tired, agitated under the veneer of calm.

"Well?" Venny asks, smile tense. For a stunned second you can't think what they want from you—you're alive, you're here, isn't that enough?

And then you pull yourself together, remembering your task, moving to their side and opening your bag. They glimpse the red box nestled at the bottom.

For a moment their face drops into something uncharacteristically unguarded as they let out a startled "Ha!" of surprise. They look up at you, disbelieving, and they're kissing you before you can think of what to say. You melt into the kiss in relief, and find it over much too soon.

Venny schools their face back to a more priestly aspect—for the benefit of anyone watching, you suppose—and asks nonchalantly if they can carry the bag. You are filled with visions of Venny giving you an apologetic look before knocking you out, and waking up with neither bag nor Venny, now they have what they wanted.

You hand it over anyway, and to your relief, Venny does not leave but squeezes your arm and begins in a low voice to discuss preparations for your journey. They say it as if there's no question of your going together, and you feel warmth spreading through you in the chill evening air.

> **If you have the status *birdsong*, turn to page 275.**
> **Otherwise, turn to page 274.**

A DIFFICULT JOURNEY

When you press them, Venny gives you a very brief account of their escape. The things left unsaid paint an unspoken picture in your mind: Venny, efficient and deadly even when limping and exhausted, inquisitors left gasping and bleeding in their wake.

In low tones like a priest murmuring advice to a stranger, Venny tells you their friends have left the city and the two of you shall have no help reaching the border. To you, this sounds calamitous, but they seem to take it in their graceful (if now-lopsided) stride, telling you with a tired smile that you both have survived through worse.

With a humble, disarming aspect of a devotee on a pilgrimage, they manage to bargain and haggle both of you into the back of rickety, slow-moving vegetable carts and onto the outer servants' seats of caravans returning hired actors and musicians home after the ball. You feel the full force of the rain and wind riding on the outside of carriages, and every bump in the road when you travel boxed in with the cargo as the goods carts judder along.

At night, you huddle together in little makeshift shelters, or farmers' stables and barns where you sleep in the straw. It feels dreamlike, like you ought to demand a clean bed and all the best food from their table—but that life is lost to you, now. When Venny invites you to share their blankets with a winsome smile, you find you don't mind the stables so much after all.

Venny never complains, sharing every hot bowl of soup or mug of wine or scrap of bread they manage to charm from the villagers and other travelers. They have a good story about their hard life in some monastery, which evolves and expands a little each time they tell it until it's a finely-tuned instrument that plays upon everyone who hears it, and every group you travel with looks upon them kindly. You watch in fascination, trying to learn the shape of the craft and use it to work on your own story.

You find yourself unable to charm the farmers, their lives and ideas a new language you do not speak. Instead, you listen to the players and merchants, learning their accents and the patterns of their voices, asking about their homes and childhoods and businesses. By the time you've drawn closer to the border, you have a good story you've borrowed and patchworked from others. Venny, of course, has been listening in. One night, listening to the rain spatter the awning of the covered wagon that bears you trundling along, Venny speaks softly in your ear. In a voice that sounds unusually hesitant and self-conscious, they say how you've surprised them—helping them escape, making it all the way into the tower, and now proving adaptable on a hard road. You drink the praise like a person dying of thirst and kiss their smile in the dark.

The truth is that even the miserable conditions seem of little consequence when Venny looks at you, sometimes. You're so used to being seen as a disappointment that every time they treat you as if you're remarkable, it thaws something inside you. You find yourself softening into something ready to be flexible—perhaps ready to be softer, or ready to be useful. **Turn to page 277.**

A COMFORTABLE TRIP

Venny leads you to an inn where a scarred servant with the burbling accent of a rural farmer is confidently organizing passage north for her merchant employer. She turns to smile at you, and with a start, you recognize it as the person who was yesterday calling herself Lady Tamar. When the merchant emerges, you recognize her as Tamar's 'servant'.

Once safely inside a carriage, Venny breaks the silence to tell you where they've been.

Venny had been seized by inquisitors looking for the red box. While you—protected by your parents' standing—had been put under house arrest, Venny had been taken to the dungeons below the keep. Venny says blithely they were 'questioned' but kept alive for a trial and public execution. You wince as you think about their new limp.

"They wanted us to know we weren't safe there," growls Tamar. Venny nods as if she'd said something about the weather, and not their own narrowly-avoided death.

"Tamar had been away from the city for a time," Venny tells you smoothly, as if to fill you in on some gossip, "and our usual channels of communication were disrupted when a few of our friends left town or were indisposed. When she discovered I hadn't been seen in a while, she was able to determine my whereabouts and retrieve me from the dungeons." They flash you a smile, like you're sharing a private joke. "So I must thank you for keeping her informed."

Tamar's brief account of her role in Venny's escape leaves many things left unsaid, painting an unspoken, efficient and deadly picture. The two women defer to Venny, and you find yourself aching to be in on their secrets, a real part of whatever's going on.

After two days, the women leave on another route, giving Venny a meaningful nod that communicates something you don't grasp. They seem to have paid for the rest of your passage to Estovar—you stop at inns each night to share a room with only a small fire, simple food and rough sheets that are not what you're used to. You keep quiet, trying to rearrange yourself into acceptance.

Venny charms information from innkeeps and travelers by pretending to know very little about the political situation thanks to "their time in the monastery." You watch them with interest as they hone their story to a finely-tuned instrument, extracting just what they need to know without attracting too many difficult questions about either of you. At first, Venny tells everyone you're a chaperone who has sworn a vow of silence—but by the time you approach the border, you've developed your own story and have a double act that Venny seems rather proud of. Your chest swells with each pleased or affectionate look.

Although surprised, they seem genuinely impressed that you made it through the tower and assured their rescue—even if the information you passed to Lady Tamar had been largely accidental. Nobody else has ever looked at you with anything but disappointment. The long journey through the tower all seems worth it. **Turn to <u>page 277.</u>**

VENNY'S MISSION—RENDEZVOUS

That night at sunset, you wait in the side-street by the small inn where you arranged to meet the prisoner, red box stuffed down in the bottom of your bag.

You see a large figure limp around a corner leaning on a cane. They're wearing plain, old-fashioned robes in the pale colors of a sun church devotee from the north, with dark eye makeup, short-cropped hair and big wooden jewelery completing the impression. They look and carry themself so convincingly that it takes you until their somber face breaks into a sharp smile to realize it's the person from the dungeons.

"Well?" Venny asks, face in a tense smile.

You hand over a plain sack, and they glimpse the red box inside. They let out a startled "Ha!" of surprise, and stow it away under their robes so fast that you barely see where.

"I can hardly believe it," they say, face suddenly softened into a wide, unguarded grin. "Several people—*experienced* people," they say with a wink and little fluid gesture that you take to mean Venny was one of them, "have tried and failed to do what you have." They lean closer, warm and serious and confidential. "You cannot know what a service you have done the world, how many lives may have been saved." Stepping away, Venny looks you up and down appraisingly, still looking a little baffled that you actually made it out with the box, and seems to gather themself.

"Right," they say, instantly schooling their features into something more closed off and businesslike, and reaching into a bag at their side. "All that remains is for me to do is to thank you—and I wanted to give you this." They pull out a large book that lands heavily in your hands. "Have a read through when you get home. I think you shall find it very rewarding." Using their stick, they swivel gracefully back out into the main street, manner falling into one of a serious, slow devotee and hobbling away before you can say anything.

When you get back to your room, you open the book and find the pages have been cut away to conceal a small bag—inside you find:
+ **A glittering black jewel**

Suddenly drained of adrenaline now the exchange is over, and exhausted and battered from your sleepless night in the tower, you duck into the inn next door. You pay for a room with a window, eat and drink whatever you want, and fall into bed, where you sleep better than you have in months, waking early and contented the next morning.

> If you're the **thief, turn to page 282.**
> If you're the **acolyte, turn to page 286.**
> If you're the **sailor AND have the status** *Toymaker's aide*, turn to page 292.
> If you're the **sailor** and **do *not*** have the status *Toymaker's aide*, turn to page 296.
> If you're playing your own character, **turn to page 269.**

THE TRAVELERS' INN

At the border with Estovar, the papers you retrieved from the princess's tower are examined. For a moment, you're suspended in nervous anticipation—then you hear the sound of a stamp. They're passed back over, and the guard waves you both through.

The proprietor of the travelers' inn beyond the gate is expecting you, greeting Venny with open arms and setting out a humble little meal on small plates that you eat happily and that tastes much better than half the expensive stuff you're used to anyway. You're given a comfortable little room that you don't seem to have to pay for, where a woman with a matching tattoo to Venny's is waiting to take the red box, assuring them it will be disposed of as they discussed.

She stands slightly nervously as you enter the room, bowing to Venny. "Venkatesh," she says formally, eyes only flicking to you for a second.

Venny waves this away, saying, "Please, Venny will do," and sinking into a chair. At this, the woman relaxes visibly like they've just said a code word, and when Venny says, "Report?" she begins a long stream of information you don't understand.

"She works," Venny tells you later, their round face lit soft in the candlelight, "for an organization called the nightjars." And then they put their mug down to look at you— their smooth, lovely voice serious in the flickering darkness. "We both do."

Venny tells you they've been all over the world working for the nightjars, gathering information and steering the course of events. "In our benefactors' favor, of course," says Venny, carefully not mentioning what benefactors, "but their interest is in peace and prosperity. History is like a great tapestry being woven: you can pull on threads to change the pattern of things." They say it with their dazzling smile, as if it's a joke.

The nightjars' work in the mountain kingdoms, they tell you wryly, has now ended. But Venny will set up somewhere new—somewhere quieter, now that they're getting older. Somewhere that another person willing to cooperate with the nightjars might live, too.

Their eyes are dark in the candlelit room. They don't look old to you, but the smile they flash you is tired. You think of how long their wounds from the dungeons will take to really heal, and all the other little scars that your fingers have traced so many times across their body. They do not touch you as they say this, but their hand rests on the bed where you sit, close enough to touch. Close enough to reach out and hold if you wanted to.

> **Go with Venny.** You want to be part of this greater purpose, part of the secrets and shaping the world—and you want to do it by their side. **Turn to page 279.**

> **Decide to move on.** You don't want ties with deception any longer. Tell Venny you can't go with them and want to make your own way in the world. **Turn to page 283.**

NIGHTBIRDS' CALL

As evening falls, you try to ask quietly and subtly around, and it does not work.

You keep the red box on you, down at the bottom of your bag—too afraid to leave it unattended. It feels like a beacon, and you're sure eyes are following it around the room as you try to listen in to conversations at alehouses and taverns, moving quietly through the narrow streets of the lower city.

When you try to make conversation hinting at what you have to sell, most people do not seem to understand you. Only one person you find in the corner of an inn seems to light with familiarity and asks you to join her for a drink. The battle-scarred figure stands a head taller than you and will not tell you her name, keeping her face hidden in shadows as she watches you sip your drink. She tells you she's *extremely* interested, insisting on a meeting place at midnight and holding your arm too tightly until you promise to meet her there.

You hurry out into the night, wondering in a panic whether you can escape her and what to do, and find your head and limbs strangely sluggish.

Two figures dressed head to toe in black peel away from either side of the doorway and seem to have no desire to keep themselves hidden as they follow you, ten paces behind. Trying to focus, you duck into side-streets and weave through alleys—but find that far from shaking them off, a third figure has appeared behind you when you glance back. Suddenly you turn a corner and there's another ahead of you, identically dressed.

You freeze, head slow and swimming, wondering whether to run. The one ahead holds something to their mouth and makes a noise that sounds like the rattle of birdsong—the call, you think, of a nightjar.

You find yourself suddenly surrounded, gloved hands on your limbs and over your mouth, a knife at your throat. You try to struggle and find your arms too weak and slow. You see the world dull in a blur—the night sky above as it starts to spin, a little tattoo visible on the wrist of your captor where the glove meets sleeve, their wrist moving as they hold your mouth closed and pull the knife across your neck.

As you sink to the floor, you see them find what they're looking for at the bottom of the bag. The red box, you think slowly, as one of them slips it away into the folds of their clothing—too important for witnesses to be left alive or murders to be kept secret.

They disperse into the night, leaving you to die on the dirty cobblestones. The world fades to black—at least one thing you retrieved from the tower has made it back to the people who wanted it.

Your journey ends here.

THE LIBERTINE'S FATE: AN AGENT IN ESTOVAR

You have never been able to say no to Venny.

Their smile is open and lovely when you say yes, spilling out of them as if they're letting their guard slip. The exact familiar wrinkle of their cheeks pulls at things inside you that you thought you'd buried long ago.

The next day, you spend a long, slow morning in bed, then take a modest carriage out toward the coast. The carriage is heading far, far away from the mountains and the seat and life you were supposed to inherit there. As you watch the clouds sweep across open sky and each mile of road rolls away beneath you, you feel as if you might laugh with relief.

The night falls and the days give way to forests and rain that smells like moss where it lands, and your thoughts turn to your life ahead of you. You think about the way Venny navigates the world and wonder who you should endear yourself to when you arrive. When Venny, watching you fondly from under the brim of their hat, asks you what you're thinking about, you ask them to tell you everything about the place you're going, and what name you should go by.

Venny looks so proud of you that you feel as if your chest might burst.

You come up with your name and story together—the one you will use for now—and Venny reads you facts and details from a book, then drills you on them over and over.

You roll into the glittering canal city that sits at the mouth of the Es river nervous and excited, eager to learn and hopelessly lost to the looks Venny gives you when you say something funny or unexpected. It feels as if the world is open to you for the first time in your life, and you finally have a purpose you have shaped for yourself.

Venny introduces you to society there carefully, using your new name. You slowly build connections, making the contacts you should—appearing a bumbling fool *mostly* only when you have planned on it, and using it to keep yourself always underestimated. You learn the common language there but don't let on, and overhear as much as possible to report back to Venny in the evenings. Together, you plan and scheme and talk, sharing setbacks and triumphs and long whispered conversations.

Venny somehow finds rooms with a hidden entrance where they can slip in unseen from tunnels, where warm wind blows in from the ocean, and you now only sleep in past noon on Sundays.

Something slowly grows inside you, a feeling you thought lost years ago when your father made you cut your hair and give away your dog. You still flinch when you do something wrong, some part of your brain still anticipating disappointed fury—and instead you are greeted by Venny, wrapping you in their arms, or Venny, frowning and nodding and thinking how to turn everything back in your favor.

The nightjars' game intrigues you and draws you in, and after some years you find yourself growing truly useful and good at something. Your heart swells and sings at working for the cause and seeing its incremental progress—crises averted and money diverted toward worthy causes. The intricate tangle gradually unravels in your mind until you can see the whole game board clearly and all its players, to be influenced and shifted or maneuvered around.

War never breaks out in Estovar in your lifetime—the box has been disposed of, a nightjar agent tells you conspiratorially as she reports to Venny, before she joins you for dinner and becomes someone you consider a friend. Some years later, when you are a full-fledged nightjar and granted your tattoo, Venny tells you other agents disposed of the box's contents in secret, for some years using its outer casing to leverage new open trade routes and causing the prosperity of the cities all along the border. You visit one of them for a summer festival, moving among the food stalls and hearing the poets speak under the fluttering flags of the makeshift structures. In the evening, you sit with Venny and watch the sun sink below the horizon as the sounds of wooden flutes and children playing, which meander up toward you from the grassy fields below. It feels very good to see the results of your long-ago journey into the tower taking root and flourishing into something you can see.

In the mountains, there are whisperings of a new merchant among the western assembly with the clipped tones of a kingdoms accent. So the nightjars spread new rumors about your demise in the tower, which you hear are swallowed eagerly by old acquaintances happy to gossip about your ending. You think how glad you are to have new acquaintances. Your family is relieved to gradually forget you, and Venny is happy to arrange financial difficulties for your father, who finds himself miserable and humiliated at his inability to maintain the lifestyle he was used to.

In the sprawling city at the mouth of the river Es, you grow used to the seasons and only having one set of fine clothes. You eventually make friends as well as contacts, and after some pleading, Venny even lets you keep a well-trained puppy. (You often hear Venny in the next room talking to the dog lovingly and slipping her treats when they think you can't hear.)

Venny still disappears for days at a time, but now you know where they are, and that nowadays, their errands are peaceable. Days later, you'll see them wandering in the shade of the cusped archways past the lapping green-blue water, whispering in the ears of the council. They scan the balconies of fruit trees where they know you'll be waiting, and when they catch your eye, they flash the small, private smile they save only for you. You listen for their tread on the secret stairs in the night, and your heart always dances to hear it—even though by now you know they will always, always come back to you.

THE END

VICTORIOUS

You slip back through the streets of the lower city like sinking into a warm bath.

It is early morning, and the familiar sounds of the town are disrupted by all the traders who came through for the ball setting up their makeshift market.

There's a mix of fine goods and rough tools, elaborate pastries and simple fare. If you have anything valuable taken from the tower, you know this will be a good place to sell it without having to wait or rely on your usual third parties, and you wind through the familiar traders you know and the visitors that you don't to find the most likely buyers.

> **- If you have a glittering jewel** or **a huge gemstone:**
> You move through the crowd to haggle at a stall selling pendants, fossils and magical contraptions built around crystals. The proceeds are enough to afford a new full set of clean, warm, well-made clothes, along with a pig to roast and a barrel of ale for the celebrations you plan to hold back in the old inn that used to shelter you as a child.

> **- If you have an enchanted longsword:**
> You find an old woman selling strange and unusual weapons and artifacts hidden secretively away behind a curtain in a small, unassuming caravan. She seems extremely interested in buying the sword, and hands over a heavy purse. You check to find it is real gold all the way through, and weighing it in your hand, judge it will be enough to fix the leaky rooftops all along the rickety tenements, install proper guttering, along with pipes for a new tap for the whole street, where the water is clean and free from the chance of disease.

As you move through back to your part of the city, you keep the opal crown shrouded in the folds of your cloak. This is your own prize.

> **If you have the status** *firestarter*, **turn to** page 300.
> **Otherwise**, turn to page 302.

THE LIBERTINE'S FATE: THE OPEN ROAD

Venny has brought you a long way: over the border and through trials and missions and the space Between worlds, where you found yourself capable of more than you realized. Thanks to Venny, you found your family's low evaluation of your worth was not the only one.

Venny has honed you like a knife from restless, unfledged recklessness to purposeful sedition—and you have loved them as they did it. But you're not sure you want to be a tool in another's hand any longer.

Now gratifyingly far away from your family and unwanted responsibilities, you are free of the tower and free of your parents—the bittersweet realization you could be free of the influence of Venny, too, feels like a weight lifting off your chest. The road stretches away from the border into the unknown, and for the first time in your life, you have a chance to travel it without the pressure of anyone pushing you in any direction. You don't want to be caught in the mesh of secrets any longer, tied to a person who only told you what they were getting you into when it suited their purposes.

You hold Venny for one last night and think they're too clever not to realize it's a goodbye. Their face looks soft and tired in the morning, lit in a shaft of sunlight that springs stark from the window to dance in their dark eyes. For a moment, their face breaks and is undone, and then they regain the composure that always seems at their fingertips. "You're not coming with me," they say, sad and calm again, and you don't need to reply for both of you to understand.

Among the assembled vehicles leaving that morning, there is a caravan of actors and musicians heading out along the winding westerly road toward the coast. Before the sun reaches the top of its arc, you have left on it without looking back.

The caravan is heading far, far away from the mountains and the seat and life you were supposed to inherit there. You sit up with the luggage in a cloak that's growing travel-worn, tipping back your head to watch the clouds sweep across the wide open sky, the birds calling overhead. Beside the trundling caravan, thick orange-blossom trees and river-reeds sway the wind, and you feel as if you could sing—like you could run alongside the carriage and out through the fields, like a weight is lifting from you with each mile of road that rolls away beneath. For the first time in your life, the world is truly open to you, and you feel as if you want to be open back.

Some of the players inside clamber up to join you in the sun, and respond with enthusiasm when you ask about the shows they're traveling to perform. You feel around and adopt the role of someone who had dreamed of acting in their childhood but whose family disapproved so strongly it was squashed miserably out of them—but over the next few weeks, you realize the role has a great splash of truth running through its core in all the important parts.

(Continues on next page)

In the evenings, the players share their meals with you. You watch them rehearse and find yourself caught breathlessly in moments of poetry in the performance.

The players love nothing more than an appreciative audience, and they love to draw out your sharpest and most dramatic comments to laugh over them. Over the weeks they bring you inside the caravan when it rains and ask you to read lines and share drinks and take sides in good-natured arguments about their next play. One of their number has left, they tell you, and they're short an actor: trying to combine two parts to solve it has proved difficult.

One night you blurt out that you have no set work at your destination and volunteer yourself for the part with a flourishing speech. Ignoring the flourishes, one of your most fond and protective new companions asks about your lack of destination with interest and concern, and you find yourself replying truthfully. You sketch the story of you and Venny—with none of the incriminating details—at a drunken and sympathetic fireside, and they agree to bring you aboard in a moment of midnight camaraderie.

In the town where you set up, you manage the part well enough that they let you stay on, and it's when they allocate roles for the next season that you find your place in the craft. You discover you shine at playing the villain.

Your parents and the people at court had always handed you the role without much thought, often simply for not fitting their expectations of what a person ought to be. But the more you speak and break bread with people who do not sneer at any sign of exuberance or vulnerability, the more you realize you'd been wearing the role like a cloak to hide what was underneath. You were *made* cruel and sharp, and you have the ability to make yourself softer again—it feels as if the lid of a stubborn jar were loosened by Venny's care and the disorientation of the Between, when everything but your thoughts was stripped away. You've had a lifetime of experience playing up to the role of the scoundrel, but over the years, you find with relief it is only a role: one you find yourself able to take off when you leave the stage.

You draw out the very worst of the court and your father in your performances as if to exorcise him and find the truth of it a great relief. You dedicate yourself to rehearsal and learning your lines more than you've dedicated yourself to anything in your life. And your unwavering commitment to the roles, as well as to the troupe, cements your place as a part of it. Made flexible, now, you force yourself to sincerely apologize after fighting with any of them, and you accept the humble work of helping with cooking and carrying and mending.

Your livelihood is precarious, but your group travels wherever there is work and good company. You move people, and you mean something to people. You never become famous, but something you never expected happens: you become happy.

THE END

FREE FROM THE THRALL

You walk the streets of the mountain city in a daze, still reeling in the strange feeling of freedom, your mind full and buzzing, exhausted in relief at its freedom from *the Key*.

In the lower town, people are spilling out into the morning streets, winding around the laughing children and market stalls in and out of houses. The city teems with a cacophony of life, the shouts of families you have never met and the smell of foods unfamiliar to you. With a pang, it strikes you how very far from the Great Library you are, and from all the comforts and structure and honor it grants in exchange for your service.

Blinkered by *the Key*, you hadn't thought of the town as anything beyond the place that held it. Now you begin to see it as a living, breathing organism, noticing all the things people are doing and thinking back to the people you met in the weeks before the ball. The booksellers you spoke with had remarked on your knowledge and your handwriting, asking if you worked as a scribe. One offered you work in translation and—it dawns upon you, your cheeks heating—was very sweet to you indeed, and may also have been offering companionship.

As you walk the cold stone streets, you are heartsick with the weight of missing the library—but at the same time, your head swims with possibilities, more choices than you have ever had before.

> **If you have papers retrieved from the tower** to send to the Great Library, you arrange everything immediately before you can forget, making a careful copy and posting them swiftly and anonymously by a reliable service. You feel relief in your assurance that you have done a good, important thing for the world.

You return to the simple room that's been kept for you—surprised to find it still there, still the same after all you've been through. Your world that had seemed narrowed to a tiny point, focused wholly around *the Key*, suddenly blooms outwards.

> **Return to the Great Library.** You think of the shelves and scrolls of your beloved home, curling under the domes. You think of your mentors and friends and the people you'd wish to be more than friends. You ache to get away from this damp, gloomy corner of the map and return. You may not have chosen it as a child, but you will choose it now—you will not abandon your post. **Turn to page 287.**

> **Do not return to the Great Library.** You think of the glimpses of other lives and worlds you saw in the Between and the unknown owners of the objects in the requisition room. You think of this windswept mountain town and its people's strange customs, the subtle feel of their unfamiliar gestures, the smell of the rain and the food sold on street corners. How many of their stories will not be cataloged? *The Key* narrowed down your world to a point, but the library, too, narrowed your world before that. How much more could you learn in the world outside of it? **Turn to page 290.**

THE ROAD TO THE GREAT LIBRARY

- If you have a glittering jewel or **a huge gemstone:**
You manage to sell what you have in a market busy with servants and travelers and caravans who came for the ball, counting the coins and adding them to your pouch.

The road is long but you ration the money carefully. When the weather is bad, you travel inside the simple merchant wagons that will take you for a low price and stay dry and warm in a new set of clothes suited for the miserable climate. When the weather is better, you wrap yourself in your cloak and ride on the outside seats of post-carriages, whisked along and shielded just enough from the bitter wind to enjoy the rocky hills and barren moors that sweep by either side.

You travel in slow barges where the owners laugh at your many questions, eat bowls of food you can't identify and scribble notes in lovely leather-bound journals you bought for the purpose. The further north you move, the more you see recognition in people's eyes when you explain you're an acolyte of the Great Library, and the more eager they are to tell you their stories and explain the customs and history of their hometowns. You copy it down, cataloging it all carefully. **Turn to <u>page 288.</u>**

Otherwise:
The road is long and hard. With barely any money to smooth the trip, you end up riding crammed between sacks of some sort of edible tuber, piled on rickety carts whose tops are open so your robes get soaked through in the cold rain. You spend more than one night with nowhere to sleep in bleak little traveling towns, and once, you decide to walk through the night to the next place you might be able to find a ride, just for something to do and to keep you warm.

By the end of the first week, you meet other travelers, curious about how far you have come from home, who see your inexperience and help you on your way. Now, you trek on foot on the days you do not find passage and sleep exhausted in the straw of strong-smelling barns. The nights are long and dark, but you share food and find yourself enthralled by stories of their lives—when it is dry and one of your fellow travelers has a candle, you scribble their stories on every slip of paper and ragged notebook you were able to get before you left. The travelers are good-natured about repeating themselves and seem pleased at the idea of featuring in some account that will be read far and wide.

Eventually you pass out of the mountains, leaving traveling companions behind to find new ones and write down their stories. You make your way over hills that avoid the great walls and gates that mark the edge of the country and its checkpoints. You travel on rafts down wide rivers with people who ask you to write letters down for them in exchange for teaching you to fish, and by boat and foot and trundling cart you make your way eventually back to your homeland. **Turn to <u>page 288.</u>**

ACOLYTE'S FATE: RETURN TO THE GREAT LIBRARY

You walk the last stretch of the uneven road up into the mountains, and in the setting sun, you see the glint of the familiar spires and domes. Having never left before, you've never so strongly felt the sensation of coming home.

Your seniors are cold and unsmiling to see you, but even their strict demeanor cannot hide their surprise at your return and the long story you report to them. After the first ten minutes, they stop you to bring in scribes to write everything down, and you take out your notes to hand over, as neatly and accurately dated as you can manage. You hand over the three books you found in the tower and stowed away in your cloak, books written in languages you strongly suspect are from other worlds. As she carefully turns the pages, the more senior acolyte's eyes widen as her mind turns from disbelief to a hunger to study them and add them to the collection.

Late, late into the evening when your story is done, you are brought solemnly to a disciplinary chamber where you sleep alone. You crawl into the plain and familiar bed and sleep better than you ever have in your life.

You are kept in silence and isolation for the next month, escorted to and from a room where you fulfill menial duties, transcribing damaged texts as penance for your desertion. But as you are walked from one place to another, you hear people around you whispering excitedly, and sometimes see your friends trying to catch your eye or the long-limbed youth whose attention you most want beaming at you as you're escorted away. You stand tall, and once or twice, smile back without anyone catching you.

Even the most scrupulous of the acolytes seem a little unsure what to make of you, and after a month you are allowed back to the common areas and dormitories where your friends whoop and cheer and pull you into their arms. Everyone wants to hear stories, and you acquiesce, speaking quietly and shyly, but glowing and getting better each time at capturing the feel of the thing you describe.

You return to the dance of the library, and when someone is needed to deliver messages or receive shipments of books donated that must be collected further afield, they begin to send you. And sometimes, the people you collect the texts from smile when they see you, recognizing you from descriptions that spread through the scholars' world.

For you are The Great Library's brightest star, returned. You are their new ambassador—the acolyte who traveled all the way south pulled by the thrall of a terrible artifact, only to overcome it and seal it safely away. And after seeing each country and the Between itself, what did you do but struggle all your way home by your own wits, keeping meticulous records all the way and turning yourself in to come back to your post. What could show more loyalty and admirable discipline of mind?

Over time, you are exonerated for your abandonment, forgiven and reinstated as the Great Library's most promising young acolyte. People speak as if you could do anything, and you feel as if you could. You will go on to advocate for greater freedoms for young initiates, visiting days for families where you finally see your mother again, and sponsored field trips to spread knowledge and bring it home. You will succeed at all of it, buoyed on by the tales of your journey into the tower.

But for now, you slip like a fish returned to a river along the corridors under the grand dome and up its enchanted ladders, putting everything in its right place, back where you belong.

THE END

ACOLYTE'S FATE: THE WORLD OUTSIDE THE ARCHIVES

You were chosen—first by the Great Library, then by *the Key,* and have so far only ever lived the life that was chosen for you. Now, a new expanse of possibility stretches before you, and you reach out into it, like a plant that flourishes in the space of a fallen tree.

You stay in the little mountain city for three years. You make friends and read its books and fall in love. You learn some of the language and customs and to like the moss patties and fried tubers sold on street corners. You write it all down, and when you run out of space in your notebooks, you make copies of your writing and have them bound in volumes in the back room of the little office where you help translate and proofread. You send them under a pseudonym to the Great Library along with the books you found in the tower and imagine where they will be shelved and who might pull them down to read them. With this done, you pack up and sell off your things and set off further south, high up into the mountains where the maps in the Great Library cut off.

You wrap yourself in warm cloaks, sturdy boots and caravans where you can. You are growing used to the weather by now.

You meet other travelers. Some are delighted at your book-studied, halting speech in their obscure tongue, where you mispronounce and misunderstand every other word. They invite you up into the structures they travel in, strapped to huge bovine creatures covered in shaggy hair and greatly attached to their masters. You are let into warm stone dwellings on long dark nights where everyone shares stories and is excited to have you copying theirs down.

You stay in the houses of goat farmers who you understand to be distant cousins or old acquaintances of the people you travel with, who all seem used to moving great distances looking for work outside the harvest season. You hear songs around fires that have never been written down and meet people who speak languages never listed in any guide. You meet whole villages where people keep the old faiths whose rules are not written, who keep the enchanted candles burning in the hollowed-out rocks that mark the roads across the high moors and black jagged mountains. They listen eagerly and seriously to stories about the Between and bring you fried flatbreads full of spiced unidentifiable vegetables and cups of blackberry wine. You write it all carefully down.

You return to the mountain city next season, weatherbeaten and smiling. Again, you send your writings along to the library—and, at the bookbinder's encouragement, make a little run of copies to be sold. They sell well among the communities whose families and partners hail from over the mountains, and you find yourself with the money to go wherever you like.

You look over a map of the whole known world, and instead of the memorizing and cross-checking of your time as an acolyte, you trace its rivers and long to feel them lapping at your ankles. You look out over its seas and want to feel the storms and lulls of the crossing, to see the harbors marked with dots alive and breathing, bobbing with ships and loud with birds and laughter. You see the plains and want to lie in them, watching clouds drift on endless skies, feeling the bumps in the roads that snake through them. You want to cross the lake neatly penned around the Lazurite Court and hear the streets and sounds and music played in the carefully-inked shapes of Estovar and the far islands and out in the unmapped lands beyond the shores over the crevasse.

You've heard the call of *the Key* and survived it. You've saved the world, and now you will see whatever you want of it. The open road is what calls to you now, and you will answer.

THE END

SAILOR'S FATE: TOYMAKER'S AIDE

You return to your father at the guesthouse, where he seems to be slowly recovering his strength. He seems as content as he can be in his dazed state, and well-looked after.

You remain for a few more days, visiting and preparing in the daytime and sleeping and recovering in the crowded bunkhouse at night. The noise and movement of bodies around you reminds you of normality, helping you shake the strange desolation of the place Between that seems to have sunk into your father.

You check diligently in on him. Mostly he sleeps and stares into space, avoiding leaving the room, but he seems to be able to eat and wash himself and smile at the people who come in to bring him food. On the day your preparations are ready, your father gives you a watery but genuine smile as he sees you come in. There's a plate of food empty beside him, and he looks clean, warm and comfortable, even if he still will not speak. You feel as if your heart swells with relief every time you see him, real and present in the ordinary world, still here. You think he'll be strong enough for the long journey home.

   - **If you have a glittering jewel** or **a huge gemstone:**
   You manage to sell them at a jewelery stall in the market for what seems like a good price. The proceeds are enough to afford a new set of clean, warm, well-made clothes for you and your father, as well as safe passage out of the city all the way back to the little town on the coast where your mother and brother are waiting.

   - **If you have an enchanted longsword:**
   You find an old woman selling strange and unusual weapons and artifacts hidden secretively away behind a curtain in a small, unassuming caravan. She seems extremely interested in buying the sword and hands over a heavy purse. Counting it out in private, you find you can afford not only good new clothes for yourself and your father but also to move him to a comfortable room in a more expensive inn, where he can rest in a soft bed for a few days before beginning the long journey. You can also buy presents to bring back for your mother and brother, as well as fruit and dried meat, sweets and tea with a little travel kettle that supplement your food on the long ride home.

If you have none of these, you live and eat plainly, rationing money from odd jobs to earn just enough for a long, hard passage south. It will get you both home, and that's the important thing.

Your mother weeps when she sees him, and more when she sees him changed. Your little brother can't understand what's wrong with his dad, why he won't always reply or listen to what he's saying. The mood is fraught, both happy and awful. Your mother takes her violin with a shaky smile but does not play it. She hugs you and does not let go for a long time.

Your brother is left with family friends for now, so he can stay in school and not have to see your father so often, not yet. Every time his dad doesn't reply or will not hold him, you see his little hands ball into fists, his small face drop into disappointment.

You find an old, run-down cottage out along the coast whose owner takes pity on your mother and gives it to her for next to nothing. When the three of you first arrive, you find it bleak and cold. To you that seems to match the state of things well.

You move into action for something to do in the still little house: gradually you clean each corner, fix the roof, scrub the floors, and gather the materials to make rag rugs and patchwork curtains that bring color into the bare rooms. You pick up occasional work in the nearby village, and save up for blankets and strong tea and biscuits, chipped old kitchenware and enough firewood to get by. It's not the same as the home you had, but it becomes warm and comfortable enough. At least it is quiet, and you're together.

Your father comes back to the world in slow pieces.

He will never enchant again. Sometimes, you see his hands move in the air, trying to guide their way to the seams in all things, to peel back reality and let a little of the space Between in. But he has lost the trick of it, had it all drained out of him—and he always returns his big hands to his lap, as if forgetting what he was doing halfway.

Your mother teaches him to churn butter and feed the goats. Some days you find him standing on the top of the cliffs, staring out at the sea. Sometimes, he watches the great long creatures that wind beneath its surface and the gulls that wheel overhead. Other times, the sea is still or misted, and he gazes out into nothing. He does not reply when you ask what he's looking at.

After a while, he's well enough to chop vegetables and use an awl for sewing leather, and not too long after you see him whittling at driftwood. There's muscle memory in his clever hands. At first, he makes things that your mother watches emerge from the wood with sad eyes—you recognize them as fragments of things he has seen in the Between. The carving draws all his attention for hours at a time, and the results are intricate and abstract. In them you sometimes see echoes of elongated colossal figures on a horizon, mists and memories. He makes beautiful, incomprehensible, garbled figurines that your mother lines up on shelves until the shelf space runs out. You hear her crying in the night and you wonder if he notices.

Then one day, you take a boat out over the waters with the shell-divers, who need experienced hands for a few days. You feel guilty but free to be out of that sad, quiet house, back among the spray and shouts and motion of the water. When you come home, you see your father has placed a big hand over your mother's where they sit by the fire. You see the edges of a smile tugging at her cheeks.

(Continues on next page)

Now, he carves the sea serpents and the birds and miniatures of the clifftops. He makes little wooden simulacrums of the kettle, with all its dents replicated exactly. He spends a long time on a tiny model of violin, small enough for the palm of your hand, and when it is finished, he leaves it on the lid of a pot your mother uses every day.

She laughs when she sees it, and keeps on laughing so long it turns to tears. He looks shyly up to meet her eye and gives her the hint of a smile.

She begins to play the violin again after that day.

The violin, spellbound long ago by your father to sound sweet, has soaked up the magic that poured from the Between into your old ruined house. It sounds otherworldly and ringing, and as she plays, flowers and seashells, pearls and ribbons and sea glass and conkers bubble into the world around her feet. She learns to control them by the melody and takes the fiddle into town where children are delighted to watch. When their parents notice, too, she is invited into taverns in the village and the next one over. She makes friends and drinking companions and sells the pearls for yarn and dresses, for hats and things to send away to your brother back in town.

Your father does not regain his speech entirely as it was before, but he comes slowly back to himself—to a new, quiet, deliberate self that diligently keeps house and watches the waves and wraps your mother in his big arms. When your brother returns, your father listens to him carefully, even if he seldom replies. Each time your brother visits, little carved figures in the shapes of animals are waiting for him on the pallet set up for him on the floor. Your brother clutches them tight and does not let go, holding them to his chest as he falls asleep.

One day you will go away to sea again—on voyages shorter and longer, on big-bellied merchant ships that move slow like islands along the far coast, and on batten-sailed racers that dance from town to town, carrying the post and the news. You will meet friends, lovers and teachers, survive storms and darken in the northern sun. You will move through the world fearless, like someone who has known the space Between worlds and come out the other side; careful, like someone who knows how precious a life is.

But for now you watch your mother make butterflies and thistles and sea glass at her feet, playing an old melody and wearing the echo of an old smile. Beside her, your father has paused where he sits fixing nets, and he looks up at her like he's never seen anything so wonderful—like he's never seen the ancient things that called out to him from the place beyond.

The evening air blows chill through the long grass, and you hear the kettle start to whistle on the stovetop. Your father stands to move to it, instinctively—relearning his new place in his new home.

THE END

SAILOR'S FATE: THE CALL OF THE OCEAN

You move through the streets of the city, considering your next steps.

In the lower town, you find a market set up by traders who came through for the ball and have been slow leaving. It's busy with servants and travelers and caravans, and there's a mix of fine goods and simple fare—if you have anything taken from the tower, you realize this would be a good place to sell it.

- If you have a glittering jewel or a huge gemstone:

Moving through the crowd, you see someone at a stall selling pendants, fossils and crystals, who seems keen to buy them from you. The proceeds are enough to afford a new set of clean, warm, well-made clothes, and safe passage out of the city all the way back to the little town on the coast where your mother and brother are waiting.

- If you have an enchanted longsword:

You find an old woman selling strange and unusual weapons and artifacts hidden secretively away behind a curtain in a small, unassuming caravan. She seems extremely interested in buying the sword and hands over a heavy purse. Counting it out in private, you find you can afford good new clothes for yourself and your brother, along with some fine lace and silk that you bundle away in a parcel for your mother, stowing it all in a fine new leather traveling-case. You pay for a good room to rest for the night before beginning the long journey, which you take by the fast mail carriage, buoyed by provisions bought with your prize: fruit and dried meat, sweets and tea, with a little travel kettle to supplement your food on the journey.

If you have none of these, you have to beg and barter your slow way home, half-walking and often damp and cold.

Either way, you make the long journey back home, relieved to be leaving the tower behind you with each mile.

Grief still lies heavy on your limbs as you travel down over the hills toward the sea, but you find yourself thoughtful. You'd set out into the tower as if it were repentance, punishment for not being there when your family most needed you. You were careless with your wretched body. But in the Between, you had to hold on tightly to life to make it through the chaos of magic. You emerged determined to go on.

If you could endure that, you think, you can survive the space your father has left in your life. Just as summer storms blow through without warning, it seems strange and magical things work their way into the world here and there, and little can be done to stop them. After a storm, there's nothing to do but mend sails.

Your mother takes her violin with a shaky smile, but does not play it, not yet. She hugs you and does not let go for a long time. "It's very good to have you back," she tells you, arms tight. "For a while I thought—it seemed as if I'd lost both of you."

The little fishing town you grew up in seems loud with memories, full of the yawning space where your father should be. Everything reminds you of him, and your mother says she feels the same, whispering the admission after dark once your little brother has cried himself to sleep. He's stopped asking when Dad will be back or when you can all go home, but he hasn't stopped crying.

You look half-heartedly for new work, but think yourself unable to seriously consider anything beyond odd jobs unloading cargo at the docks—not while your diminished family needs you so much. You think of the swirling memories of the Between, of all the places out in the world. For all your time at sea, you haven't got to know much but the briefest of glimpses of city ports on your limited shore leave. And here you are, tied to your little harbor hometown again—only now, every doorway and friendly face is haunted by the memory of your father.

One day, you set down your crates and pause to rest at the top of a gangplank, and notice a huge merchant ship coming to anchor in the bay, its round hull low in the water with cargo. You recognize the unusual vessel as one that usually crawls along the coast on the other side of the ocean.

When its crew come to shore, you learn a far-off magical harvest has gone awry, creating an abundance too great to be sold off at home. They're making a one-off trip to sell the excess, and you're hired to unload dried fruits you've never heard of, peppery herbs and dark, sweet wine that jingles in its crates. A ship so large, you realize, can't be filled by your little harbor town, and will return emptier than it left.

A wiry, freckled sailor who turns out to be second mate buys you a drink in a crowded tavern by the docks. She tells you she's looking for hands to replace the crew staying in the east to seek their fortune, along with any passengers or travelers they can take. The price is far lower than that of any usual crossing, and when you ask after the destination, you find it's not so far from the city your mother grew up in.

When you tell your mother, she nods, businesslike, barely needing your full explanation to come to the same conclusion. She goes to count every scrap of money the two of you have been able to bring in and save and finds it's enough.

You pack up your few possessions into bags that you cram into a cabin on board the huge merchant ship. It's for the best, she keeps telling your brother, but he looks cold and miserable as the ship pulls away from the coast. The three of you watch the little harbor town that used to be home disappear into the misty distance on a rainy, mizzling morning, and it's a bitter relief to see it go.

After a few days, your brother has been gradually cheered by the other travelers slipping him biscuits and pinching his cheeks, and he forms a new habit of tearing across the deck yelling whenever he sees the distant shapes of sea serpents and great leviathan creatures away on the horizon. You hold him up so he can see better, and it pulls at your heart to see him laughing again as his hair whips in the wind, sadness momentarily forgotten.

One night, your mother brings out the violin and begins to play—not one of the old, bawdy shanties, but a mournful, lovely ballad that she does not sing along to.

The sailors and passengers gather around.

The violin, spellbound long ago by your father to sound sweet, has soaked up the magic that poured from the Between into your old ruined house. It sounds otherworldly and ringing, and as she plays, ribbons and seashells, pearls and coral and seaweed and sea glass bubble into the world around her feet.

Her swells of emotion seem to guide the enchantment, and as the days go by, she learns to control them by the melody. It seems to soothe her to pour her grief into something, to have a place to shape all the love for your father that has no place to go.

She plays sweet, soaring songs, and shimmering fabric billows from the air around her in a swirl; high haunting melodies send sparkling blue crystals shooting up from the deck at her feet; lullabies send your brother to sleep as beds of night-blooming flowers spring up to cushion him.

Once you are landed on the far coast and she sees the cliffs of her childhood, long-missed pastries and spiced buns and the faces of long-lost aunts, she slowly learns to play reels and jigs again. She plays in snow and mist and shafts of sunset of her own creation to the delight of children in the street; she is hired out to make gardens bloom and crops thrive. She sells the pearls and crystals and makes a little life for herself in one of the homes she had always dreamed of, high up on the cliff where the view extends for miles in every direction.

Your brother slowly, cautiously makes friends of his second cousins and learns to read. You move furniture and haul goods at the docks, and buy your mother comfortable cushions and colorful pots and pans and roof-tiles enchanted for durability. You have enough to live in a house of fellow workers in the town below, but there is always room for you with your family on the squashy old sofa after you visit for dinner.

One day, you will go away to sea again—on voyages shorter and longer, on the big-bellied merchant ships that move like islands along the coast, and on batten-sailed racers that dance from town to town, carrying the post and the news. You will make friends and learn to truly smile again, survive storms and darken in the northern sun. You will move through the world fearless, like someone who has known the space Between worlds and come out the other side, and you will return to your little family, diminished but still held fiercely together, steadfast in the face of the cruelty of fate.

Things are not the same, but you have found a place to begin again, and perhaps one day, to build new and happy memories.

THE END

THE THIEF'S FATE: REVENGE AND GLORY

High above, the remains of the tower still smolder, smoke curling upward from its wet remains. The bodies of those lost are burned with the rites of the sun church: flags hung along the battlements, prayers burned for eight nights at the site of the thing everyone is calling "the accident." The guests who died are remembered somberly in all the towns and villas they came from, wept over by families, mourned in grand state funerals, or built great crypts and monuments that serve one political goal or another. The servants who died are only able to be mourned quietly by people with new holes in their lives. Their absence is felt like a missed step on the stairs every time their loved ones see their name, their old clothes or favorite color.

Strange things go on in the ruins—one day a purple moss growing from a strange contraption that cannot be moved will cover the stones, sprouting ferns and trees and causing the keep to finally be fully abandoned. It will become a site where children play, and people will say you can hear laughter and music if you stand in just the right spot, see wisps of golden dancers and hear the ring of bells. They will say, too, that if you clamber up over the stones to the highest point on a clear day and squint just right, you can see a strange shimmer in the air right above you, like a great crack that splits the sky.

For now, frantically scrawled missives are appearing on the desks of spellbinders all over the kingdoms. In the wake of their panicked discussions and the public outcry around the tower's destruction, the post of royal spellbinder will be abolished, and its inquisitors disbanded as a new and more lenient coterie is elected in its stead.

Unknowing of the fate that awaits them, the last inquisitors that survived the tower's collapse now clamber through the ruins, struggling to control the survivors and mourners that take the spinning, humming trinkets from the wreckage of the tower and bring them home. Several give up entirely, casting away their masks of office and starting away from the city on a long road to a different future.

A treaty intended between several countries is never signed, its signatories dead and missing after the ball, the diagrams and materials intended for magical weapons it included now lost. Magic will be set back centuries, some say, if not further—and others toast to it. They know it may mean safer centuries to come.

But you know none of this.

You are walking, triumphant, through the streets of the lower city—*your* city—watching the distant smoke rise from the skyline. You place the opal crown on your head and step into the little inn, a conqueror. People cheer and laugh and lose their bets and you buy drinks until half the crowded room is on the floor.

You leave the opal crown high up on the spire of a building you think nobody else could reach, and it attracts gaggles of people from all over that try to claim it before the authorities retrieve it, furious and humiliated. The bounty on your head is raised tenfold, and whispers spread from the little inn all across the city that you were the one who burned the tower. Good, you think. You want them to know.

Nothing can truly surpass your one most famous and glorious heist. Rebel groups in other cities use your name as inspiration in their bloody feuds, and some are even successful—you take credit but never get involved.

And yet, the bitter pit in your stomach never quite fills. You go on to more and more reckless prizes, closer shaves and more daring escapes. Each revenge seems to fall short, to leave a more yawning void in its wake—it is never enough, and nothing you can do can really be good enough to make things better. You work alone, and when you try to work together with others, they always fall—captured or dead, or worse. You are wanted and dangerous to know, and find you must cut yourself away from the families you grew up around to keep them safe.

Before you die and long after, people know your name. They sing it in songs and whisper it in bedtime stories and cautionary tales.

You can see the end of your path, sure and certain, in each narrow escape—an inevitable but spectacular end waiting just around the next corner. One day they will catch you, but first, you will be glorious.

THE END

THE THIEF'S FATE: A SEED OF HOPE

Faced with the chance of more violence at the top of the tower, you turned away from it, and it has planted a seed of hope in you.

You are welcomed warmly into the inn where your survival has lost everyone their bets. They gather around and ask for stories of the tower, which you tell happily, softening some parts for the children that have spilled out from the tenements to huddle at your feet and listen. At the end, you bring out the opal crown to cheers and gasps and yelling from the children, until the ones with homes to go to are shooed and cajoled back home, and the ones without are given supper and blankets.

Watching them, you remember all the little kindnesses in your harsh childhood. When the wind swept down from the mountains and the cobbles slicked with ice, old Maud used to let you in at the side-door to the basement kitchens of the inn. You would curl on the warm stone in front of the hearth and scrub potatoes in exchange for the dregs of bowls of potage to lick clean. No gift or trophy you could ever steal now could be as sweet, you think.

The crown has been your finale, but now you slip it away instead of showing it off, keeping it as a rumor and the enforcers and inquisitors far from your door. The swirl of memories in the mists of the Between have made you think about all the things forgotten in your life, pushed aside in the pursuit of raising yourself up and the chase for revenge.

Tonight, you ask around quietly to find out more about the opal crown, and tomorrow, you make plans to approach things differently.

You go for small prizes that will not be missed and can be easily sold on. You make regular, but not spectacular money, and put work into the squat little inn until it always has plenty of food and a whole room of little beds for children with nowhere to sleep or a home where they can't stay warm or safe. You find the people who really need work and find them things to do at the inn so that old Maud can retire, well-fed and chattering happily to guests by the fire.

You trace the war the crown was taken in and find it was not so long ago as you thought. Much of your information comes from a wizened old woman who survived it. You source maps and find the city-state it's thought to have come from and decide to turn your daring and adaptability toward a long journey.

You slip among caravans as they leave the city after the ball, out over the border into Estovar. You travel down the great river Es in a fishing barge and turn your quick hands to gutting to earn your way. In the beautiful canal city at the mouth of the river, you turn to careful pickpocketing from those who can afford it—enough for passage across the great wide ocean that laps turquoise at the white stone of the harbor.

You find yourself quick in the rigging and good at palming cards—you meet sailors and crooks and travel memorably with pirates traversing the warm waters of the northern islands. You tell them about the tower and warmly speak about the street you grew up in, but never the opal crown in the hidden pocket sewn into your jacket.

In the lands over the ocean, you find colorful towns huddled on cliffsides, bustling markets and new foods. Above the harbor where you finally make anchor is the biggest city you've ever seen, its strange and lovely structures stretching upward along the sides of a ravine and built all across the bridges that cross it. In the dark water of the deep bay, great slow ships the size of buildings loom above you, their hulls curving far down into the ocean where they carry bolts of cloth and dried herbs in their bellies as they journey south toward the crevasse.

You find you have to buy yourself a ticket, a thin wooden slip, to get onto one of the carriages headed inland. And you find these are coaches, with seats for ten inside and more for those who'll brave the weather on top. They're pulled by whole teams of horses, slimmer and faster than the ones back home, sure-footed on the scree as they climb the great broad road heading inland. You meet tinkers and merchants and nomads on the road, who bring you with them when your money runs out on your last stretch to your destination. On an island at the center of a green lake so wide it may as well be the sea, a sprawling city fans out in stepped layers that reach up toward its highest tier: the many-layered building of the Lazurite Court.

You spend a while in the city, watching and listening and waiting, learning the way things work the best you can in a land so totally strange. You make inquiries at serious little offices where there are more tickets and long waits wherever you turn. Whenever you try to speak to someone important, you are handed over to someone else. You find yourself frustrated with dead ends and layers of court formality and climb your way over rooftops into the walled gardens of palaces until you can speak with the people that glide among the exquisitely cultivated gardens yourself. You have to make your escape once or twice, but eventually you find someone you can speak to for long enough to show them the crown. Their eyes widen behind their fan and you find yourself ushered into gilded waiting rooms painted with landscapes to sit and wait until someone from the Shining Council of the Wise itself is brought before you.

You present her with the crown and answer all her questions about how you came by it. She brings a translator to be sure she understands correctly—that you are not from any official delegation from any of the kingdoms, but rather, she says, speaking your language perfectly but slowly, "You are someone who has been failed by them?"

A scribe is sent to write your statement, and you stay in the city for several months as the Shining Council deliberates, befriending more of the children and traders than the scholars of the court in their elaborate dress. Eventually, you are brought into a beautiful room and told how very grateful they are for the return of the crown, *and* that you're to swear to secrecy, to keep the peace between their lands and your kingdoms.

They pay your way all the distance back to the city in the mountains, and send you with a small delegation that peels off at each stage, a bubbly junior scholar, and bars of a shimmering magical substance and trunks of beautiful fabric. You trade the bars and cloth in Estovar for a small fortune—not much to a city named for its gemstones, perhaps, but more than you could ever imagine.

The scholar points out features of the landscape eagerly and excitedly gets you to try new food and tiny glasses of strong, unfamiliar drinks until you become firm friends. She makes notes of everything and stays with you all the way home, where she organizes your money and goods and starts to make notes on the city, too.

You arrive back to the little inn, stooping through doors of the rickety tenements to surprise and delight from people who thought you gone forever. The scholar is only here to bring knowledge back to her home city—technically—and says she expects to stay only for a few years. But she has bright eyes and big ideas, and she looks carefully at the drafty windows of the tenements, and tours the poorhouses and hospitals with serious, focused concern.

The money from the Lazurite Court does not transform the lower city overnight, and sometimes projects falter or fail—but other times, they flourish. People in your neighborhood have learned long ago not to question where your money comes from, and when your influence spreads further, they seed rumors about pirates or long-lost aunts. You do nothing to curb them and let your secret recede into the shadows.

Your name as a daring thief is gradually forgotten, but you rekindle the connections with the families that raised you and work with representatives from each family and community to change the place you grew up. You build warmer homes and more efficient drainage and sewers; you work on systems to get people clean water and good boots; you help people looking for places to organize schools and care for their children when they're out working in the shops or fields. You store food for hard winters and sure up roofs and chimney stacks that may fail in the storms.

You are welcome at many tables and a regular at the little inn, where children know your name and ask to hear stories about Estovar and pirates and the city on the lake. One cold autumn morning, you see a carriage moving slowly through the neighborhood and see your old master frowning up at the sured-up, scrubbed-clean tenements. You have now purchased all the deeds to give to the inhabitants. You see his nose wrinkle at the new houses being built down the street, as if unable to understand where they're coming from. In the warm little inn, one of the families you used to live with is waiting to meet you for breakfast to celebrate one of the children's birthdays. Your old master sits in the carriage alone. You flash him a smile as you walk past the carriage, hoping he remembers the missing silverware. Either way, you think you are satisfied with your revenge.

THE END

CHARACTER SHEETS

THE THIEF

Skills

Strength: 3

Agility: 6

Charisma: 4

Logic: 3

(If your stamina reaches 0, your journey ends.)

Stamina: 5

When you see '*add to your inventory*,' write it here.

When you see '*gain the status*,' write it down here.

Inventory

Status

Notes

CHARACTER SHEETS

THE SAILOR

Skills

Strength: 6

Agility: 4

Charisma: 1

Logic: 2

(If your stamina reaches 0, your journey ends.)

Stamina: 6

When you see '*add to your inventory,*' write it here.

When you see '*gain the status,*' write it down here.

Inventory

Status

Notes

CHARACTER SHEETS

THE LIBERTINE

Skills

Strength: 1

Agility: 2

Charisma: 5

Logic: 4

(If your stamina reaches 0, your journey ends.)

Stamina: 3

When you see '*add to your inventory*,' write it here.

When you see '*gain the status*,' write it down here.

Inventory

Status

Notes

CHARACTER SHEETS

THE ACOLYTE

Skills

Strength: 2

Agility: 1

Charisma: 3

Logic: 6

(If your stamina reaches 0, your journey ends.)

Stamina: 4

When you see '*add to your inventory,*' write it here.

When you see '*gain the status,*' write it down here.

Inventory

Status

Notes

ACHIEVEMENTS *checklist:*

Ending connoisseur

BRAVADO
Find five different pages with 'your journey ends.'

BURN IT DOWN
Destroy the tower and escape alive

UH OH!
Destroy the world

SHAKESPEARIAN
Die dramatically in front of a large audience

CALLBACK
Die in the dungeons

KEY PLAYER
Die destroying *the Key*

MEMENTO
Escape the tower but lose all your memories

DREAMER
Get lost forever in the Between

THAT'S ON ME
Die at your clone's hand

TEEMWORK
Escape the tower to spread the gift

It's more about the friends you make along the way

**MAGIC PALS**
Speak to a junior, minor and senior spellbinder.

HERO AMONG ISOPODS
Gain the status: *friend to the king of woodlice*

FASHION ICON
Get new clothes

JUST GOOD SENSE
Run from a monster

WHO NEEDS IT
Survive the tower without ever having any money, jewels or gemstones

MATRICIDE
Become the new Mother

**BEYOND THE VEIL**
Talk to a ghost

MOST WANTED
Kill or help kill an inquisitor

THAT'S MESSED UP
Eat your clone

**MONSTER GF**
Kiss the princess

Main character energy

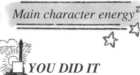**YOU DID IT**
Escape the tower

LOBSTER DINNER
Sail over the crevasse

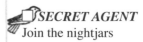**REPATRIATOR II**
Travel to the Lazurite Court

SECRET AGENT
Join the nightjars

**INDEFATIGABLE**
Escape the tower with a higher stamina than you started with

LOADED
Find 2 different jewels and a huge gemstone

REUNION
Reach 'THE END' with the status *toymaker's aide.*

PROTAGONIST
Survive and reach 'THE END' playing the acolyte.

DESTINY MAKER
Destroy *the Key* **and** leave the tower alive with the cure recipe.

OPTIONAL EXTRA: CREATE YOUR OWN CHARACTER

PLEASE NOTE: Before making your own character, it's **highly recommended you try playing most of the book characters first**. Each has special endings that will give you more of an idea of the world of *Into the Tower* and can't be reached other ways. **You'll be making up your character's own beginning and ending.** Knowing the plot and world will help form your own story!

To make your character, look at the character sheets provided—you can rip them out, print them out, or make your own versions. As long as you have a note of your skills, inventory, and status, you can use any method that suits you to draw, type or record as much or little of your thoughts and story as you want.

There are **prompt tables** on the next pages that can help you build your character.

1. Create your character.
Find a 'create your own character' sheet example at page 314, and a blank to use at page 316—or online at **hari-illustration.com/itt**

> • **Roll a 6-sided dice** to get a value for each skill, as well as a starting value for stamina. Write these down on your character sheet, along with:
>
> - Who's the character you're playing? What's your background?
> - What's the object you want from the tower?
> (Prompts for both on the next page.)
>
> • **One weapon** and **one piece of clothing** from the table below that your character will start with, and write them down in your inventory.

	Weapon	Item
1	A concealed knife	A long blue robe (Fine clothes)
2	A long, battered sword	Plain servant's clothes
3	An ornate dagger (poisoned)	A dark cloak
4	No weapon	A pouch of 50 gold pieces

(To pick at random, use a 4-sided dice or an online dice roller. You can also flip a coin twice, where 1= Two heads, 2 = Heads-tails, 3= Tails-heads, 4 = Two tails.)

Have a look at the next few pages for ideas for getting the most out of your play. Then, when you're ready to start, **turn to page 24 to begin.**

(Continued on next page)

2. The Between (page 167)

When you reach page 167, you'll be prompted to follow the thief route. Write down what memories your character would be thinking of. What is it they're trying to get home to? What are they most afraid of or motivated by at this stage on their journey?

3. Out of the tower (page 264)

If you make it to this page, you've successfully finished the game! You'll be directed to a page with final prompts, where you can think about and note down what your character would do once they have retrieved their item from the tower.

CHARACTER PROMPT TABLES

Prompts: *What are your skills?*

Roll a 6-sided dice to get a value for your character's stamina and each of their skills. You can make up your own character based on these, or for any skills that are 4 or above, choose reasons from the tables below.

(To pick at random, use a 4-sided dice, an online dice roller, or flipping a coin twice.)

	High strength. You have built your physical strength by . . .	**High agility.** You have honed your speed and reflexes by . . .
1	Working in a warehouse or a bakery	Hunting in the forest
2	Doing a lot of hiking or traveling	Picking pockets or performing card tricks
3	Hitting the gym	Waiting tables
4	Training as an athlete or soldier	Keeping your very energetic toddler out of danger

If your character has **low strength or agility**, are they unused to physical activity day-to-day, or exhausted after working a physically strenuous job for many years? Do they have disabilities or health problems that make some tasks more difficult, but the item in the tower is so important that they want to (or are forced to) venture in anyway?

	High charisma. You . . .	**High logic.** You . . .
1	Are disarmingly honest and friendly	Absolutely love pub quizzes and being right
2	Barely speak and seem extremely wise	Are a rogue spellbinder obsessed with how magic works
3	Work hard to seem devastatingly charming	Work as a private investigator by night
4	Are too intimidating to question	Like books more than people

(See the skills table on page 2 for ideas about low charisma or logic characters.)

CREATE YOUR OWN CHARACTER, *continued*

Prompts: *What item are you looking for in the requisition room?*
Is it something your character previously used to own, feels they have a right to or has never seen before and wants to take for themself? Is it something expensive they want to sell, something of sentimental value, or a document or magical item that might give them ownership over property—or control over land, magical technology or other people?

You can make up your own, choose from the table below or roll a 6-sided dice to pick at random:

1	**A magical family sword** without which you cannot inherit your fortune and title. Do you like your family? Have you only just discovered you're heir to a fortune?
2	**An enchanted protective ring** that belonged to someone who passed away and is of great emotional value to you. Who was it, and what does the ring protect from?
3	**A mysterious shimmering cloak that makes the wearer unusually lucky** that you claim rightfully belongs to you. Does it? How do you know about it?
4	**A spellbook deemed dangerous** You are an apprentice to a wizard of dubious moral character who has tasked you to retrieve the book. What's in it? Do you give it back if you find it, or use it yourself?
5	**Scrolls of magical research** You are a distraught university student whose research has been confiscated. You'll fail your degree if you don't have anything to hand in. What are you studying? Was it really dangerous or not?
6	**Ancient cursed bone dice that predict the future** You work for a courier who had a very expensive cursed package seized at customs. If you don't get it back, your awful contract means you'll be in debt to your terrible employer forever. Have you used the dice? If so, what did you see, and do you expect it come to pass? Will giving the dice back curse your employer?

CREATE YOUR OWN CHARACTER: Example

NAME: Linda (she/her)

SKILLS: Number (1d6) Why?

Strength	4	Crush on a fitness instructor at the magic gym has meant she's developed incredible quads
Agility	3	From chasing around her 3 year old nephew stopping him from drinking potions in her very child-unfriendly flat
Charisma	2	Extremely honest in a way that doesn't always go down well
Logic	1	Acts on what she feels is right

Stamina: 4

1. Character background:

Linda works in a cake shop and mostly stays out of all that magic business. She is saving up to put a deposit down on a cottage so she can fully provide for her wonderful dog, Gavin, who doesn't appreciate her tiny flat.

Portrait / appearance

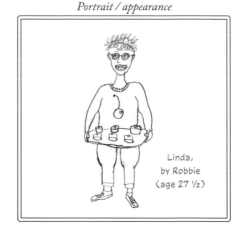

Linda,
by Robbie
(age 27 ½)

Magical item they're looking for:

One day, tragedy strikes when her terrible cousin who went into wizardry comes to visit, and captures Gavin in an orb of power 'as a joke'. Before Linda can retrieve her beloved dog, the forbidden soul-trapping orb is detected by the local inquisitor and confiscated. Linda's quest is to venture into the tower to get her dog back.

Personality

Optimistic —X———————— Cynical
Cautious ——————X——— Reckless
Frantic —X———————— Calm
Bumbling ———————————X Stylish
Heist novice X———————— heist expert

very chatty

gets excited easily

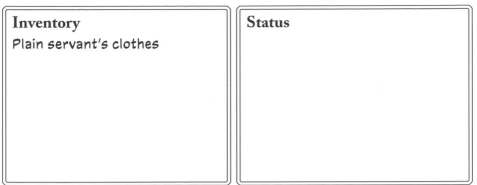

Inventory

Plain servant's clothes

Status

Adventure notes

2. What does your character see in the Between?

Linda sees beautiful memories she and her dog have shared together and almost gives up all hope of seeing him again. Then she remembers her terrible cousin and realizes he's definitely an evil wizard. Motivated by revenge, she pulls herself together and vows to track him down and trap HIM in the orb instead when she gets out of the tower.

3. Out of the tower: what does your character do if they escape?

Linda works out how to use the soul-trapping orb and releases Gavin, who is very glad to see her and now magically infused with ancient powers. She figures out how to use the orb of power to infuse her cakes with the essence of summer and happiness, and the magical cake shop becomes the most famous in the country. She buys a lovely cottage and lives happily there. On the weekends, with the help of her dog's new powers, which help him smell magic, they hunt down evil wizards to seal them away in other dimensions in the orb, starting with her cousin.

CREATE YOUR OWN CHARACTER SHEET

NAME:

SKILLS: Number (1d6)   Why?

Strength		
Agility		
Charisma		
Logic		

Stamina:

1. Character background:

Portrait / appearance

Magical item they're looking for:

Personality

Optimistic ———————— Cynical

Cautious ———————— Reckless

Frantic ———————— Calm

Bumbling ———————— Stylish

Heist novice ———————— heist expert

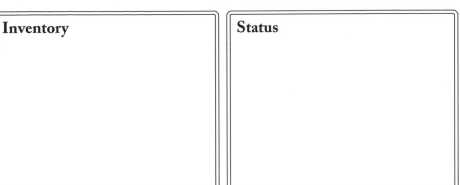

Adventure notes

2. What does your character see in the Between?

3. Out of the tower: what does your character do if they escape?

HELLO, WE MADE THIS

Author & illustrator—Hari Conner
hari-illustration.com | @HariDraws

Illustrator: Cover; player characters, and the junior spellbinder; the castle and tower (p30, 38, 41, 54, 174); the requisition room (p231); the tessellation room (p155-156); the mountain city (p5, 8, 260, 264, 301); the Great Library (p21, 289); and additional locations, endings and objects.

Hari is an award-winning comics artist and author who enjoys tabletop games, fantasy books large enough to be used as improvised weapons, and being a very squishy wizard.

Hari is also the author of *Into the Dungeon*, a shorter dungeon crawl choose-your-own-path book, as well as of various webcomics and graphic novels.

You can find out more about their other books at **hari-illustration.com**.

Illustrators:

Tiffany Baxter: The guards (p33, 64, 66) and the procession, including design work (p176, 178)
tiffanybaxter.com | @TiffBaxterIllus

Anine Bösenberg: *The sailor* call of the ocean & toymaker endings (p295-99), the toymaker's story (p210), ruined house (p13) and enchanted violin (p255)
anineillustration.com | @AnineBosenberg

Alexander Chacón: The twilight forest (p192, 198) and endless meadow (p206)
instagram.com/avantaron | @Avantaron

Kateřina Čupová: *The acolyte* world outside the archives ending (p291), the castle kitchen (p47) and memories in the Between (p167, 169, 170, 173)
katkacupova.wixsite.com/portfolio | @Chechulalala (twitter)

Shazleen Khan: The magical goods dealer (p49), glass flower merchant (p52) and the woman with the silver hair (p117, 118).
shazleenkhan.com | @ShazleenMKhan (twitter)

Ashley McCammon: Lady Tamar (p34)
avmccammon.com | @Draculing

Rowan MacColl: The ball, masks and golden halls (p101, 102, 111, 144), the girl with the teeth (p194, 196) and Orla's ghost (p148, 152)
rowanmaccoll.com | @SkulkingFoxes

Felix Miall: 'Taking them down with you' (p40)
felixmiall.com | @FelixMiall (twitter)

Sajan Rai: The dark planet and impossible building (p180, 182), the Mother of bearers (p185-189), colossal creatures (p137, 205) and the end of the world (p259)
sajanrai.co.uk | @PlanetSmudge (twitter)

Faye Stacey: Ball guests: the prince and the spellbinder (p124, 126) and the dignitaries (p121, 122)
fayestacey-illustration.co.uk | @Pppondi (twitter)

Danielle Taphanel: *The thief* seed of hope ending (p304)
danielletaphanel.com | @Treelet

Korinna Mei Veropoulou: The tapestries (p130, 132)
korinnamei.myportfolio.com | @KorinnaMei

Peter Violini: The inquisitors (p93, 95, 97, 109)
peterviolini.com | @Petarvee

Letty Wilson: The King of Woodlice (p164, 168, 267), the creature in the undertunnels (p73) and the princess, the smiling woman and bearers of gifts, including design work (p113, 115, 233, 238, 240)
toadlett.com | @Toadlett

Val / Bishop Wise: Venny (p85-90, 98, 273) and *the libertine* agent in Estovar and open road endings (p281, 285)
valkwise.com | @ValKWise

Special thanks:

To **Emmett Nahil** for developmental, mechanical and structural feedback and edits; to all playtesters and in particular **Alexi Conman** for your detailed help, to Sam for testing the first draft and Es for playing as Gowron; and to my long-time DM Robbie for being the 'person who never draws' to draw Linda. Thanks to my agent Jess Mileo, and to Katie Gould and everyone else at AMU RPGs for making the book possible.

Into the Tower: A Choose-Your-Own-Path Book copyright © 2023 by Hari Conner. All rights reserved. Printed in China. No part of this book may be used or reproduced in any manner whatsoever without written permission except in the case of reprints in the context of reviews.

Andrews McMeel Publishing
a division of Andrews McMeel Universal
1130 Walnut Street, Kansas City, Missouri 64106

www.andrewsmcmeel.com

23 24 25 26 27 RLP 10 9 8 7 6 5 4 3 2 1

ISBN: 978-1-5248-8386-7

Library of Congress Control Number: 2023932023

Editor: Katie Gould
Production Editor: Jennifer Straub
Production Manager: Chuck Harper
Art Director: Hari Conner

ATTENTION: SCHOOLS AND BUSINESSES

Andrews McMeel books are available at quantity discounts with bulk purchase for educational, business, or sales promotional use. For information, please e-mail the Andrews McMeel Publishing Special Sales Department: sales@amuniversal.com.